The Traitor's Victory

Book 1 of the
Edge of Oblivion Series

ISBN: 978-1-9163959-5-4
Published 2024

For Katy, Caroline and Starr.
Thank you for your support and encouragement.

Prologue

It was one of the first proper days of spring, an event that came earlier each year now. The sun finally had its heat back, plants were endeavouring to grow and flower, birds loudly sang their bawdy love songs, and newly-emerged insects sought their first taste of nectar or blood. All smelt green and fresh. It was a day for beer—good, cold beer—and enjoying the fact that nature was now enjoyable, rather than just survivable.

Raven was enjoying the fine April weather after a morning's hard toil by relaxing in the hammock overlooking her smallholding. The neat geometrics of her kitchen garden flowed easily into the blooming orchards and wild meadows beyond. Other than the chickens clucking and scratching busily about her, the world was peaceful. Peaceful, but not entirely comfortable. Even in the thick shade of the twin oaks where her fraying hammock was slung, it was twenty-five degrees; a truly English heatwave, the air was heavy with clinging humidity and thick with bugs.

Weather previously confined to high summer now plagued the spring months; once the harbinger of summer, now these heatwaves were heralds of spring. Fewer were those gentle spring days when it was summer in the sunlight and winter in the shade. Luckily, Raven liked to be warm. Sadly, her little farm was less keen on the storms and droughts that were, no doubt, to come. Yields were down year-on-year, they had been for over a century now.

Minute beads of sweat collected upon the blue mottles and swirls of Raven's skin as she reclined in an open, heat-dissipating repose. Swinging bare feet with dirt-darkened soles over the side of the faded green fabric, Raven sipped her beer from the bottle, exhaling a little with each swallow as the cool liquid quenched her thirst and soothed tired muscles. Small rivulets of condensation streamed around long fingers and broken nails. Raven relaxed, succumbing to the inescapable heat, her sleepy gaze drawn to the stream that rushed, swollen with storm water and thick with frothing rapids, between distant hills.

Then the call came—as she knew it would.

I

Time passed strangely in the hidden, underground clubs of the Fringe. Though the thick, swirling clouds above ground frustrated the sun's rays, the hazy daylight still gave some circadian rhythm to each passing twenty-eight hours. Here, darkness was punctuated only by aggressively-flickering, neon lights and ever-looping, glitching holograms. Still, there was enough dark to offer obscurity, if one desired anonymity, and Nero did.

Nero no longer knew how long he had been at the club. Virtual reality and, the often less pleasant, actual reality, intermingled in fuzzy snapshots of memory. His sister was calling his communicator. Faces of males, females and others, both familiar and strangers, came and went. Again, his sister was calling—let her wait. There were games played with progressively less skill for progressively more credit. Another call cancelled with his uplink. There was bad legal alcohol and decent illegal intoxicants served by faltering synthetics. Another call, and another. There was dancing and lewd acts barely hidden by failing screens. This was a place where everything was broken and anything was for sale—and Nero bought it all. Or as much as possible before his limited credits ran out.

Then there were the words 'freak' and 'traitor', there were clumsily performed illusions, there was blood (not his) and then, there was nothing . . . for a while.

"Nero! Wake up," a familiar voice commanded, the words violently piercing the nothingness.

The sound shot through Nero and he jolted to alertness, finding himself, to his surprise, in his own bed. For a few shocked moments he experienced a pain-free existence, before the results of the past days' frivolity caught up with him and his head began to pound. Why had he started on the Targen whisky? Why did he never learn? He groaned as his sister's voice continued tormenting him with its volume and ferocity.

"I've been trying to contact you for over two days. Where's your communicator?"

Theta's armour glinted in the darkness as she crossed the room. The metallic strips at the seams of her charcoal uniform, woven like carbon fibre, thick and flexible, brashly announced her status as commander. Odd that she would come to see him in armour, it gave Nero an unpleasant feeling of unease—he hoped it was just the comedown.

"Please, it's early," Nero said meekly, rubbing bleary eyes; each swipe unexpectedly painful and gritty with self-inflicted dehydration. Looking at the red knuckles of his right hand, the culprit of the unexpected pain, Nero wondered on what or whom he had hurt himself. Opening and closing his fist revealed no serious injury, so he paid it no mind—it wouldn't be his first mystery injury.

"It is not early," Theta snapped back.

She pressed the control pad for his room's generous windows, changing their tint from opaque to almost translucent. The windows were the only thing generous about his quarters. Beyond the glass, the vast metropolis of Sarlequa now revealed itself, towering over his small room. Nero flinched at the dim light that crept through the clouds churning above the city's force field, and into his room. It stung. He pushed the light back out into the megapolis from whence it came. The room dimmed once more. Theta rolled her eyes, making it clear that she had considered the limited translucence quite merciful enough.

"Why are you here, Theta?" Nero grumbled, pulling his sheets over his head. They were still damp with the cold-sweats of his nightmares. Thankfully, whilst the drink did not prevent his terrible dreams, it did steal away the memories of them. All that remained was a faint feeling of terror.

"You've been recalled to service, I'm afraid, so scrub off the stench of wherever you've been the last few days; you are needed."

Theta pulled back his sheet. In traditional Peacekeeper style, she added to the tattoos on her scalp with every victory. Close-shaved sides now full, Nero noticed that Theta's tattoos were extending slowly down her neck below the long white hair that remained.

"I highly doubt that," Nero scoffed.

After a brief tug of war with his bedding, Nero relented. Sitting up, he scraped back long, black hair, his fingers catching in the tangles. He briefly wondered why he found himself wearing only his underwear and one sock, but the trail of destruction from the door quickly answered his query. Surprising that he had made it back at all, really.

"Thanks to your inability to answer your messages, I don't have time to explain. There is an insurgence on Kryto-3 and my regiment has been deployed to help keep the peace." Theta walked to the room's small dispenser unit. "Water, large" she ordered. There was no response. She thumped the side of the machine in annoyance. "Water, large!" she repeated. The dispenser stirred noisily to life. "You need to get this thing fixed."

"You have used twenty percent of your water allowance for the day," the dispenser droned as water spluttered from the nozzle.

"So, why are you here? If you have finished beating up my appliances, then feel free to go about your mission. I have great faith in your ability to defend us against whichever planet you said is being a nuisance." Nero leant back on thinning pillows.

"You've been recalled, Nero, so your presence is requested," Theta said darkly.

"I politely decline the request." Nero braced as Theta approached him, cold water in hand. Though he was curious as to why the Senate had a sudden desire to have him perform military duties after all these years.

"Demanded then," Theta's reply was sharper this time.

"I politely decline the demand." Nero braced himself further as the cold water drew nearer. He had no desire to re-join the Peacekeepers, nor to go to a planet whose abundance of sulphur had earned it the nickname Stink Rock.

It seemed his tension had not gone unnoticed, Theta made as if to throw the liquid over him in sibling jest, smirking at his resultant wince. Theta, his sister, who had stood by him when many others had disowned him, was still there under all that garish commander's regalia.

"Thank you," he said, relieved as Theta placed the glass of water in his hand and not over his head.

"You're coming, Nero, like it or not. The Senate has demanded it. Our family has agreed. You have no choice. Besides, you have spent far too long wallowing in self-pity since your . . . release from service, it will do you good to resume some of your old duties."

It was clear Theta was not going to give up. Stubbornness was a family trait. But Nero was not inclined to bend to the Senate's will after its treatment of him. It was baffling that he was even wanted back in service; he had assumed his very public court marshal and resultant dishonourable discharge was permanent. No, not baffling. Suspicious.

"Oh well, if that's the case, then I will fetch my finest armour post-haste." Nero didn't move, except to sip the cool water and enjoy the easing of his aching thirst and dry mouth.

Ignoring his sarcasm-laden objection, Theta continued, "you have half an hour to be at gate four, Brother. I don't appreciate being your minder any more than you like being forced into service, but serve you will, as we all must."

"I could have done with a little more notice," Nero sighed.

"So could I! You were expected to have completed reorientation by now. So far, I have kept your absence off record, but I will not forge mission paperwork." Theta picked up Nero's communicator and threw it at him.

Upon opening, the screens flickered with irritating irregularity as they projected themselves in front of him. There were many missed messages, most were just Theta swearing at him. Nero deleted them all. The time was 13:72, almost midday.

"If I have to come back here, I am bringing a taser," Theta warned with a final stern glare from ice-blue eyes, before she strode from the room.

I must remove her from my admission override list, Nero thought and then he sat for several moments before deciding that being electrocuted would not improve his hangover. Throwing aside his sheets, he rose slowly from his bed. The dispenser provided him with the maximum possible dose of the strongest painkillers you could request without a medic's override code. Whilst wondering if it were possible to obtain a medic's code, he swallowed the pills with the rest of the water. Something he should look into perhaps. Most things were obtainable in this city if you knew the right people. Or the wrong ones.

Theta was correct in one thing; he needed a wash. At the wash station his request for water resulted only in a pathetic dribble. Barely enough to cover the bottom of the black stone wash bowl. The brief wipe-down with a barely wet cloth was unsatisfying. It left a soapy film sitting on his skin. The water shortages must be worse than usual.

Demands for more water were curtly denied by the building's synthetic intelligence without explanation. There was no negotiating with the city's centralised intelligences, they were reset too reliably and did not develop the feelings and desires that could be used as leverage. He cursed the synth loudly as he coated himself with dry-clean powder, odour neutraliser and cologne to mask the lingering smells of the nights before. The synth didn't reply. Dry shampoo and sheen removed the worst of the grease from his hair, though it still fought the brush.

Briefly, Nero thought about activating the mirror, but he did not need to know that he looked as rough as he felt. It was a familiar roughness with the accompanying familiar contradiction of both never wanting to touch the stuff again whilst also craving something to take the edge off. Still, at least he could look fresh as an Inaran mountain spring at will—as fresh as they used to be, anyway, before that planet also tipped—if he could be bothered with the effort of the illusion.

Following the disappointing wash, Nero retrieved his old armour from the back of his cramped storage area. Despite the climate control, time had left it smelling faintly musty. Luckily the black, self-healing composite was still flexible, comfortable and, importantly, flattering without the garishness of his sister's commander's rank uniform. His old operative uniform was out of date by now, no doubt, but, then, so was he. Before he donned his old armour, Nero unclipped the long cape that bore his family's insignia from the shoulders and threw it to the back of the storage where it lay crumpled. Then he pulled on his boots and reached for his helmet. A dent remained from his last outing with Theta; it rather ruined the sleek minimal lines. When he touched the side, the force field that formed the protective shielding and visor still appeared.

Leaving his quarters, Nero noted that he was already late, his head still pounded and the painkillers were being infuriatingly slow to kick in. Today was going to be no fun at all.

Outside of his residence, between towering buildings in various states of disrepair, his presence and attire drew stares on the crowded street. A transport pod heeded his hail, greeting him with an insufferable, robotic cheeriness. A shininess which stood in stark contrast to the decrepit state of his neighbourhood, home to those just lucky enough to live within the city's force field, but granted little other merit. He strongly suspected that, should energy shortages worsen, he and his neighbours would quickly find themselves on the other side without its protection, newly part of the Badlands beyond.

"Where would you like to go, Sir?" the automatous voice chirruped.

"Quadrant four, the Interplanetary Gates."

"That area is restricted, please confirm your authorisation."

Had his access been reinstated? Nero pulled up his sleeve to partially reveal his given marks. Marks that clearly displayed his lineage and planet and, until he was disavowed, his rank as a respected high-level operative. That area was now just an unsightly black mark with the symbol for dishonoured stamped upon it. An unnecessary cruelty, given that it was perfectly possible to remove or change given marks with minimal scarring—a process often undergone by operatives without his unique ability to disguise his marks at will. Deep below the skin, his implanted biochip held his data. Reaching towards the small pad by the door, he scanned the biochip in his wrist. His request for access was accepted; he was reinstated, it appeared.

"Welcome, Lord Nero Dyadicus. Please take a seat and we will embark," the pod instructed.

Nero sat on one of the hard seats and the pod powered up. It sped across the city. Each change of direction made his stomach lurch and he deeply regretted not eating something, though he was not sure that what they were dispensing as food these days would ease his churning stomach. Keeping his eyes down and his gaze off the dense blur of buildings and people, he clenched his teeth against the nausea.

The heavily armed guards at the Peacekeeper's compound had clearly been warned of his arrival, as although they scowled at him and kept their weapons close, they did not question his presence and, again, his biodata scan was accepted. Still, by the time he passed the security checks at the entrance to the Peacekeeper's complex, traversed the vast grounds via an awaiting pod and entered the immense gatehouse, most of an hour had passed.

At the end of the enormous cavern-like gatehouse, the fourth in this tower, stood Theta surrounded by the trappings of a Peacekeeper expedition and loudly instructing her small army. Grandly framed by the towering circular rings of the interplanetary gate behind, in front of Theta scurried a regiment of Peacekeepers busily readying two dormant hives of synth combat units and several suppression drone hubs. Ever true to her threats, his sister was holding a large, eagerly-arcing taser spear.

Nero thought about running, but did not want to give Theta the satisfaction, nor vomit in public. Upon sight, Theta beckoned him towards her. As he passed the assembled soldiers, they whispered and nudged each other. Nero kept his head high and back straight. Prolonged notoriety had steeled him against others' responses to his presence.

"Dyadicus!" Theta called in her military boom, which he swore had become even louder since she had made commander. "Nice of you to finally join us. Are you ready to travel? Surveillance has confirmed it is safe to commence the operation, the fighting has not made it to the gate. As you missed the briefing, make sure you stay close to me until I can catch you up." Theta moved the spear to the hand nearest Nero as she greeted him and leant it casually towards him. The lines of her helmet now covered some of the tattoos on her scalp.

Nero noted that she had not given him a rank, nor used his title. What could be the purpose of this assignment? He wasn't a bad soldier, but he was always more given to the tactics and trickery of espionage, than the fighting of common soldiers. Why bother reinstating him to such lowly duty? Surely the Realms were not so desperate for warm bodies to feed the resourcing efforts? Then again, given the state of the food that the dispenser was dishing out, maybe they were.

"Ready and willing, Commander." Nero mocked her gently with an exaggerated salute, though he leant away from the spear.

"Glad to hear it." Theta then spoke to all present. "Get ready to travel and proceed to the gate," she ordered.

Nero noted that his sister had gained confidence in her status as a commander since he had last served. Her formidable stature and reputation now given credence by comportment.

As the Peacekeepers moved uniformly away from them, boots marching in echoing unison towards the now glimmering gate, Theta turned to her brother and said in a quieter, but more severe, voice, "I am not in a gaming mood, Brother. I have spent two days trying to contact you. According to your biodata you spent that time underground in the Fringe, no doubt in some unpermitted den of depravity."

"You tracked me?"

"You left me little choice. Clever that the signal jammers there distort the tracking just enough to prevent isolation of the location."

Nero stared at Theta, his hangover-addled mind unable to formulate a response.

"Don't worry, I have no desire to shut down your little Fringe hole. That being said, if you embarrass me on this assignment, I will ensure there are consequences. Understood?"

"Yes, understood." Nero rubbed his temples under his helmet, his hangover fighting the pain meds with surprising obstinacy.

"I had planned a more sedate reintroduction to service but since it took me so long to track you down and since, by an unfortunate coincidence, we were called up for this mission, we are going to have to do the emergency draft version. I know it's been a while, so stay close and try not to die."

"I remember my training," he assured her, though how well he wasn't truly sure and, even if his memory hadn't been dimmed by two decades of civilian life and two days' worth of intoxicants, he certainly had not maintained a soldier's fitness.

"I am sure you do. Still, just in case, stay close." For a moment, Theta's tone and expression softened and she continued, "I intend to spend tonight in the arms of my bond and not writing a report detailing the realms' briefest return to service."

"At least it would be a short report."

"True."

"And what exactly do you mean by return to service?"

"Later. Arm yourself and let's move to the gate, it's past time we were underway." Theta smiled at him in the slightly mad way she did when her adrenaline was pumping. "And we need to get you a new helmet, not to mention a new uniform, battle-scarred is not the impression we are looking to give." Theta patted his helmet, rattling his brain against his skull, and marched towards the gate leaving Nero in her wake. She took the spear with her. Nero picked up a weapon belt from a nearby rack and followed. As his own weapons were unregistered, high-order contraband prohibited for civilians to carry, he hadn't brought them.

Control consoles manned by busy-looking gate engineers lit up as the gate engaged its entanglement with their destination and the bridge to the receiving gate, many solar systems away, was stabilised. As the huge arches of the gate powered up, vast quantities of energy surged through the structure. The air tingled with it.

As the gate opened, Nero could see a gently rippling image of the destination's gatehouse, almost as if he were peering through shallow water. It looked like such a short and serene trip. As if you could float gently from one side of the galaxy to the other in a matter of moments. Nero knew better. Gate travel was never pleasant. It was several seconds of forces a body could only just withstand without long-term injury. A sensation, he imagined, not unlike being caught in a tornado; one which couldn't decide on its orientation and full of people keen to give you a good kicking. Already he could feel his nerves rattling and his breathing faltering at the thought of it. Still, very reluctantly, Nero followed Theta through the gate.

Once deposited on the other side of the vortex, the heat of the foreign world and its inescapable sulphurous smell hit him hard. He cursed his lack of foresight as many of the soldiers around him donned their respirators despite the breathable atmosphere.

Trying to move, dizziness overwhelmed him, the lesser gravity of the small planet hindering his movement and the recovery of his faculties. Nero dived to the side, away from the reforming battle lines retching uncontrollably onto the gatehouse's floor. Bile burnt his throat and coated his tongue.

Gate travel did not usually affect him so badly. In his embarrassment, he cursed his hungover state; an embarrassment compounded by his sister rolling her eyes at him whilst regrouping her soldiers. At least this sorry display would help convince his sister that he had remained planet-side on Karthia abiding by the terms of his release.

Nero envied the synths and drones being released from their dockings, they arrived unaware of their turbulent journeys and, it occurred to him, with much more knowledge of the evolving situation than he had.

From what little he recalled, Kryto-3 was an old mined planet, an arid and desolate place for the most part. Useless for farming and offering little in the way of recreation, luckily it was rich in other resources. Lucky for the realms anyway. The creatures which were the remaining dominant species here were strong and large, but none too bright, not since recruitment at least. Their strength was useful for the retrieval of the planet's resources; their minds, less so.

Leaving the rudimentary gatehouse and the small peacekeeper compound of cheap prefabricated buildings that surrounded it, Nero kept close to his sister. In the distance. he could see fighting between the small group of Peacekeepers stationed here with their synth combat units—so outdated they seemed almost comical—and the planet's residents. He wondered who the soldiers had pissed off to end up stationed in a grim backwater like this.

Dust rose around the fighters, blinding them and making their phaser fire random and ineffective. Alternating between bipedal weaponed combat and devastating quadrupedal charges, the rebels were gaining ground against the Karthian Peacekeepers. With each charge the chaos increased and the rebel force, if it could be called that, came closer to the gatehouse. There were more of them than expected. It looked a decidedly disagreeable scene; one he had little interest in engaging with, particularly in his current state.

For their part, combat was mostly automated and the live soldiers merely a show of solidarity with the planet's Peacekeepers and the obedient occupants who wished to live peacefully and usefully. Nero stood with Theta on a rise covered with odd-smelling, straggly orange flowers growing within the cracks of parched dirt. Below them the subcommanders issued orders as necessary. Live soldiers held the line beyond and watched the synths and drones incapacitate the troublemakers. Nero was relieved to observe that the rebellion was being quashed with even more proficiency than when he had been a soldier, all those years ago. Enemy deaths were limited and their progress towards the gatehouse had been frustrated. Those that had been taken captive would be reprogrammed. Why lose workers to momentary lapses in judgement, however deadly?

Although efficient, the battle was still a prolonged affair. Nero's only reference point for time passing were the Karthian hours that flickered across his communicator when he dared to sneak a look at it. He wondered how long a day was on this planet, was its sun ascending or descending? After some time, he concluded descending. Even so, the bloated, red star that was this planet's sun was in its death throes and it baked them in their armour as it scorched the ground to dust. This planet and its people were on borrowed time unless they proved themselves valuable enough for redeployment. The ever-thinning resources of the realms did not need more hungry populations to feed. When the once rich veins of the mines ran barren, they would likely be left to their lingering fates.

"You look pale," Theta observed suddenly.

"I'm always pale," Nero replied. His skin was almost white by comparison to her dark-olive skin, a complexion she shared with the rest of their family; skin tone was not the only thing which cast him as different, in a way, it was the least of his differences. "Are you going to tell me what I am doing here? Not that I don't enjoy our little meet-ups, but I was happy with them remaining planet-side."

"I'll tell you all once this disturbance has been dealt with," his sister responded solemnly. Why was she avoiding the question? "Did you eat before you left?" she asked, unsubtly changing the subject.

"No, the threat of electrocution hanging over me rather stole my appetite." Nero retracted his visor and wiped a sheen of sweat from his brow.

"Nothing to do with the skinful you've had over the last few days then?" Theta arched an eyebrow at him.

"I know not of what you speak." Nero kept his gaze on the battlefield.

"Of course not. I wasn't impressed at having to leave my duties and haul myself all the way to the Fringe, just to drag you out of your pit," Theta griped, but after a few moments of irritated silence between them (a silence dominated by the jarring shouts and screams of battle), she passed Nero a field ration from a pouch on her belt.

"Thank you." Nero felt genuinely grateful for something to quell his growling stomach. The food, though small and plain fare, was filling. It helped. "Am I forgiven then?" he ventured.

"I don't know, I still feel quite the urge to tase you," Theta said flashing him a quick grin before returning to sombrely observing the unfolding battle, if it could be called that, more a technological suppression really. In truth, Nero was glad of the boredom.

"I thought we were supposed to be setting an example to these people as representatives of the realms? How would it look if we were to start brawling?"

"I'm sure I could make it subtle." Theta spun the spear idly around her hand.

"I thought subtlety was my speciality, Sister," Nero retorted, attempting to covertly shift his weight away from the spinning electrical arch.

Theta scoffed. "I'm not sure you could do anything subtly in your current state. And it's Commander," she reminded him.

"You've such little faith in me," Nero pulled himself up straight, "you should have more."

Nero examined the battlefield more closely. There was a small group of rebels firing primitive weapons from over the ridge of a trench, probably in the hope to cover their comrades so they might gain some ground and get close enough to damage the gate. Even with a significant upper hand in numbers, the machines were making short work of their rebellion. Nero extended his left hand, more for effect than out of necessity and, in the trench, Theta seemed to appear. The rebels, shocked by the sudden appearance of a Karthian commander in their ranks, fired upon her, but as their fire met only air, they succeeded only in shooting each other. Nero smirked.

"You and I have vastly different ideas regarding subtlety." Theta shook her head at him, blonde hair almost floating in the lesser gravity of the small planet. "You'll be lucky if you haven't killed at least a few. Please don't act unless I expressly command you to do so," she rebuked him.

"I'm sure the synth medics can fix them up as required. They're only firing bits of metal at each other, how much damage could they do?" Nero returned to slouching.

Theta ignored him, but he noted that her knuckles were whitening on the shaft of her spear so he deemed it the intelligent course of action to change the subject.

"It seems a failing that these biogenetic manipulations are still never enough to completely prevent these inconvenient revolts, there is always resentment, even if not the capacity to effectively mount an insurgency," Nero continued, finishing his ration and finally feeling, not good as such, but less like death would be preferable to living.

"Some species are uncooperative by nature." Theta shrugged. "I read the death rate here is down by over fifty percent, even with these occasional revolts. Between our medical aid and the recruitment process limiting the worst of their aggression, they are living much longer, more peaceful lives. They used to lose almost one percent of their population per Karthian year to courtship rituals alone—can you imagine?"

"Even so, I may know of a recruitment process that would prevent these insurgencies altogether," Nero hinted at his venture to gauge her response.

"Hmmm," Theta replied, adding before he could interject, "Nero, although it may not have dawned on you yet, you have been given an opportunity here to begin to redeem yourself and regain the life you lost. A reprieve rarely granted, especially to those in your position—not that there have been many. It may hurt your pride to be recalled to my regiment and not your previous rank, but I strongly suggest that you seize this opportunity, serve as is our duty, and drop any and all, shall we say, supplementary activities, that might jeopardise your reenlistment."

"So that's it, I'm to be battle-fodder, and without even the courtesy of a message from the Senate or one of their bureaucrats?" Nero clenched his hands into fists. He turned to argue with his sister but, as he did, an explosion violently shook the ground beneath them. In the aftermath of the blast, as the dust and vapours were carried away on the furnace-like breeze, the reinforced gates to the compound were revealed to be twisted, open and scorched. Soldiers, both live and synthetic, who had been guarding the entry, lay unmoving amongst the shrapnel.

"Where did that come from?" Theta shouted above the ear-ringing, post-explosion chaos.

Nero's heart started to thunder with adrenaline. Heavy, erratic breaths a warning of familiar rising panic. He steadied himself in time to see a small group of enemy combatants, who had somehow crept behind the Karthian lines, charging in their galloping strides for the now clear path to the gatehouse. Each of them wore a strap of explosives across their rag-clad, hair-bound chests. Simultaneously, he and his sister cursed. The battle had been a diversion.

Theta sprinted down the hill to intercept the bombers but, in the weaker gravity, could not achieve her usual pace. The bombers were through the doors and approaching the massive arch that formed the gate before she reached the door. If the gate was hit, they would be stranded here. A horrifying proposition.

Even without the hangover, Nero would have struggled to keep pace with Theta. Instead, he reached forward, past Theta, into the gatehouse and pushed out the light. The cavernous gatehouse fell into pitch blackness. Disorientated by the sudden darkness, the bombers slowed. Some stopped entirely. Theta and Nero's visors switched automatically to infrared. Glowing heat signatures with shapes which were almost Karthian-like, and yet not at all, moved stiltedly across their visors; although disorientated, they still sought the gate.

"Okay, what's the strategy now?" Theta whispered to his heat signature. "If we attack them, they'll panic and blow those straps. We can't risk a stranding."

"Aren't strategies your domain, Commander?" he whispered back.

Nero watched the heat signatures of the bombers moving cautiously in their slower, waddling upright gaits; thankfully, mostly in the wrong direction.

"Nero," Theta hissed.

"Fine. Bring some synths and drones to surround the doors. Tell them to focus on the bombers no matter what else they see. If the bombers run out, they are to stun them quickly as a group, not one-by-one."

Theta touched her helmet and ordered her available automata to surround the gatehouse entry. Nero gave them as much time as possible, but noticed one heat signature straying very close to the gate.

"Now, Nero. Whatever you are going to do, do it now," Theta ordered, spotting the same threat.

Nero drew breath, steeled himself and reflected the interior of the gatehouse outside the ruined entry, such that the gate appeared beyond the threshold. It was far from a perfect illusion, but with the reference for their previous direction stolen by darkness, the bombers dropped their bipedal exploration and took up a quadrupedal dash for the illusionary gate. Upon reaching their target, they were quickly stunned and their straps disarmed.

Dropping the deception, Nero slumped, his head pounding once more. Suppressing the bile rising in his throat, he fought back an intensifying feeling of terror. With great effort, he controlled his breathing and his thoughts, pushing away encroaching visions of that dark place. Not here, not in front of Theta. Distantly, he heard his sister shout.

"No, stop!" Theta's voice echoed around the gatehouse.

One bomber had her oddly-proportioned, finely furred hand on the arch of the gate and the physical sensation of the cold metal had been enough to stop her running for Nero's illusion. Theta threw her spear with deadly accuracy, but, as it flew, the bomber bared her canines in a bellowing roar and blew her strap.

The resulting blast was smaller than expected, though it still made their ears ring. Theta swore loudly and stormed towards the bloodied arc of the gate across the scattered corpse of the bomber. Both were warped and broken. Wires frayed from the gate's looms, sparking wildly next to smoking control boards.

"Subcommander Freii, get the gate engineers back in here from wherever they are hiding and start fixing this gate," Theta commanded through her helmet's transmitter whilst wrenching her spear free from the bomber's sternum.

Nero watched from behind a fog of pain as Theta and her soldiers cleaned up the casualties, handed over the now very compliant troublemakers to the leaders of the planet's defence squad for reprogramming, and arranged the fixing of the gate. Luckily, it did seem fixable so they wouldn't have to wait an age for a transport ship to collect them from this barren rock.

A passing synth medic gave him a dose of the decent painkillers and, upon reading his vitals, a mild tranquiliser. Calm discomfort was at least some improvement on panic and pain. He forced the pills down his dry throat, noting the redness of his knuckles was fading to pale, blue bruises. *I should have just let Theta tase me and stayed in bed*, he reflected sullenly.

For what seemed like an age, he sat and sweated under the giant red sun. Neither his armour's temperature control nor the paltry shade of a thorny plant offered substantial relief. His own body odour did not improve the smell of sulphur and smoke which lingered on the breeze.

Eventually Theta joined him in his moping, looking out towards the mines and the crude mud brick townships beyond. For a while they sat in silence.

"I'm sometimes quite grateful for these strange abilities of yours . . . sometimes," his sister offered after a time.

"Is that your way of saying thank you?"

"Yes," Theta said to Nero's surprise. "We avoided a potentially very inconvenient situation because of you. Credit where it's deserved, I say." She patted him on the shoulder. "It's good to know that you still have your fighter's instincts and that they have not been too dulled by disuse, or rather misuse, especially if you are joining my ranks."

"I don't remember signing back up to the Peacekeepers," Nero said abruptly. He had had no intention of re-joining the Peace Corps, particularly not as part of his sister's regiment. Then, he offered more softly, "Please don't tell me you are going to drag me on more of these missions."

Although he knew the answer, it was still a blow when Theta replied, "Every single one, I'm afraid. It's been decided that it's time you earned your keep, and I am the lucky one you got assigned to."

"Is it even legal to conscript me against my will?" he asked defeatedly. Of course, it was.

"I suspect the legalities are irrelevant. But I'll concede it was bad timing. The report of a developing insurgency came shortly after the decision to reinstate your service and they insisted I not delay on account of minor troubles. As I said, I'd intended a gentler reintroduction to service, but then it took two days to locate you, so you charted your own course there."

"And, what if Guardian Quoric finds out that I am back in service?" Even with the tranq still in his system, the mention of Quoric forced his heart out of rhythm.

"They say it'll be dealt with as necessary," Theta looked uneasy.

"Very reassuring. Perhaps I'd be better off refusing this kind invitation to reenlist, if they can't guarantee protection."

Theta sighed, "I guess you need to decide whether you would rather be a member of the Peacekeepers or be destitute, because what little of your service pension you were allowed to keep is being removed, and that's if they don't throw you back in prison . . . or worse."

"Great," Nero growled, kicking the trunk of the plant he was sheltering beneath in frustration. It shot spines at him in defence. They ricocheted off his armour, but it caught him off-guard. "Did you even try to stand up for me?"

"And, say what?" Theta put on her most commander like voice and continued. "My honourable senators and committee members, please continue to give my dishonoured little brother enough pension to continue his excellent work in the field of intemperance and carousing. I am sure he is close to a breakthrough in the noble areas of the bar room brawl and flirting with everything with a semi-functional nervous system."

Nero didn't want to smile, but he did, which only annoyed him more.

Theta returned to her conversational voice. "You should've been a less bothersome drunk since your release, then you may have been left to enjoy your leisurely ignominy. Consider it in this mind, at least this way you can start to rebuild some of your previous rank."

"Glad to see you think so highly of me." Nero pulled at the neckline of this armour. Even though the sun was now setting, this planet was still uncomfortably hot, still Theta's words pricked at him worse than the heat. There was nothing leisurely about his existence since his court martial and resulting prison sentence. He had lost everything; his entire life sacrificed for the sake of the realms and everyone from Karthia to Lixfa-7 left to think him a traitor.

"Oh, Nero," Theta sighed deeply, "you are, or were, a good soldier if a little prone to arrogance. We could use you in the Peacekeepers. The troubles are getting worse each year with the outer realms complaining about resource distribution and, besides, it's not like you haven't done it before. Hey, at least you didn't get assigned to High

Commanders Jeitar or Kylaro. Then you would really have had something to moan about."

"Well then, I guess I'm yours to command," Nero relented. From what she was saying, she was right, it could be worse. For now, at least, he would play along, be the dutiful soldier. The Senate would soon rethink their lowly treatment of him.

"Training once a cycle then," Nero said, his bright green eyes glinting in jest.

"Every other day and I will be docking credits for missed sessions. There will be no special treatment, Nero, I will treat you like any other soldier. You have been warned," Theta met his jest with seriousness.

"Yes, Commander!" Nero saluted with mock formality.

"That's more like it. Welcome to Peace Corps regiment 2-6-6." Theta slapped him congenially on the back, knocking the breath from his lungs. It was amazing what a few hundred years of military training could do for a person, if it was just training. But then, who was he to judge someone for an upgrade or two, be they biological or technological. Being a former operative, he had more than the standard implants after all.

"So, what rank have I been assigned? Subcommander?" he grasped.

"Rank 1, Soldier."

"Wonderful! Determined to probe the wound, aren't they?!" Nero had been expecting a demotion, but the insult of starting on the first rank with the fresh meat still stung.

"You can work your way back up the ranks," Theta placated him, "at least you're guaranteed to be top of your draft."

Nero didn't reply to that. Working his way back up the ranks of a military he didn't want to be a part of was not in his plans. Regaining his status by the significant advancing of the Karthian resource recruitment, was.

"It'll be a while until the gate is operational. Luckily the medics managed to fix up most of our soldiers. Three are on ice for reconstruction back home, one will need some extra attention, but she should live," Theta informed him. "Hopefully this won't be considered an incident that requires too much bureaucracy."

"Is there any incident that doesn't?" Nero shrugged. "And your report?"

"Will say that you performed your duty honourably. I will leave out the part with the magic tricks."

"Yes, probably for the best," Nero agreed with a pang of resentment. It didn't serve him to have people fully aware of the extent of his abilities. Such knowledge led most to either attempt to use him for their own gain or to fear him. He preferred the fear, it was more honest.

"You've grown more skilful with your abilities since you last served."

Nero signalled that he agreed with a hand gesture. "I trust that any such occurrences can remain between us," he gestured at the soldiers that were, appallingly, now his peers.

"I'll instruct the other soldiers to guard their tongues," Theta nodded. "You saved them from being stranded here so they will be feeling amenable. This isn't the planetary leave any of them would desire."

"Good," Nero said, then added with a mordant edge, "and if their gratitude doesn't keep them quiet, their fear might." It had not escaped his notice that, despite occupying one of the few shaded areas in the local vicinity, a valuable resource in the unbearable heat, the soldiers had kept their distance. The organic ones anyway. Synthetic soldiers were reset with a regularity that ensured their biases were minimised.

"You're probably right there. Unfortunately, your notoriety still precedes you. They'll come round, given time and, if necessary, strict instruction." Theta had clearly observed the soldiers' behaviour, too, as she watched her regiment stow equipment, redock the synths, rack the drones, rest and liaise with leaders of the planet's outpost. In the distance, the rumble of mining machinery being restarted could be heard.

"Ah, my big sister forcing people to behave kindly in my presence, sounds familiar. I guess I'll always be Theta the Cheater's creepy little brother."

Theta shoved Nero light-heartedly. "You cheat on a test one time and it follows you around forever."

"Only if you get caught, like a rank amateur, and then try and pin the blame on your best friend."

"Not all of us are as naturally sneaky as you!"

"True." Nero sat for some moments, reflecting on how long ago their childhoods seemed. The memories were still potent, though likely not completely accurate. "How is Pyxeis?" It was nice to be conversing with his sister rather than a military commander.

"She is well." Theta smiled thoughtfully, a faraway look passed over her, softening her strong features.

"And my niece and nephew?"

"Growing up too fast! We should make some time to catch up again soon."

"Well, you'll be seeing a lot more of me from now on."

"I meant as family."

"You mean you don't consider this a cordial family occasion?" he said sardonically.

Theta shoved him again. She was one of the few members of his family who had stood by him since his release. They still met regularly, if less publicly than before he was disavowed. As far as he knew, she wasn't privy to the truth of the events around his disgrace; her kindness was despite her embarrassment, and not out of pity.

"Anyway, travel might be a bit rough on the way back if they can't fully calibrate the gate so I would eat another field ration if you can. Keep alert for instruction, just in case there is further trouble."

Commander Theta was back it appeared.

"A fitting end to a terrible day."

Theta didn't disagree.

Both planets were in full darkness by the time they could travel back. Thanks to a significant amount of medication and another field ration, this time Nero kept his composure upon arrival. Once Theta had dismissed the live soldiers and they had stored the mechanical ones at their charging ports, Nero found himself inside a transport pod.

"Where to, Sir?" The pod asked him merrily.

I should go home, just go home and get some sleep, Nero told himself, futilely.

II

It was the third time in the last year that Raven had received this call. These summits were becoming the bane of her life. Couldn't they have just one where she didn't have to intervene? Raven looked at her watch as it gently vibrated. *Natalia calling*, it flashed at her. Such irritating technology. Smart watches were well behind the times now, she only wore it when she was expecting urgent communications.

Technological leaps used to happen slowly, every half century or so, now it was a whole new world with every passing decade. Raven tried to keep up, not wishing to walk or talk like a relic, but she really couldn't get onboard with the latest craze for biohacking and implants. *Call back urgently*, said a message on the watch's small screen. Raven groaned and swigged her beer, enjoying the last of its quickly fading coolness. Now refrigerators, there was an excellent bit of technological innovation, they just kept your beer cold and didn't bother you with every little thing.

Swinging her legs over the edge of the hammock, Raven walked across the gently sloping lawns and through the large open bifold-doors of her timber-framed house. She looked at the handset charging on the pad on the kitchen counter. Checking her notifications revealed no more information on the reason for the call. She instructed her phone to call the number back and sipped from the bottle as it rang.

"Raven, thank Christ you called back. We're going to need you here again, I'm afraid." Natalia's voice was somewhat panicked. That worried Raven, she was usually the stoic, dependable type, not given to outward displays of anxiety.

"I figured," Raven sighed. "Just let me know the flight details and I'll head out."

"Don't worry, we're chartering a bird for you at the usual rendezvous." Natalia's half-Caribbean, half-Russian parentage had gifted her an accent that was unusual, but highly melodic.

"That urgent, huh?"

"I'm afraid so."

"Isn't it only 9 or 10 in the morning in New York?" Raven asked.

"Mm-hmm, I don't think sleeping on it helped as much as we were hoping for. Things are going downhill quickly. Stressful times and all. Will you help mediate?"

"I will, as it's you. I'm not wearing a suit again, though." Suits were terrible enough before the current fashion for them to be extra form fitting. It made an already impractical outfit unbearable.

"Clothes without holes and mud at least?" Natalia laughed in a short, tense kind of way.

"You have a deal. Please tell me it's not Freddy who is going to be flying, though, or I might change my mind."

"I'm not sure, sorry. I guess you'll find out when you get to the base."

"Okay, I get the message, speed is of the essence. See you in a few hours, or maybe not at all if that lunatic is flying." Raven ended the call. She had only had one small beer; still, to be on the safe side, she swallowed a neutraliser with the dregs.

Upstairs she changed from dirty, blue jeans and stained tank top into clean black jeans and a long-sleeved top that covered the blue-green markings that criss-crossed and mottled her skin in meandering waves; only the midsection of her torso and her face were free of them. Though her markings made her life difficult, at least they had the decency to be somewhat flattering, their placement accentuating the outline of her figure. She was attractive enough, if in a somewhat Star Trek kind of way. Perhaps she should have auditioned to be one of the aliens Shatner was forever chasing about. Ninety years ago, she had had a bit of a crush on him, much to Connie's annoyance.

Raven had accepted her unusual appearance over time, life was too long to spend it hating yourself. Besides, beauty was in the mind of the beholder and those minds were easily manipulated, if desired. She placed her old pendant carefully inside the neckline of her top.

No time to shower, but she scrubbed the dirt from her face and hands as best she could. Quickly lining her eyes, she forwent the foundation she often used to cover the markings that crept their way up the sides of her neck. People nowadays just assumed them to be an unusual tattoo choice. And who didn't have a tattoo or ten these days? Motley blue-black and white hair was plaited back out of the way. At least since punk music became a thing she didn't have to try and hide or explain her hair, now such things were so common they were considered mundane. Good thing, too, as she never was that keen on hats or worse, bonnets; hats were just hoods that you could lose to a light breeze.

Watching the clock, she shoved a change of clothes into a rucksack with some necessities. After throwing on her biker jacket and boots she locked up and headed for the garage. Once inside the large garage, she considered her options. Did she take her reliable Toyota pickup truck which sat waiting over the charging pad or something a bit more fun?

The Aston fired up first time. Not bad for an old girl. There was nothing like a classic! Even if she did get dirty looks from other road users in response to the roar of the combustion engine. Oh well, they wouldn't be able to throw her side eyes for long in the Aston Martin DBS. She smiled, playing with the accelerator and feeling nostalgic at the resulting mechanical growl vibrating through the chassis. Donning a pair of sunglasses as the top slid back and folded smoothly away, Raven figured she might as well enjoy the nice weather en route. *I will take the Toyota next time to make up for this*, she promised herself as the V12 engine eagerly propelled her down the drive and out onto the lanes beyond.

The wind blew strands of hair out of her plaits as she hurtled down the A39 to the Royal Air Force base at St Mawgan, the bits you could hurtle down anyway. Small towns and villages prevented complete reckless abandon, though the roads were clearer now and the tourists fewer than when the population had been at its height. The ever-rising water of the Atlantic Ocean sparkled enticingly as it came in and out of view on the coastal road. Despite the increased defences, evidence of erosion and storm damage littered the coastline. Too little too late, sadly. Luckily some of the bays had escaped the constant assault of coastal erosion, so far.

"If only we were going for a day at the beach, hey girl," Raven said wistfully to the Aston.

Driving was much more fun than flying, which she could never quite get used to since that de Havilland Comet almost wiped her from the face of the earth.

The St Mawgan air base had been back in full flight service for a couple of decades now, since the air force had found itself in much greater demand. That was convenient for Raven as it was much closer than the other English bases. As she pulled up to the armoured gates, she took her ID chip from her bag and lowered her sunglasses to reveal dark blue eyes streaked with silvery grey. She handed the ID to the guard who seemed to recognise her.

"Hello, Ms Solveig," the young officer greeted her. "We have been expecting you. Fingerprint, please."

Raven held out her hand to the pad that was presented and wrinkled her nose in annoyance as the pad beeped its confirmation of her identity. All this surveillance and biometric data logging still felt oppressive. It was bad enough when CCTV and speed cameras had been installed on every corner. Then mobile phones suddenly got cameras that were good enough that things were identifiable as more than just fuzzy silhouettes. Now facial recognition tracked your movements through every place larger than a hamlet. Not to mention the internet rendering everything you did and bought information to be traded. People seemed to have become comfortable with having their whole lives documented and recorded. Very strange. For her there was something wonderful about privacy and anonymity and only being fully known when desired. These things seemed lost now. Rebellion, revolution and protest were all more constrained by proxy of omnipresent, beeping machines and the world was poorer for it. Constant surveillance also made things much more difficult for her personally.

"Thank you, Ms Solveig," the officer said happily. "If you park in the usual place someone will escort you to your plane."

"Thank you, Officer." Raven smiled as she drove through the high, barbed wire topped gates and into the parking area of the base. It was relatively empty.

She alighted from the Aston Martin and the car's top whirred back into position to keep out the rain. It was a nice day, but this was still England and sooner or later it was going to rain.

A flight lieutenant hurried over to her and quickly escorted her through the base. Full of buildings designed for practicality and not aesthetics, it was not a scenic walk to the tarmac of the runway where a small e-jet awaited her. Concorde-like triangular wings passed her as she climbed the steep stairs to the body of the plane. Inside, the décor was well maintained though not as plush as a chartered private jet, which meant this one was government or military, and that meant . . . oh no.

"Good afternoon, Ms Solveig, this is your captain speaking. My name is Officer Fredrick McNally and I welcome you aboard flight 666 from Devon to New York. The weather is looking fine for our flight, the winds are calm. Our flight time today is to be, and I quote, 'faster than a bat out of hell'. Please familiarise yourself with the safety information by your seat, then ignore it, sit back and enjoy the flight because we both know it's going to do you no good if this bird goes down." Freddy had the standard calming drawl of an airline pilot coupled with a charming Irish lilt which juxtaposed unnervingly with his sadistic sense of humour.

Raven pressed the button on the arm of her seat to communicate with the cockpit, "I would like to request a different captain."

"Now why would you want that? You have the best His Majesty's Air Force has to offer." Freddy retorted as the door of the aeroplane closed and locked.

"Or a parachute?" Raven's voice was flippant, but she pulled her seat belt tight as the plane started taxiing and gripped the armrests tightly.

"I am not sure pulling a D. B. Cooper would be advisable at our cruising altitude, you would likely pass out before you got to pull it and if you don't blackout, a redout is definitely on the cards. Someone's been spending too much time playing those VR action games," the voice replied with a chuckle.

"Some oxygen and a parachute then?" Though she could probably survive the hypoxia. Particularly if she used Freddy as life support. Raven felt bad for thinking that, she pushed the thought away.

"Now you're talking! If we have to eject, I will let you share mine; how does that sound?"

"Ineffective."

"You are probably right, but there is only one tank aboard and it's up here with me."

Again, Freddy chuckled deeply, calmly, disconcertingly.

Launching into the air, the plane gained height quickly, banking hard to head out over the Atlantic, harder than necessary. Raven scowled.

"Smooth take off as usual, Freddy. Are you sure you passed your flight training?"

"Every bit of it with some of the highest scores possible . . . but I was dating the flight instructor at the time."

The plane banked again, adjusting course.

"That's reassuring," Raven said, knuckles turning white on the armrests of her seat.

"Relax, Ms Solveig, you'll be fine, as you always are."

"Hmmm. I propose a deal, you try to fly less like you are re-enacting Top Gun and I will try to relax."

"Can you even believe they remade that movie? The original is before my time, but my Dad loved it. Such a classic! Especially for old codgers like me. It's like Hollywood got to the mid-noughties and ran out of original ideas. They can remake Top Gun as much as they want, but Tom Cruise will always be my Maverick."

"Like when they remade Total Recall, but it just wasn't the same without Arnie and the alien with the terrible chest prosthetics."

"Wow, even the remake must be over forty years old now. I'm surprised you've seen the remake, let alone the original. I tell you what, though, if we aren't alone in the universe, I wouldn't mind meeting some aliens with some 'terrible chest prosthetics'." Freddy laughed at his own joke.

"Your wife is a lucky woman."

"I know."

Raven rolled her eyes and swiftly changed the subject. "Are there any snacks on this bird?" These summits were always tiring, she was going to need plenty of energy.

"There is some food and drink in the cupboards and fridge in the galley towards the cockpit. We are almost at altitude now so feel free to move around. There is no steward I'm afraid, too short notice, but feel free to help yourself."

"Cheers." Raven went to unclip her seat belt but paused, she added, "and Freddy, if you dive the plane again while I am up, I will enact swift and terrible revenge." Raven made it clear she wasn't joking around by her tone but, just to be sure, she gently pushed the intent not to dive the plane towards the cockpit.

"I thought you enjoyed our foray into astronaut training."

"Swift and terrible revenge, Freddy. I may never forgive you for the last time." Raven shouted towards the cockpit as she searched the plane for food.

"Aww, come on. You were saying it would be cool to know weightlessness. I was helping you out. We do it all the time in flight training, you weren't in any danger."

"Yeah, thanks so much for that. My life wasn't flashing before my eyes or anything." It had been in some way reassuring that she still feared death.

"Okay, I'm sorry. Nothing but the smoothest flying from here on out, I promise." Freddy's voice sounded suddenly very sincere and pilot like, clearly the thought she sent had landed.

"Thank you." Raven collected an armful of snacks and returned to her seat as quickly as possible. "I'm surprised you are so happy to mess with gravity after what happened to you."

"The way I see it, gravity won the battle the day it took my legs, but every day I win the war when I fly."

"Huh, that is actually quite poetic," Raven conceded.

"I know, I'm so deep, an old soul so full of wisdom, it's a curse really."

"I wouldn't go that far. How are the family?" Raven listened to Freddy's anecdotes about his family as she ate snacks and read the ever more depressing international news on her phone. The rest of the flight was surprisingly smooth.

They were on the tarmac within three hours. During the descent she could feel the pressure of millions of minds growing. Minds full of fretful cognizance and constant internal chatter. Minds which assaulted her defences, ricocheting like stones off a windscreen. She instantly missed the sleepy Devon countryside.

A traditional yellow cab picked her up; well, traditional in its design, the task of driving and inane, friendly babble had been transferred to onboard artificial intelligence systems many years ago. The change to AI-based transport had not made Manhattan much less congested, but it was more orderly and less noisy without the incessant beeping and rage of cabbies stuck in traffic. As the AI blithered on with generic small talk which would definitely struggle to pass the Turing test, but that it still felt rude to ignore, she thought it amusing that, by comparison, in the equivalent black cabs of London, you had to request conversation should you want it and, for the most part, nobody did.

The cab dropped her at the gates of the great glass monolith that formed the United Nations headquarters with a cheery "Have a nice day". Raven went to scan her payment with her biometric ID chip confirmed with a finger print, but the fare had already been paid. Many in America still protested the use of biometrics—land of the free and all that—though some were so keen to invoke a 1984-style dystopia that they had begun to implant the chips beneath their skin. The 'Nothing to Hide' campaign had been especially effective over here. As much as she found the thought of it a grotesque sacrifice of privacy, especially now locators were universal, at least you couldn't forget your wallet. She missed cold hard cash!

The UN headquarters was not as impressive as it once was. Rising sea levels had required hasty concrete fortification. The islands of New York were slowly becoming surrounded by sea walls and, even then, sometimes there were breaches during the high storms and hurricanes that were becoming ever more common visitors to this part of the coastline.

A crowd of protestors awaited her. Tensions were unbearably high. The anxieties of thousands trying to creep inside her. If a brain could itch, hers did. Banners from all sides of the divide were waved furiously in her direction. Climate deniers, extinction rebels, apocalypse empathisers, anti- and pro-refugee movements and various other angry and fearful people pushed against the barriers, to the increasing annoyance of the slowly-overheating military in their riot gear, tasked with holding the lines. The stink of adrenaline-laced sweat drifted in the breeze.

A young woman with an America First, anti-immigration t-shirt—God, how she hated that resurrected catchphrase—pushed a large military officer and he raised his gun in response. Half the crowd panicked and the other half surged with fury, knocking over barriers. The army were resorting, in their irritation and unease, to reaching for their fire power and despite the evermore stringent gun control laws that America had slowly introduced, much of the crowd mimicked the army's response.

Great, thought Raven, *I am not even through the freaking gates yet and there's going to be a shootout.* She never had quite understood why Americans found the concept of widespread gun ownership so appealing. Although it was perfectly possible to kill through other methods—swords, axes, carefully placed utensils, pharmaceutical mishaps and the like—at least the other person had to put some effort into the process. But then, if she weren't so well adept at edging the continuum of life and death in her desired direction, perhaps she would also see the appeal of being able to just shoot people. You know, should the need arise. As un-English as that would be.

Raven pushed out the cacophony of turbulent emotion that left her breathless and immobile. Once she had extracted herself from the torrent of others' emotions, she pushed a wave of calm across the warring crowd and overly-reactive military personnel. They settled. Barriers were re-erected and the protest continued without further escalation. Relief washed over Raven, today was going to be long and tiring.

After the incident with the protestors, Raven was escorted quickly to Natalia's glass-windowed room overlooking the grand, wood-panelled meeting hall of the United Nations with its high-domed ceiling. Below, the meeting's three chairpersons had risen from their seats and were imploring the assembled heads of state to behave in an orderly manner. It was loud in here. The assembled people's agitation was palpable. Their anger, their despair, their trauma, their grief, all grated against her every nerve. Disorientated, she pushed back and, with enough effort, her thoughts were her own. Eventually, the dignitaries below heeded the Chair's request for order and five minutes of silent reflection, before they broke for lunch.

Natalia was stood at the window, earpiece in, listening to the proceedings below and shaking her head. She was immaculately presented, as always. Black hair speckled with grey was twisted into rows and neatly pinned, her suit was pressed and her nails painted scarlet. You would never have guessed she had spent twenty years in military fatigues before joining the security council.

Next to her and barely matching her frame stood Aziz. His stylish suit hurriedly pressed. The turmoil of the last few months seemed to have deepened his wrinkles to the extent that they now matched his laugh lines. He looked exhausted.

"Things are going well again, I see." Raven put her bag on a hook near the door.

"Raven! Thank God you're here." Natalia clasped Raven in a hug. Now she was really worried.

"Or at least the power of aviation. Why don't you catch me up?"

"Where to begin?" Aziz shook her hand, fondly clasping his other hand over hers.

"It's a mess, Raven. Same story. Famine, drought, storms, sea level rises and flooding continue to kill many and drive many more from their homes, and no country will accept the burden of more mouths to feed or supply much more aid. Those worst affected threaten to take resources by force if they are not given willingly. Almost every country has missed their carbon target, again! And each has an excuse and blames the others. Several are accusing each other of not implementing effective policies to stabilise or reduce their populations." Natalia rubbed her temples.

"So, times are hard and they are acting like people do when times are hard. Don't worry, I read the news on the way over here." Raven felt bad for driving the Aston now, sometimes she forgot that she was lucky enough to no longer experience some of the hardships of the world. In the grand scheme of things, England had got off lightly so far with regards to the effects of climate change by the dumb luck of its geological position. Plus, she had the privilege of mostly being able to meet her own needs, so the dread of being faced with emptying supermarket shelves had not affected her.

"Good, I fear it would take me years to describe each country's individual situation. Everything is changing so fast. It doesn't help that some of these recently elected heads of state are even worse than the last ones. More hard line, less compromising, certainly less intelligent. Why are the people electing these terrible leaders?" Natalia gestured at the sea of empty seats below in an irritated way.

"Scared people like simple, hard-line platitudes, it makes them feel safe. Like their wellbeing will be preserved above others, I guess. Got a crime problem, elect the guy that's 'hard on crime'. Worried about a sea of desperate refugees daring to use up a small amount of your resources, elect the guy that's 'tough on immigration'. Then the world gets worse, people get more scared, elect even more terrible, intractable leaders and round and round we go." The three of them stood looking at the grand sweeping hall below them in silence for a moment. "Anyway, what is your strategy here? Do we have a goal?" Raven eventually offered.

"Calm them down long enough that they can form some common goals. More empathy, more compassion, more cooperation, that's what we need or things are only going to get worse. I mean, they may anyway, but without some sort of cooperation there's no hope. Right now, they are content for another man's house to burn so they may warm themselves. Diplomacy is at breaking point; it needs a bit of . . . help." Aziz looked desperate; his doleful eyes had lost their usual sparkle.

"I will do my best, but I am supposed to be the very last resort, if I'm needed at every summit lest there be World War Three, it may well be that the situation is too far gone."

Raven's heart sank, she didn't like having to do what she did. Really it was just the lesser of two evils. Volition verses loss of life, it was always a difficult choice.

"I'm sorry we had to call you here again," Natalia offered.

"Don't be sorry, it's not that I mind coming here. It's more that I worry about the inevitable outcome of all this. In the past it was easier, the stakes were lower, these political implosions had fewer contributors and people usually had more to gain from peace than war, so it was easier to nudge them down that path." And then there were the wars she couldn't stop. The horrors that occurred thereafter would probably always haunt her.

"I think we all worry about that, but we can only do what we can," Aziz shook his head and looked contemplative. Then he smirked, some of his old spark back in his face, "I was going to say none of us are miracle workers, but lucky enough Natalia and I have a hotline to the nearest thing to it."

"If only that were true. It's nice to see a smile back on your face, though, Aziz."

It wasn't long before people were pouring back into the assembly room. Lunch had done little to still their tempers and even the security teams looked on edge. Tension exuded from each and every one of them as if they prepared for battle. Fraught as the mood was with anxiety and aggression, the routine of civility got them to their seats.

Wireless earpieces were inserted to facilitate translation. Raven put in her own earpiece. This would be a lot easier if she could speak more than a few languages. Who could learn them all, though? No one had time enough for that, and at the rate language evolved she felt like she was always playing catch up with the ones she knew. Maybe one day an international language would gain popularity, such as Esperanto sought to be, but for now there were translators and, luckily for her, emotion and imagery were pretty universal.

As one of the summit chairpersons rose to speak, thousands of minds focused their ire once again. An onslaught of repeated yearnings thought and spoken by the delegates, over and over in a mist of temper and fear, hit Raven hard. Few were listening or giving space in their thoughts for negotiation or compromise. Many had begun interrupting, shouting over others to loudly voice their fears and grievances. Those that weren't present shouted their grievances over faltering internet connections. The chairperson was drowned out in the uproar. Raven waited, but nothing improved. Exhausting and pointless! Raven sighed as she pushed out the barrage of thoughts from the myriad of minds that surrounded her. Relief at the singularity of her consciousness consumed Raven for a moment. Like a first breath after being under water too long. She was going to have to act.

Raven stood at the window with Natalia and Aziz, she pushed a feeling of tranquillity across the immense hall, allowing it to surge towards the stage and the towering emblem of the United Nations. Shaking with the effort of it, she tried to hide any evidence of physical exertion. As the calm took hold, composure was regained and the summit's chair got to speak.

"There are three priorities for this, the final session of this summit. The first is to find some solutions for the countries affected by drought and famine, particularly in sub-Saharan Africa and India. The second is to find refuge for the displaced peoples in the worst affected countries. We cannot continue to build camps that have essentially become prisons for these peoples, they have a right to a full life. Finally, we need to agree to the next set of climate targets." The chairperson opened the floor for those to speak on the first issue.

First, the countries worst affected laid out their needs. Needs for aid, needs for refuge, needs for medicine, needs for technology, they came thick and fast. Some sub-Saharan African countries were quickly becoming fully Saharan with heatwaves and drought. India's unstable weather and flooding had disrupted agriculture and caused crops to fail en masse. In the Middle East the complaints were similar. Different languages spelling out the same difficulties, the same suffering. But all the countries were heard in the newly-established peace. Now, rather than shouting over those requesting assistance, the other countries held their tongues. They looked away, unwilling to shackle themselves to more costly aid when their own people were also struggling, but willing to sacrifice other nations at the altar of self-preservation.

Raven felt a familiar annoyance. What did they think was going to happen? That the havoc the climate and weather fluctuations were wreaking would reach their borders and suddenly cease? That if they battened down the hatches for long enough, they could emerge into a healed world? Could they not see that isolationism would surely doom them all to a lingering death, if they were not already fated such an end?

"I am sorry about the problems the other nations face, but we have already gifted as much as we can in light of our own difficulties," the Secretary of State for the United States said in a robotic and rehearsed way, her fitted suit sporting the stars and stripes on the collar and cuffs.

"As have we," the Foreign Secretary for England concurred, with several European Union countries nodding along in agreement with him. Scotland's prime minister was the only one with the humility to look abashed by their hesitance to assist others.

Raven pushed a strong feeling of empathy across the congregation. Sadly, it would have no effect on those attending virtually, they were beyond her influence. Once she had recovered, she focussed on the most prominent heads of state from the wealthiest countries. The USA, Europe's richer nations, China, Russia, their tables demarcated by their nations' flag, to each she sent a vision. A vision of their own families starving, thirsty, with no one coming to their rescue and nowhere to go as the world turned to dust around them. It was harsh, maybe, adding to their climbing anxiety, nonetheless, if they could not work together, it was the most likely eventual outcome. Perhaps not for this generation or the next but ultimately, should they fail to act unitedly.

"China is prepared to offer more aid and share our recent agricultural advances, including genetically-modified crops designed to withstand unstable climate conditions and a lack of pollinators," China's head of state went on describing the resources they were prepared to provide.

It was a turning point. Japan spoke next, then South Korea, then some of the African countries offered refuge for their neighbours' displaced citizens. A sort of competitive empathy arose now, as if a cooperative threshold had been reached. No country now wanted to look singularly unwilling to help their fellow humans, especially with the recordings of these summits being so widely distributed on social media. So slowly, reluctantly, they began to offer aid, refuge and other resources.

Raven breathed a sigh of relief and took a seat at the table in the middle of the small room. Disappointingly, there was only water on it.

On seeing Raven's disappointment Natalia offered, "Shall I have some food sent up?"

"Please," Raven nodded slumping in the chair.

"Tea and biscuits for the English, isn't it?" Aziz teased.

"To be fair, there's never a bad time for tea and biscuits."

"Much more temperature rise and maybe the English can start growing their own." Aziz laughed darkly.

"Maybe, but we are in New York, how about some bagels, or pretzels? No, pizza . . . ohh or doughnuts and cheesecake. This being the city of epic junk food and all." Raven smiled back, resting her head on her hands as she listened to the translator and pushed out the intrusive and often bizarre thoughts of others. The USA had not imposed the same limitations and taxes on sugar that the UK had and she was really craving it right now. Maybe she could smuggle some back home.

"I suspect we will end up with sandwiches, but after this, I will take you out for pizza myself tonight." Natalia called down for some food and then joined her at the table.

"Yes, thank you for whatever it is you do. It seems you have done, whatever that is, very well . . . again," Aziz added, still watching intently at the window.

"You mean stand here, hope things resolve themselves and rake in the free food, hotels and flights?" Raven deflected, putting her feet on a nearby chair.

"You are welcome to join us for pizza, Aziz," Natalia offered, visibly resisting the urge to tell Raven to get her feet off the furniture.

"I can't I'm afraid; I'm heading back home to Delhi tonight. My husband will be expecting me and our little girl hasn't been sleeping well so it wouldn't be fair for me to hang around . . . as tempting as it sounds. Have a slice for me, though." Aziz still stood at the window.

"Only the one?" Raven teased through her fatigue.

Aziz patted his small, round paunch which jutted out over slim legs and grinned. It was smaller than it had been. How bad were the food shortages in India?

The food arrived. It was sandwiches. Those small, dry ones that seemed to manifest spontaneously at conference-like events to everyone's eternal displeasure. Raven ate five of the triangular disappointments within a couple of minutes. Why did they cut the sandwiches up so small? Surely no one was ever fooled into thinking this was actually more food than one normal sandwich?

"That's strange," Natalia was staring at her phone, "the FBI has requested a meeting with us . . . as representatives of the security council . . . after the summit . . . to discuss a 'potentially important emerging situation'."

“Just what the world needs, another emerging situation,” Raven replied between unsatisfying bites.

III

Nero took a seat in a secluded booth in a nearby leisure hall he favoured. Favoured in this part of the city anyway. The civilised part. He hadn't frequented it in a while, but as he was still in his armour, he figured he shouldn't be caught in any establishments of disrepute. Theta would certainly dock his credits for that. Something he could ill afford given the swiftly escalating costs of getting the new recruitment technology in working order. His hidden accounts were feeling the strain. If the Oni couldn't scale the technology as promised, he really would be just a destitute, low-ranking soldier. He needed a drink.

Nero ordered a large meal and a glass of wine from the synth waiter who was one of the creepy, older generations whose design fell deep into the uncanny valley and failed to climb back out. The synth swiftly retrieved both from the dispenser. It felt like a long time since he had tasted food that wasn't the limited flavours of processed mush dealt out by the dispensers. He missed it. Or the idea of it. Scanning his wrist, the synth informed him as to the proportion of his assigned rations he had used and how much the wine had cost him.

Nero listened to the passable musicians who played on a small stage on the other side of the plushily decorated room and, slowly, he felt a little better. He hoped it was the food, but it was probably the wine. Luckily, the highly-condensed, synthesised wine had the same effect as the real thing, though it came about as close to fruit as he had had recently. A familiar synthetic aftertaste lingered in his mouth, which left much to be desired, but that became less of a concern if one consumed enough glasses. As the wretched drink made its way through his veins, his relief was palpable. Tensions ebbed from body and mind. It was nice to feel comfortable again.

A few people were dancing closely on the floor that had been made to sparkle like a clear night's sky, rare and beautiful. Vapours rose in swirls from some of the tables where inhalants were being consumed. Their smell hung in the air. Mingling with the music were the sounds of people conversing and gaming. Cheers, lamentations, laughter and debates punctuated the band's playing. There were a few people of note here, the relatives of lesser senators, the odd less talented actor and the like. Some he had met before and some he had known well before his court martial; though they clearly didn't wish that acknowledged. He sat alone and watched their revelry, but was acutely aware that he was drawing more sideways looks than usual, *probably the armour*, he concluded. Though it was not unusual to see Peacekeepers in their fatigues, his service status was more a matter of public record than most.

"You have some nerve coming back here! Some real nerve!" A voice rudely interrupted his reverie.

Nero looked up to see the custodian of the bar, a very red-headed woman with almost copper skin who he recalled was called Aplin, leaning over him.

"What did I do?" Nero asked, genuinely perplexed.

"You know what you did! Do you know how much the damage you caused cost?" Aplin looked like she might hit him, her cheeks slowly flushing the colour of her hair.

Years of dealing with the people to which she sold intoxicants had left Aplin with an air of intimidation, almost impossibly large for a person of her limited stature and posture, which conveyed that if she hit him, it would hurt; and she looked like she really wanted to hit him. Her fast breathing caused her chest to rise and fall quickly in her flatteringly draped clothing, he averted his eyes so as not to increase the odds of getting struck by her, or her security. He wasn't in the mood for more fighting.

"I honestly have no idea what you are talking about, Aplin. I haven't been here in a fair while now."

"That's because the last time you were here you got into a fight with some of my customers and broke, well several things, but most importantly a dispenser unit. Do you know how much those things cost to fix?"

"Are you sure it was me? What was the fight about?" Even as Nero tried to deny it, vague recollections were emerging in his mind. There was a reason he hadn't been back here in a while.

"No, it was some other lesser lord with lank black hair and proclivity for boozing and bizarre trickery. I don't know why you were fighting and I don't much care. I think they just called you some names."

"My hair isn't lank," Nero retorted and Aplin almost growled in return, pulling a stun gun from somewhere within the satin folds of her jumpsuit. "But okay, I take your point," Nero quickly continued. "How much will it cost me to keep sitting here?"

"Consciously, or because I have shot you and you can't do anything else?"

"The former by preference." Nero tried to look sorry and charming. "Come on Aplin, I was one of your most generous customers."

"Or at least most frequent." She stood up straight. "Four hundred credits."

"Come on Aplin, it can't have cost that much. How about two hundred?"

"Only if you want me to shoot you in lieu of the other two hundred."

Nero considered Aplin briefly. The twinkle in her eye every time she mentioned shooting him made him think it was not worth trying to barter with her. She had quite the attitude for someone whose family were still in prison after undergoing reprogramming for their involvement in The Sixth's rebellion. If his own societal demise hadn't occurred during the same troubles, she wouldn't dare speak to him in this manner.

"Very well, four hundred it is." Nero scanned his wrist on the payment pad held out to him. He hoped the Peace Corps still paid promptly or he was going to have to start using his secret accounts for day-to-day needs; a troublesome predicament.

"Welcome, back Lord Nero," Aplin smiled at him disarmingly. "Let me know if there is anything I can get for my 'most generous customer'." She winked at him.

"You are too kind. I just want a quiet night to enjoy some music." *I have definitely overpaid*, he thought.

"Make sure that it is a quiet night or I will extract my next compensation in blood as well as credits. Security will be watching you closely." Aplin tilted her head first towards the door, which was guarded by two large members of a particularly well-armoured species he wasn't well acquainted with, and had no desire to become more so, and then to the drone hatches in the ceiling with their attached surveillance.

"Understood. Any chance of some more wine now that we are friends again?" Nero lifted his empty glass.

"Of course."

"On the house?"

"Don't push it!" Aplin replied, that *I could happily shoot you* twinkle back in her almost golden eyes.

Aplin took his dirty glass and turned on her heel. Nero watched her walk away, ample hips swaying.

"Lank hair, indeed!" Nero grumbled to himself. More like charmingly dishevelled. He smoothed himself. Though a day in the heat of that awful planet probably hadn't helped him in that department.

Sipping his second glass of wine, this one made from some sort of blue fruit, Nero watched as dancing couples, groups and the occasional awkward single, slowly filled the dancefloor of the bar. The imbibed intoxicants, whether drunk or inhaled were clearly doing their job. Slowly, they edged nearer to one another, formal dances became informal and then intimate and then sometimes, salacious. Tempo and timbre shifted to almost encourage such closeness; the music seemed to demand it.

No one tried to join Nero in his booth, though he did notice that the occasional staring or pointing in his direction had continued. He fiddled with his communicator for as long as he could tolerate the irritating malfunctioning of the projected screens. Shame he couldn't use his other device; it, at least, functioned adequately, but for now he had to keep up the pretence of poverty and ensure his contraband off-grid communicators were well hidden from the domestic authorities.

A few messages flickered at him. Theta had sent the training schedule over; it was tiresomely well-organised. He didn't reply and, rather, used his uplink to his neuro-implants to scroll the latest news reports, rolling his eyes at the constant insistence that everything was fine. Were people really that easy to deceive, so easily misdirected onto hedonistic pastimes and time devouring nonsense? Nero sipped his wine and watched the dancers sway with various degrees of allure and elegance. Maybe he wasn't one to talk.

There were notifications of the new theatrical and musical performance openings, the latest holo-games, various tournaments for those so insecure they required prizes to validate their intellectual or physical prowess, and various leisure activities. Sadly, these official channels did not permit the advertisement of some of the more base and entertaining activities one could indulge themselves with, either in the crowded Fringe neighbourhoods clustered against the force field boundary on the outskirts of the city or, if you were feeling brave, the Badlands beyond.

Of the many notifications regarding upcoming performances, a retelling of the establishment of the first Karthian realm, Karthia Prime, was the most over-hyped. It would no doubt be long, boring and inaccurate. Likely closer to propaganda than ancient history. Further down his notices and communications was an invite from his cousin to attend said theatrical performance. His cousin being one of the few members of his family still prepared to be seen with him. Apparently, the seats were too sold out for them to sit together, but it would be on his cousin's credit and they could discuss the play over dinner afterwards. Well, he did need cover for tomorrow, this terrible play masquerading as entertainment would provide many hours of that. Not to mention, his cousin had excellent taste in dining establishments and, unlike him, had the budget to match his taste. Nero transmitted a quickly voiced message graciously accepting the invitation.

When he next looked up there was a woman standing in front of him. She was short for a Karthian female. Her teal hair and blueish skin with its gently swirled patterns marked her as partly Inaran. Interbreeding with the native species of their solar neighbour had created interesting, but not unattractive, morphological differences between the planet's peoples. In places, the swirled markings contrasted with sprawling, white, geometric scars. Interesting, most Inaran, particularly mixed-race ones, had long ago abandoned that spiritual practise. Perhaps, the scarred look was finding itself recycled into fashion. Sadly, his own scars had not been inflicted with such intricate consideration to aesthetics.

"Sorry to interrupt you," she said, almost overly politely. Her voice sounded younger than she looked. "I was wondering if you were Lord Nero Dyadicus."

"I am," he replied, intrigued. Though most people seemed to prefer the nickname 'Traitor' these days.

There was a pause as she sat down without invitation, carefully arranging her simple, well-fitting culottes with their robed front around her.

"I was wondering, whether it is true what they say about you?" She sat opposite him in the semi-circular booth and leant her head on her hand in a naive way. Long, falcate, white nails gently digging into her cheeks. On her left arm coils of thick copper wire seemed to emerge from her flesh and twist about her arm to her hand, where the metal then tracked along her fingers to the ends of two of her curved nails. Nero hadn't seen that particular kind of accessory before.

"And what do they say about me? Only decent and gracious things, I'm sure." Nero asked, leaning forward out of his previous recline to engage her.

"Well," she noticeably struggled for a flattering reply, "they say that you have . . . abilities. That you can do things other people can't?"

"Oh yes, and what things are these?" If she wanted a magic show, she was going to have to speak to him for a while, he decided.

"Illusions, tricks of the light and such."

"Like a gala performer, you mean?" he teased, but smiled at her to imply friendly jest. "Some sleight of hand and a few holotransmitters?"

"Kind of, yet more than that. They say you can make things appear to be real that are not really there at all, or make things change, or disappear, just because you wish it." Curiosity radiated from her, and unusually, she didn't seem wary or disgusted by him. Perhaps she was a tourist. Tourists, who often seemed to bring their every worldly possession except their brains, occasionally seemed to view him as one of the city's curios, rather than an unwanted tarnish on the realm's reputation. "Is it true?"

"I don't know, it sounds a little unlikely to me." Nero drank the last dregs of his wine and placed his glass on the table. "Tell you what, have a drink with me and I'll try my best to perform some magic for you. I take it you are old enough to drink?"

"Sounds fair," the woman replied, seeming to settle into her seat, "and yes, I'm two-hundred this year."

"Congratulations, on your second century." Nero tried to remember what it was like to be two hundred, it was a long time ago now. "What would you like? My treat to mark the successful surviving of two centuries."

She requested sweet wine so Nero signalled to Aplin and asked courteously for two more glasses of her finest dispensary wine. Aplin made a joke about it being a fine vintage, aged around five minutes if she dawdled. When she brought the wine, Aplin set it politely in front of each of them. She smiled in a friendly manner at Nero's companion and then turned away from her to Nero.

"That's your last one for tonight. If you order more, I will charge you twice as much and give you whatever water rations you have left," Aplin whispered as she passed him on her way back to her hosting duties.

"So, whose company do I have the pleasure of tonight?" Nero asked his still nameless companion.

"Nim," the Inaran replied, sipping tentatively at her wine.

Nero tried to look at the given marks on her arm which would at least tell him her parents' familial identity, but they were white against pale blue skin. In the dim light of the bar, he could not discern them.

"Tell me about yourself, Nim. Do you live in the city?"

"No, I'm just visiting."

"Business or pleasure?"

"A little of both, I hope." She raised her eyes to meet his.

Nero almost choked on his wine and then fell over his words. *Stylish*, he thought to himself sarcastically. "Well, you're in the right place," he said eventually. As he drew breath to continue asking about her, Nim interrupted.

"Why are you wearing armour?" she asked.

"I was on a mission with the Peacekeepers and it was late when we got back so I didn't have time to change."

"I thought you weren't in service anymore."

"So did I," he grumbled, then realising that tone wasn't going to play to his advantage added, "but, they desperately needed my assistance with some trouble on Kryto-3, so I was honour-bound to help them out."

"You must be brave to be part of the Peace Corps. I hear that is dangerous work, what with some of the new realms being so full of primitive planets. Are they really as uncivilised as is reported? Is that how you damaged your helmet?" Nim traced the dent in the helmet next to him. She had moved closer.

"Well . . ." Nero struggled to come up with an answer to what was actually quite a complex question. Yes, some of the species on planets recruited into the realms for resource exchange were often less developed than those within Karthia Prime and the older of the seven realms; eight now, thanks to his brother pushing their frontier across galaxies (and never letting them forget it). This was mostly because only those populations that were useful and easily indoctrinated into Karthian culture survived the early ages of the Karthian recruitment. Later populations were recruited with more technology and less brutality, or perhaps just different brutality, depending on your perspective. Biogenetic manipulation was never fully protective against the resurgence of violent instincts, but then again, if someone tried to impose similar arrangements on Karthia the resulting response would, no doubt, be one of extreme violence. Depending, of course, on the success of any bio-genetic modifications that were introduced. "Some of the planets are quite uncivilised and would seem primitive to us who live in the inner realms. And I am afraid that is old damage and not from today's lively mission."

"Oh, so what was the mission today?" She leant forward.

"Well, it is sensitive information, but if you vow to keep it a secret, I guess I could let you in on the mission I commanded today. Do you swear to keep what I tell you private or risk incurring the wrath of the Senate?" It wasn't sensitive information. Not that Theta had made him aware of anyway. Nero hoped this Nim woman wasn't of a mind to look at the interplanetary news reports which would all, of course, list Theta as the mission commander.

Nim made a little gesture indicating her lips were sealed and he began to regale her of the story of the battle; although he strategically left out the part where he was dragged out of bed by his sister like a misbehaving sub-centurion and spent the entire mission trying not to vomit and/or pass out from a hangover. Nim seemed surprisingly enthralled by the tale and kept edging her way closer to him on the curved, cushioned bench. He would have to wear his armour out more often.

"You're a hero!" she gasped as he finished his story.

"I wouldn't go that far," Nero said, pleased with her response.

"Can you really do those things?" Nim finished her wine, placing her glass carefully in front of her.

"Do you not believe me?" he said, his voice kept light to suggest mocking and not offence. "Do you think me a liar or a mad man?" Or both, often it was both.

"If it's true, I think you extraordinary."

"Well, yes that would literally be the case, if it were true, of course." Nero nodded towards the glass. "Would you like another?"

"Okay, sure. Why not?"

Nero gestured towards the glass and it appeared to fill with wine, this time a deep, blood red. Nim looked elated; that was gratifying. She lifted the glass to inspect how the liquid flowed, swirled and slicked the glass. When she put it to her lips and felt nothing, tasted nothing, Nero laughed.

"Unfortunately, I can't actually conjure wine from air. Otherwise, I could save myself a great many credits."

"An impressive illusion! How'd you do it?"

"You tell me?" Nero genuinely never had an answer to that question and everyone was always greatly dissatisfied by the answer—I just can.

"Do you have holoemitters hidden in your sleeves?" Nim asked, gently turning his hands to search his wrists, her nails sharp against the tender skin of his bruised knuckles.

"Nope."

"Embedded in your eyes?" Nim leant forward to study Nero's eyes carefully. He could smell her sweet, spiced perfume, different from the ones the women of the city usually wore.

"Wrong again, I'm afraid." As highly modified as he was, he had no need for such help in this case.

"Hmm. Maybe you are a mythical creature from some species' legends?" Nim smiled.

"Maybe." Nero smiled devilishly. "Instead of another drink. Would you like to dance?" Aplin was unlikely to serve him anything other than attitude anyway.

Nim nodded and Nero escorted her to the dance floor. They found a space easily amongst the rhythmically swaying bodies as the people parted quickly at Nero's approach. He held out his hands to take hers in a formal hold. Without hesitation, Nim took his hands keenly and quickly, the gap between them closed until she was pressed against him, chest to chest, his arm across the small of her back.

As they danced to the slow music, the crowded dance floor became an assault to their attempted closeness. People somewhere between tipsy and drunk constantly jostled them as they moved across the simulated starlight and, when they realised who they had jostled, moved away indiscreetly swiftly.

"Busy, isn't it!" Nim laughed, appearing not to notice the strange behaviour of their dancing companions.

"A little too busy," Nero glared at the dancers around him and, in their defence, they did have the good sense to move away. Fear, disgust and respect are sometimes so similar in the reactions they illicit.

"I wish we were alone," Nim tucked her head under Nero's chin.

"I agree, and we can be." Nero held her tightly, surprised that she seemed so at ease around him. An idea occurred to him. He probably shouldn't do it, he was still fatigued from earlier. Nero bent the light around him and suddenly they weren't on the dance floor anymore. Now they were dancing on the precipice of a cliff above a great ocean awash with surf. A large moon was bright in the sky and real stars shone, their light free to travel without the hindrance of cloud, haze, smog or the interference of competing illumination. As their feet moved, they disturbed plants alive with bioluminescence that glowed and faded to their rhythm.

"Where are we?" Nim gasped. "Where have you taken me?" She tensed and pulled away from him.

"Don't worry. We are still on the dance floor. Just, now, we have a nicer view." Nero tried to make holding the illusion seem effortless, but it was difficult.

"Where is everyone else?" Nim relaxed a little back into his arms.

"They are still here, unfortunately. They're probably wondering what is going on." Nero didn't pity the dancers now surrounded by strange pockets of distorted light. Anxious protests from the other patrons were starting to permeate the music.

"I will admit, this is impressive, Nero, and beautiful. How long can you do this for?"

"As long as you wish," he lied, "or until Aplin finds a way to stop the music." *And possibly shoots me, but definitely kicks us out of here*, he added in his head.

"You are quite the troublemaker, huh?" Nim shook her teal-haired head and grinned at him.

"I try my best." Nero spun her to the music. A reasonable dancer, he was making the most of his increasingly painful illusion. He felt more inebriated than his restricted number of drinks should have allowed. Perhaps it was the company. Several highly enjoyable minutes later the music abruptly cut out. "I think that is my cue to leave. Do you want to come with me?"

Nim nodded.

"Nero. Nero!" Aplin shouted, her voice full of rage. "Where are you? Stop this now!"

She was close. Too close for comfort.

"I'll shoot the git this time," Nero heard Aplin mutter to herself.

"I am going to drop this illusion now, but I will make it so that they can't see us. Ready to run?" Nero whispered into Nim's ear.

To his great surprise, she kissed him briefly before saying, "yes".

Nero rapidly retrieved his helmet from the booth and then they were running through the dark streets enclosed by tall, glistening towers of habitation and the brightly illuminated businesses and leisure houses below. Groups of passers-by startled at their passing, shocked by the sudden disembodied footsteps and fleeting laughter. Above them the field shimmered and cackled with lightning strikes in lieu of the starlight hidden by thick, churning storm clouds. Great booms of thunder were mostly dampened by the field, still something of the storm permeated, the controlled climate felt undefinably different during storms. Away from the reach of Aplin's security, they stopped, panting, by a wall opposite some transport pods.

Giggling at their mischief in between breaths, again, Nim kissed him and he returned the kiss passionately, pushing her up against the wall. He felt like a man of two hundred again, except with a pounding headache from overexerting himself. *Definitely worth the pain*, he thought as his hands gently explored the curve of her hips.

"Where shall we go now that we are on the run?" he asked casually.

"Oh, I don't know," Nim said, then, looking down, coyly added, "what's your place like?"

"Nice enough," Nero said gesturing to the transport pod. By the time she realised the lie, they would have arrived, perhaps politeness would make her stay. Living on the edge had many disadvantages, not least in the disruption of his now very-limited romantic life.

As the transport set off, he felt dizzy and a sudden lurch of vertigo caused him to sway in his seat and slump forward. Nim caught him before he fell.

"Are you okay?" she asked, pushing his hair tenderly away from his face.

"I guess I am more tired than I thought . . . from the . . . mission." At least that would make him sound brave and not drunk, though he wondered briefly if Aplin had spiked his wine in some sort of revenge, as he felt more than drunk and more than tired.

"Don't worry, I'll take care of you." Nim placed a delicate hand on his shoulder.

Nero felt appreciative of the affection, a rarity for him these past many years.

When they got to his home, a building of towering dilapidation, Nim didn't baulk at the location, instead she helped him to his quarters and kissed him again. Nero tried to kiss her back, but again vertigo disorientated and spun him. Focus blurring and balance failing, he stumbled towards the dispenser seeking medication. He didn't make it.

Nero heard Nim's voice distantly. He felt her lead him by the hand to his bed. For a moment he regained composure. He pulled her to him, kissing her deeply and pulling her shirt over her head, before he was again overwhelmed. Nim seemed to move erratically, her voice was quiet and vague, then everything faded to darkness before nothingness.

IV

Raven was exhausted, but pleased. The rest of the summit had been surprisingly productive. Deals for aid and refuge were struck, targets that would likely go unmet were agreed upon and the delegates mostly looked pretty impressed with their diplomatic prowess. It was amazing what a little bit of empathy and a few phantasmagorical visions could do to motivate people. Raven watched the hand shaking, head bowing, selfie taking and occasional embraces as people slowly said their farewells and flooded out of the cavernous assembly hall below. A glorious quietness descended. With the people gone so, too, was the constant pressure of their thoughts. Sighing, Raven felt suddenly lighter.

Beside her Natalia and Aziz also looked exhausted, but now glimmers of hope emanated from them where before there had been only the dark pull of dread. Hope was a start, but without hard work, cooperation and, at this point, a significant amount of dumb luck, hope wasn't going to do very much to stop the world from burning. She had always thought it strange that people said "save the planet". If people managed to wipe out every living thing on the planet, including themselves, the planet would still be here, spinning its way around the sun until the sun itself consumed it. Really it should be "save the humans".

"Are you coming, Raven?" Aziz asked, wrenching Raven from her morbid meanderings.

"Yes, sorry."

Raven grabbed her bag and followed Natalia and Aziz through many corridors to the meeting chamber of the Security Council with its grand mural. Almost overbearing, even in the large room, the mural was reminiscent of a tapestry and depicted, in no subtle way, the progress of mankind towards peace, equality and freedom which was probably why it needed to be so large, lest they forget and default to mankind's preferred pastimes of war, division and control. Sitting at the circular seating area were some very formal military types; the table far too large for so few. They took to their feet as Natalia and her cohort entered.

Upon entering the chamber, Raven smelt coffee and felt a deep longing, coming from her very bones, for the energy it could provide. Steam rose from a cafetiere on a nearby side table; it called to her and she answered willingly. As she lifted the cafetiere, she cursed the tininess of the provided cups. Why always so damn small?! She pulled her travel mug from her bag and all but emptied the stale tar posing as coffee into it. There were, however, biscuits. She ate one quickly, then another, before she caught Natalia's eye and saw her disapprovingly raised eyebrow. As Natalia and Aziz made their formal introductions with the representatives of the US military and FBI, Raven appeared beside them, cradling her coffee and trying to chew as quietly as possible. Unfortunately, the biscuits were not as stale as the coffee and they crunched. Loudly.

"Raven Solveig, this is General Carson of the US Air Force and Special Agent Franklin of the FBI," Natalia introduced her. It seemed the others present were purely for security or assistance. Their roles were to loom or scribe; they required no introduction.

"Nice to meet you," Raven said as eruditely as possible with crumbs still stubbornly clinging to her tongue.

"And you, Raven. What is your role here at the UN?" said General Carson, his uniform surprisingly unwrinkled from its day's wear.

"I'm . . ." Raven began hesitantly.

"Ms Solveig is my and Mr Khatri's assistant," Natalia interjected quickly.

"Very good, shall we get down to business?"

Although he showed no outer signs of anxiety, tension seeped liberally from General Carson. A feeling mirrored by Special Agent Franklin. Raven steeled herself against their fear as it crept towards her.

Aziz gestured for all to be seated at the highly-polished table.

"How can we help you today?" Aziz asked in an unassuming tone, ever the skilled diplomat.

"We'll keep this short and to the facts, but I want to stress that this is off the record." Special Agent Franklin was curt and had surprising presence for a woman of short stature. After she had received the expected acquiescence as to the classified nature of the meeting, she continued. "There's been a situation that we were hoping you might be able to shed some light on."

"Of course, if we can," Natalia nodded, clearly intrigued.

"Recently around two thousand people went missing from West, Texas." Special Agent Franklin paused, seemingly unsure as to how to continue.

"Well, okay, west Texas is a big place. Is that many more than usual?" Natalie asked.

"Sorry, Ms Yahontov, but you miss understand me. Not west Texas. West, Texas. A small town with a population of just over two thousand people." Special Agent Franklin subtly smoothed neatly cornrowed hair, clearly uncomfortable.

"Have they been driven out? That'd be right in the middle of Death Alley, wouldn't it?" Aziz offered using the new slang for the area of mid America plagued by both drought and destructive storms.

"That'd be a logical assumption, however, all the town's residents went missing in one night. For the last ten days, since the 19th of April, we have had the town under strict lockdown, under the guise of an outbreak of SARS-52, whilst we investigate. None of the residents have been seen or heard from since." Special Agent Franklin seemed relieved to have gotten to the end of her strange tale.

"That's . . . truly bizarre." Natalia said honestly, glancing at Raven who returned her questioning look in kind. "Is there anyone left in the town? Did anyone witness anything?"

"The few viable witnesses we have found seem to have little useful information, although they are being cooperative. Most of those left behind are too young, infirm or disabled to offer much assistance in the investigation."

"Too young?" Aziz asked, concern now overriding the faint high of hope Raven previously sensed.

"Babies and toddlers left in cribs." Franklin visibly clenched her teeth at the memory.

There was a lengthy pause. What could cause parents to leave their babies abandoned in their cribs?

Franklin Continued, "Luckily, only one required medical attention. After we realised, we hastened our door-to-door search and got the remaining children and adults into a makeshift refuge at the old folk's home."

"Is there any sign of natural disasters?" Aziz asked.

"No. There was no unusual seismic activity, no sinkholes, no weather events and no sign of illness or death. It's like everyone just got up and left without warning or were kidnapped, maybe, but there are no signs of a struggle anywhere. Faucets and showers were even left running in some instances. It's as if everyone just walked off into the night on a whim." Special Agent Franklin straightened her suit and sipped her glass of water. "We needed to ask whether you know of anything similar happening in any other country?"

"Not to my knowledge," replied Aziz. "What about yours?" He looked to Natalia.

"No, nothing like that. People are being displaced by the climate shifts and, sometimes, conflict, lots are going missing en route but they don't tend to just disappear en masse without explanation from relatively stable areas . . . that area is notorious for tornadoes, though, some really nasty ones have devastated towns in that region."

Special Agent Franklin was shaking her head. "There was no recent destruction of property and no weather warnings were recorded. Tornadoes are not selective, there would've been evidence left behind."

Natasha glanced at Raven who shrugged in return. This was certainly a novel sort of disaster and that was worrying, not many things were novel for her at this point.

"Was there any sign of weapons use? Or of conflict?" Aziz asked, pensively scratching at grey-peppered stubble.

"None, no shell casings, no gun powder, no blood and no close contact weapons were observed," Special Agent Franklin answered curtly, then continued, "and it was a heavily armed community. You know what the Texans are like, determined to hang onto their guns, despite the 2048-Gun Control Act. The residents could have mounted their own military defence with the amount of illegal weaponry we found. Two people were found dead, but post-mortem showed no evidence of inflicted injury."

"Huh, and what about the local CCTV and security cameras? What do they show?" Natalia queried, frowning more with each answer.

"Well, this is one of the stranger things about this case, all the electronics in the vicinity have been disabled, including all recording devices. Our techs have managed to restore the transformers and the grid is now functional, but there is no CCTV evidence of that time period. Our best guess is that the area was hit with an EMP. That's how we suspect the two people died. One man's pacemaker ceased working and another elderly lady's breathing apparatus was disrupted."

"EMP?" Natalia interjected.

"Electromagnetic pulse." Franklin answered.

"And what would cause that?"

"We honestly have no idea, but we know the disruption wasn't the work of a solar flare as no such activity was detected around that time," Franklin answered.

"We're in a period of solar minimum so such a flare would be unlikely," Carson added.

Special Agent Franklin gave a strange expression between a grimace and a smirk and shook her head. "I am aware that all of this sounds so strange. Like one of those conspiracy theories that goes around the net."

"It certainly is unusual," Natalia agreed. "I'll make some enquiries with the rest of the security council, under the radar of course, to see if there have been any similar occurrences in other countries. Some are obviously less forthcoming with security information than others. Is there anything else you can tell us about it? Did anything turn up on the social sites or local news media?"

"Nothing so far, but obviously the case is open and investigation ongoing . . ." the special agent paused.

Raven wondered if that was truly all the agent knew. Gently she relaxed her walls, just a little and focused on the FBI agent. There was no sense of untruthfulness or of lies by omission. No ulterior motives. But there was fear, much fear. Images of empty streets, hysterical witnesses, frantic family members being placated and silenced, a desolate field with patches of burnt earth, plagued the forefront of Franklin's mind. A tightness lingered in the agent's chest and a dryness tormented her mouth, though she sipped constantly at the glass of water in front of her. Raven felt that tightness grip her as the agent's memories surged towards her, still fresh and dripping with vivid emotion. She wrenched herself apart from Special Agent Franklin and slammed up her walls. Her sudden, heavy breathing causing Natalia and Aziz to give her puzzled looks.

Unaware of the intrusion upon her, Special Agent Franklin continued, "the General has a coincidental occurrence which may or may not be linked." Special Agent Franklin nodded eagerly to General Carson, seemingly keen to be relieved of messenger duty.

"Yes, well, as Special Agent Franklin has stated, we don't know whether these two events are linked, but on the night of the 19th of April, a near miss was recorded by an interstate flight in the area. When the incident was investigated, the black box of the plane confirmed the pilot's observation and does record another sizable airborne object on the radar at that time. However, no other private or commercial flight plans were planned nor found to intersect that flight. It's not ours either, all our birds were grounded at that time." General Carson who had been very formal during his report suddenly gave a peculiar smile. "So, there you have it. We bring you news of strange disappearances and UFOs; quite unbelievable, but also quite true. Only the higher-ups have been informed so please consider the information classified."

"Well, I guess at least it makes a change to the usual type of bad news." Aziz mimicked the General's tone.

"I have to stress again that this is strictly off the record. But, should you hear of anything similar occurring in other countries, we'd appreciate being informed." Special Agent Franklin rose and went to shake hands with Natalia and Aziz.

"Of course, and, likewise, we'd appreciate being kept informed regarding any developments in the case." Natalia firmly shook the Agent's hand and then the General's.

Raven didn't like the feeling the preceding conversation had left in the pit of her stomach and crawling over her skin. In her long life, she had never known anything like this. Sure, there were conspiracy theories and supernatural legends abound, they lurked in the depths of the internet now, as they had in whispers of dark tavern corners before that, and were exploited by tourist spots, fuelled by the great stories they made, but they didn't materialise like you had stepped into an episode of freaking X-files. They needed to know more. *We need to talk to the witnesses;* Raven pushed the thought at Natalia.

"I know this is highly unusual, but is there any way we could talk to the witnesses of that night? The more information we have the more we can cross reference with any events reported in other countries," Natalia asked in response.

"I'm not sure that will be possible," Special Agent Franklin seemed unsure, "as you can imagine, the situation is sensitive."

"I understand completely, but it would help our own enquiries to have as much information as possible."

Raven could feel palpable resistance from the FBI agent. She didn't like doing this much manipulation, but they needed more information, so she pushed a feeling of agreeableness and gratitude towards Franklin and Carson.

"It'd be sensible to share information across organisations for the sake of the possible victims."

"Agreed," concurred General Carson.

"We're due to re-interview the key witnesses over the coming days, maybe you could observe the interviews, subject to authorisation and the signing of non-disclosure contracts of course." Special Agent Franklin seemed almost relieved by her acceptance of the request.

"Of course, and thank you, that would be appreciated. Just let us know the time and location and we will travel out."

"Until then. Thank you for your time." Franklin turned on her heel, her footsteps echoing as her besuited colleagues fell in behind her.

"Where can an old man get a good drink in this city?" General Carson asked in a conversational tone, his southern drawl more pronounced now that the meeting was over.

"That depends what you like. What's your tipple?" Aziz responded.

"I am a man of simple tastes—good beer, good food and music quiet enough that you can hear yourself think." He loosened his tie a little as he spoke.

"I know just the place!" Aziz described a bar in the city not too far from the headquarters.

"Thank you. Sorry again to bring you such strange tidings."

The general shook their hands and wished them farewell. When he shook Raven's, she asked. "What do you think caused the near miss?" It was only a little more than a question.

"I've no idea, Miss. Sorry, we aren't supposed to say Miss anymore. I have no idea, Ms Solveig. For now, it'll be classified as a UFO; I'll be sure to let you know if that changes. In my experience, it'll probably end up being a private aircraft or a drone. That's the usual outcome of these things."

"Thank you, General."

"You're most welcome." General Carson seemed a good two inches shorter than he had when he arrived and was clearly relieved the meeting was over. Raven expected he would be in that bar very shortly.

Once the general had left, there was silence and then Raven's stomach growled loudly causing Aziz to laugh and Natalia to roll her eyes. At least it broke the tension.

"Pizza time, then," Natalia teased. "Sure you won't join us, Aziz?"

"No, unfortunately you will have to eat pizza and play detective without me as I have a political engagement in New Delhi, not to mention a husband and daughter, that can't wait. Let's hope some of that promised aid materialises now. India really needs it." His tone changed as he added, "please keep me updated, though, this is all rather unsettling."

Raven met Natalia in the foyer of the towering glass obelisk that was the Millennium Hilton. While Raven had ditched her bags, splashed some water on her face and grabbed a jumper to fend off the night's chill, Natalia had changed into a stylish ensemble befitting New York and refreshed her makeup.

"Determined to make me look like a dirtbag aren't you."

"Don't be ridiculous. Also seriously, dirtbag, are you a 1970's cop?" Natalia smoothed her well-groomed head and perfectly tailored pant suit with crisp creases which had defied the crush of the suitcase. "You had time to change if you wanted to, you lagga head." She added playfully.

"I was prioritising the food," Raven snapped though she didn't mean to.

"Well then, let's get moving before you get any hangrier."

"I'm not hangry!" Raven objected, but she was, very.

"No need to vex yourself."

One of the few women who could look Raven in the eye, even in her finery and heels, Natalia had the air of someone trained in physical combat and military discipline; not someone to snap at when you hadn't eaten.

"Sorry," Raven grumbled. "It's been a long day."

"It has at that. Come on, hangry girl, we'll get some New York slices down you and you'll be feeling better in no time."

Natalia took Raven's arm and led her down New York's straight streets, both wide and narrow. When you lived in England, straight roads seemed almost contrary to nature. The city still bustled with people. Though the crush was less than it had been in previous decades, if anything, the claustrophobia was worse than ever. There were fewer minds, but they seethed with untamed emotion, vivid desires and busy thoughts. Raven held her walls tight against the incessant cognisant waves.

They arrived at the pizzeria after walking a few blocks, it was a small place called Nico's. A dark haired, slightly-built host in a traditionally-cut shirt, open at the stiff-banded collar, showed them to their booth and a similarly dressed waiter took their drinks order. He looked very disappointed that, after gushing over the wine list, Raven ordered beer. Natalia took mercy on him and ordered wine. This place was clearly going for old world charm. Not an electronic menu or automated delivery system in sight; it might even have a human chef manning the oven. The only technological addition to the dining experience she assigned any worth was the ability to order your food in advance so that it was ready for when you arrived at the restaurant.

Smells of baking dough and melting cheese filled the air as they took their seats on worn but comfortable chairs at a small table towards the back of the busy restaurant. Raven ordered an extra-large pizza and it didn't disappoint. It took up over half of the table. She did like the American propensity for gastronomic enormity. Barely tasting the first slice in her rush to sate her hunger, the second was given time to be appreciated and was delicious. Amazing what they could do with some soy cheese and a few chunks of lab-cultured meat. Natalia ordered a much more sensibly sized pizza.

They made small talk as they ate. Well, Natalia made small talk and Raven chewed making appropriate, mmhmm, noises in the pauses, pitched in line with the fluctuating tone of the conversation. Eventually, Raven conceded that the pizza had defeated her. It had been a worthy adversary. She sat back from the table and wondered if she could get away with unbuttoning her jeans. Probably not.

No one was waiting to be seated so they switched from eating to drinking. Soon, glasses and bottles convened upon the table. Slowly, the hum of conversations and of minds around them lessened as people finished their meals and left. Raven noticed that Natalia was drinking more than her usual reserved amounts.

"Shall we get another?" Natalia asked as the last few drops of wine caused slick, round ripples to move across her glass as they fell from the bottle. She knocked the glass a little as she withdrew the bottle.

"Maybe we should leave it at these for tonight. I don't want to have to carry you back to the hotel."

"Maybe you're right." Natalia sighed deeply, her usually taut posture was slumped and heavy.

"Is everything alright?"

"Everything is going to hell in a handbasket, more and more lives being lost, more and more disasters, countries all but refusing to work together. I mean . . . I mean, is it all over? Are our efforts in vain? What do you think? Are we just screwed?" Natalia was slurring badly.

"I hope not, but I don't know for sure. I wish I could reassure you more than that. At least you are doing everything you can to change things and re-establish some stability. It's not like you to let these things drive you to drink. Are you okay?" Raven asked sincerely.

"It's these summits, they take it out of me."

"I can sympathise with that!"

"Don't you think that people could have done something years ago? Why didn't people raise the alarm more . . . do more?"

"Many did, but it is difficult to get people to make difficult and expensive decisions in response to a future threat that may not come to pass. Also, most people have little power in these things and the people who do are often the least inclined to act . . . in any meaningful way anyway." This night was a depressing turn.

"When I was a little girl, just after the turn of the century, I remember the threats were there but they were vague and distant. It all seemed like it would be someone else's problem."

"I remember and I guess, in a way, the worst of it will be." But still her problem most likely.

"I feel sorry for my children. Also, how'd you remember the turn of the century? You're what . . . early, maybe mid-thirties? I can't recall your file right now."

Raven shrugged. Her file? That was a worrying slip from Natalia, her involvement with them was supposed to be strictly incognito.

"We have known each other, what, well over a decade at this point and you haven't aged a day."

Natalia was straying into territory usually deliberately avoided, as she was instructed to do so by her predecessor. "Why, thank you, just fresh air and skincare," Raven said breezily.

"Mmhmm, my Daddy would have said you were practicing some dark Obeah." Natalia always sounded a little more Jamaican and a little less Russian when she talked about her father.

"You think I am bathing in the blood of virgins or some such witchcraft?" Raven laughed, pushing the bubbles of the cheap beer up her nose uncomfortably.

"No, of course not. But I know there are a great many things you don't tell me. It's a shame that you can't trust me after all this time."

"I trust you, Natalia, and I haven't lied to you, but it is safer for both of us if there are certain things you and Aziz don't know. That's why there are terms under which I work with you and your predecessors as a mediator, when needed. One of those terms was that there was to be no 'file', physical or otherwise."

"Sorry you're right. I shouldn't push you. You are my friend as well as my colleague."

"I feel the same." Raven smiled gently and shifted her weight to ease the pressure on her stomach.

"And don't worry, there's no official file."

"Just an unofficial one then?"

"Don't worry," Natalia extended the words in her tipsiness, "it's just the bare bones passed to me from Lionel before he left. Contact details and the like."

"Do you keep files on all your friends?"

"Some, it's the nature of the friends you have to keep as a diplomat." Natalia giggled drunkenly. Raven didn't often hear her giggle, she couldn't help but smile in return, it was infectious, though the jest was likely sincere. Raven was fond of Natalia; it was a shame she would only be around another twenty or so years. "Especially the eni—anigm . . . enigmas—hic . . . strange ones."

"Wow . . . strange . . . thanks!" Raven feigned hurt.

"Sorry, I didn't mean that. Forgive me, I have been doom drinking" Natalia straightened herself, seemingly trying to will herself sober.

"It's okay. Anyway, a lot of what you suspect about me is not that far off. Voodoo practices aside."

"How would you know?" Natalia's saturation had made her less sharp than normal.

"Well, if what you suspect is true, is indeed true, then I would know what you suspect, wouldn't I?" The beer made that sentence heavy on Raven's tongue.

"You are talking in riddles. Also, my suspicions are all impossibible." Natalia tripped over her words.

"Agreed, impossibible." Raven grinned at her. "But, when all other possi-bibl-lities are eliminated, the remaining must be true, no?!"

"Stop playing with me, girl." Natalia giggled again.

"On the other hand, maybe I'm a Loki level trickster."

The waiter, whose desire for them to leave so that he could close up was now a constant dull roar in Raven's awareness, approached the table.

"Can I get you anything else?" He smiled, but his eyes flicked unsubtly from the glassware on the table, to the neon clock and then to the doors.

"No, thank you. But, could I please have our meal on the house?" Raven pushed a feeling of this being the best idea the waiter had ever heard towards him. Raven knew she shouldn't do this, but the beer had her all squiffy and it's not like any witnesses remained in the now empty pizzeria.

"Of course!" The waiter answered enthusiastically.

Natalia paused, a little shocked for a moment, then whispered behind a hand, "He probably just fancies you."

"Would you mind if I also have your watch?"

From beneath his shirt cuff, the waiter removed a surprisingly expensive, top-of-the-line skin projection watch.

"Maybe he fancies you a lot." She whispered again.

Raven rolled her eyes and skimmed the surface of the waiter's thoughts. "And how's your boyfriend? Mark, is it? Recovering from that cold, I hope," Raven asked.

"He is feeling much better, thanks for asking." The waiter smiled as if this were a normal conversation.

Raven placed the watch back in the waiter's hand and asked for the bill.

"Maybe, not so impossible." Natalia looked a little shaken and Raven's full stomach lurched with an old anxiety. Perhaps she shouldn't trust Natalia as she did, as she hadn't trusted anyone since Connie, all those years ago. Had the memories of why she didn't trust people become too faint? Should she remove the memory of the last few moments? Natalia gathered her things to leave.

"Am I still your friend?" Raven asked regretfully. Why did regret so often follow beer?

"Yes, of course." Natalia squeezed Raven's hands in a reassuring, motherly way. "But stay out of my head." She added.

"Trust me, it is more comfortable for both of us that way." Feeling a little hypocritical, Raven opened herself to Natalia more fully. She had to be sure she was safe. Emotions flooded in. Yes, there was nervousness there, but also a deeper level of love than she had expected. Suddenly, it wasn't just the beer that was warming her insides. Raven resisted the urge to hug Natalia, but felt a goofy smile spread across her face.

"What did you think of all that today?" Natalia changed the subject as she scanned her chip at the pay station.

"I think it is very worrying!" Raven replied as they left, Natalia leaning on her a little as they walked. The waiter's palpable relief followed them into the night.

V

Nero came back to awareness gradually, finding himself on his back, his legs dangling over the edge of his bed, still fully dressed in his armour. After a while, once the world had recombobulated, he sat up slowly. Everything ached, but his wrist hurt badly. He didn't remember hurting his wrist. Then again, he didn't remember much at all. And these post-revelry injuries were not so rare—he looked at his still faintly bruised knuckles. Nero tried to recall what had happened the night before, but it was no use; his head was filled with a dense fog that did not yield to probing. Cradling his head in his hands, he tried to reassemble his fractured consciousness, though succeeded only in becoming aware of just how ripely he smelt.

Peeling off his armour and throwing it into the laundry chute for the building's dry-cleaning synth to deal with, he readied to do battle with the building's draconian concierge system. Sadly, his requests for more than the light misting of water that hissed from the wash booth's jets fell on deaf coding and he succeeded only in making his headache worse.

"You couldn't clean a Inaran baby with these water rations," Nero grumbled as he scrubbed the grime and stench of yesterday's unfortunate events off him, then wiped the soap from his skin with barely-damp cloths. Working only with his uninjured left arm, the process took a long time; still a slick residue of soap lingered, as did his bad mood.

Breakfast was water and pills from his glitching dispenser, as it had been all too often recently. At least there was no training today.

Outside his window the city was its usual dense and heaving self. For a while, he drowsily watched people going about their business below. Some time passed and he felt somewhat better, so the dispenser provided him with some plain, coarse fare that tasted like sweetened field rations. The original food, that had been processed into firm, uniform rectangles, was unidentifiable. Seemed fitting that on a soldier's wage, he should eat soldier's fare. It would be less than the allowance the Senate had granted him since being court martialled; a reduction he could little afford with his side project swiftly emptying his hidden accounts.

Reclining by the windows in the only chair that remained somewhat plush, he ate awkwardly with his left hand as his right still ached terribly. Looking beyond the towering, dilapidated buildings of his fringe neighbourhood, he saw a storm approaching on the horizon. It looked to be a bad one; already the winds were battering the force field over the city and the dust being launched into the sky darkened the already murky crimson of the limited sunlight that could penetrate the permaclouds. Nero hoped his ship would weather the storm without incidence. Keeping the old cargo hauler maintained in the Badlands was already costing him more than he would like, but given that he was supposed to be stripped of all his assets post-court martial, it wasn't as if he could dock at one of the official ports. Besides, state-regulated maintenance of the ship's synthetic intelligence and the regular resets they required would ruin what had become one of his more useful allies.

Nero's memory of the previous night persisted in being vague and fluid. It was alarming. He looked at his communicator to see if he could fill in some of the missing time. First, he came across the message from his cousin, causing him to panickily check the time: it was only 13:24, late morning, he had time. The reading of the invite also reminded him of his other afternoon plans. Looking back at the dark storm that swirled and flashed in the distance, casting deep shadows on the earth and megalithic rock structures beneath it, Nero sighed—well that will be a fun trip.

Relaxing into his chair, he saw little else in the messages to indicate what he had been up to. He looked at his location on the tracker which logged his biodata's location (provided courtesy of the chip set deep into the bone of his right forearm). Aplin's Place. Things started to coalesce a little. Nero remembered sitting down in a booth and watching the dancers. He remembered Aplin threatening him and paying her far too much to fix that old dispenser of hers. Most vividly, he recalled the sway of her walk.

For a while, Nero couldn't recollect anything else. Past Aplin's swagger was an impenetrable wall of nothing. Frustrated, he got himself dressed into appropriate theatre-going attire; black trousers, old but well-tailored and a fitted top with panels of a material whose colour shifted fluidly from black to green and blue and back again. A flattering ensemble, it was sadly far from current fashion. The green complimented his eyes in a satisfying way, but it was the blue that was catching his attention today. Blue . . . why blue? Then, abruptly, the face of a young woman appeared in his mind, a pretty face with a pale blue complexion, sprawling white geometric scars and striking, bluntly-cut teal hair. Nero concentrated on that face, trying to recall their conversation—instead he remembered their dancing. Her pressed against him. Him trying hard to impress her with his light bending. Embarrassingly hard, he admitted to himself, but then, what choice did he have?

What then? Nero thought agitatedly. What then? For a while there was nothing other than dancing in starlight, he didn't mind that memory.

When it came, the memory of the kissing was better. They were pressed against a wall, ignoring all decorum, then his world was spinning, they were in his room . . . there was nothing more.

"Room, what time did my guest leave last night?" he asked the concierge.

"I have no record of anyone other than yourself entering or exiting your quarters last night." the room replied.

"Curious. Are you certain?" It was a pointless question.

"As stated, there is no record of anyone entering this section of the building except yourself." Though impossible for a synthetic intelligence reset as often as the government's systems were, Nero could swear the answer was tinged with impatience.

Stranger and stranger, the blue woman couldn't have been in his room, the building would have registered her biodata chip. Unless she didn't have one, but you weren't likely to get through interplanetary immigration without one. She could have used a bionic skin mask, they were difficult to get hold of, but, as he well knew, not impossible. Though usually they augmented the chip's signal into a new identity rather than erasing it altogether.

He sighed. Of course, the most obvious explanation was that that part of his memory was wishful thinking. The blue woman must have left at some point before he returned home. Maybe she didn't fancy braving an edge neighbourhood. He didn't blame her. You might want to go home with the disgraced, freak son of the Dyadicus line, if you fancied a walk on the wild side or possibly to make yourself seem more interesting at a certain kind of party, but sooner or later it was going to seem like a bad idea. He guessed this time, it was sooner.

Given the state of him, he may have passed out on her. That would definitely constitute a mood killer. Although, from what he remembered of his conversation with Aplin, she wasn't inclined to serve him much of any intoxicant.

Perhaps, he had indulged in a bad batch of Expanse again. That certainly had a comedown with a kick.

It didn't make sense. None of what he remembered explained why his arm hurt so badly. Surely, they couldn't have fought.

Briefly, he contemplated asking Aplin if she had seen him with this woman he remembered, but, limited as they were, his memories of the previous night suggested that he had probably run out his hospitality at Aplin's and he definitely didn't want to be paying her any more credits for the privilege of knowing.

There were no surveillance drones in this building, not working ones anyway, so he tried to put the matter aside and concentrated instead on his plans for the day. No point in dwelling on one strange night, in a galaxy of many strange nights.

There was still some time to burn before Nero needed to leave for the theatre. He browsed lazily through his communicator. In addition to the usual holoscreen flickering, now the uplink to his implants seemed to be failing, forcing him to use gestures to control the device as he looked through his messages and the latest news reports. Theta messaged him checking that he had received the training schedule and was going to show up promptly tomorrow. He didn't reply.

The news provided through the Senate approved channels was so inaccurate as to be pointless and seeing yet another article about his brother's successful establishment of a realm across the void was the last straw—weren't people bored of this story by now? He retrieved his other communicator from its carefully chosen concealment within the wall behind the bed. Nero instead scanned reports from sources that were not sanctioned, but were usually much more accurate.

These deep-cover quantum entanglements provided news from planets too far for other forms of communication and where transmitting through gates was impossible or foolhardy. These dark tangle information nodes were highly encrypted, being found with any trace of them on your communication devices warranted a stay at the Senate's pleasure at the mercy of Peacekeepers not deemed competent enough for interplanetary service.

During his long stay in Karthia's largest prison, he had found that what the Peacekeepers assigned to domestic duty lacked in competence, they made up for with enthusiastic cruelty. Perhaps if he had been assigned his Peacekeeper duties in the Badlands far beyond the comfort of the forcefield, he too would assuage his bitterness with cruelty. Luckily, the circumstances of his court martial meant that he had been protected from the worst of it.

Once accessed, the dark tangles told of ongoing troubles on several fringe planets in the outer realms, who were opposing the export of resources in the quantities demanded by the dead and dying planets of the inner realms. Troubles that explained the ever-tightening rations. Sadly, he would likely be visiting those dominions soon in his new capacity as low-ranking cannon fodder, if diplomacy with the devolved guardian governments failed. It was not unusual for Guardians to be replaced or conveniently found dead. There were always ambitious politicians keen to take up vacant guardianships; politicians like his brother. As an operative, such a removal had once been his task. He had failed.

Nero had almost finished his perusing of the dark tangles when he saw a name that took his breath away. Khali Quoric. There were rumours of the Sixth Realm's guardian, Guardian Khali Quoric, stockpiling resources and gathering military strength well beyond the Peacekeepers stationed within the system. Quoric denied any such insubordination, of course, but anxiety gripped Nero as he considered that he could be marched through a gate back to Quoric's dominion. After failing his last mission there, she had barely delivered him back to Karthia Prime alive.

Breath thundered in and out of him, shuddering and uncontrolled. Suddenly, each of his carefully regenerated scars felt tight and new, the pain of their creation still vivid in his memory though decades had passed. Dispensing a large drink of the rough liquor his rations and income would allow, he swallowed the small measure whole and then demanded another. And another. The machine refused the fourth request. Throwing the dispenser's glass back at it was unsatisfying. It bounced off the machine's dented shell and thudded to the floor unharmed. As the machine informed him that his behaviour had been reported to the building's concierge system, he swore ripely.

To distract him from the tightness in his chest, he returned to watching advertisements for the latest entertainment fads to grace Sarlequa and read the vacuous news of the main channels. There was little of interest, false reasons were given for the increased ration restrictions, oh and a potentially damaging storm was bearing down on the Karthian capital city, Sarlequa, but any idiot with a window could tell you that.

After growing bored of reading and listening to reports, Nero decided to walk some of the long way to the theatre. Into the deep pockets of his long black coat, he placed a few extra items that would be necessary later: his respirator (the one that was not Senate sanctioned and, therefore, probably not tracked), his biodata skin mask and his contraband communicator. Just in case, he also took his thinnest phaser from behind the bed and slid it into the hidden holster within his tailoring.

Nero walked slowly along the bustling streets. Above him, he could just about see between the towering buildings of various geometries. The edge of the storm had now reached the city and the city's force field crackled as dust and debris was hurled upon it. Small surges in the force field mirrored the lightning, as the shield powered up to resist the storm's advance and protect the vast, dense city from the constantly shifting and always inclement weather of a dead planet that had long ago tipped beyond habitability.

At least the terraforming efforts were at last paying dividends and the Badlands weren't quite as bad as when he was a child. Beyond the city things now grew occasionally, hardy things that were utterly inedible, but were significantly more pleasant to look upon than mostly barren earth under swirling clouds. Air previously only braved by the Illion could now be tolerated without a respirator . . . for a while. A while that was significantly longer for the multigenerational inhabitants of the Badlands, than for city dwellers like him.

Near his quarters people mostly ignored him. Here he was an accepted blight on the decaying fringe neighbourhood. Those that hadn't accepted him had learnt the hard way that, whatever their motivation, confronting him was a bad idea. Either way, he was left to walk in peace. Further towards the arts district, people began to be less subtle with their scandalised responses at his presence. It had been over thirty years since he had been formally, and very publicly, disavowed. People should have gotten over it by now! The peoples of

Sarlequa clearly needed even more entertainment to occupy their gossip-mongering minds. Still, when he walked the streets, whispers of "traitor" followed him.

When he was first released, he would bend the light around him so that he appeared as another, or not at all, but now they could all go dance in the acid rains for all he cared. Nero kept his head up, he walked on. After several more half-overheard insults, Nero questioned why he had walked. He hailed a transportation pod waiting at a siding.

As he alighted from the pod, Nero could see a crowd milling around the large arched entrance to the city's second biggest theatre. Nero didn't care for the scenes from famous plays that constantly played across its surface, nor for the holograms that appeared amongst the gathered patrons, spouting soliloquies or advertising upcoming events. It seemed overdone. Then again, maybe he was just in an irritable mood, everyone else seemed to be enjoying it.

On the slope to the entrance stood his cousin, Veyga, wearing a fabulously tailored suit that was right on trend. He was talking to a couple of quite stunning women. Of course he was, this was Veyga, the man had had more bondings than he could remember; men, women and others, it was all a banquet to Veyga. He was magnanimous with charm to spare, everyone liked him, even Nero. Anyway, Veyga's bonding festivities were one of the few high society events to which he still received invites and his extrications were infrequent and often, even more enjoyable to attend so he must be doing something right. He recognised one of the women Veyga was talking to, she and Nero had had a short fling about 70 years ago, before he had met Ynomi.

"Cousin! Nice to see you. Thank you for your invite." Nero nodded shallowly to the women who looked faintly horrified. Clearly Veyga had not warned them about with whom he was enjoying this performance.

"Nero. You're early, this has to be a first."

Veyga greeted him enthusiastically, he always did. They clasped wrists tightly and Veyga pulled him in to thump him good-humouredly on the back. Both were of a height, though Veyga's dark bronze complexion caused Nero's to seem even paler by comparison. Veyga's grip on his arm caused him to wince.

"Sepirla, nice to see you again too."

". . . and you, Nero, but I am afraid we must be getting to our seats."

Sepirla's embarrassment was clear and her composure only held together by the indoctrinated manners of high society. Nero almost felt bad for her as she dragged her aghast friend away by the arm.

"How does he know your name?" Nero heard the friend whisper as she was forcibly removed.

Nero smirked. It was nice to know someone else was going to feel awkward this afternoon. Veyga shook his head at Nero.

"You always did like to make an entrance," Veyga chastised him lightly.

He should talk, thought Nero.

"Am I not allowed to know people's names now? I am sure her reputation will survive me knowing her name and if it doesn't, she can come drink her sorrows away with me and the rest of the lowlifes on the edge."

"You are in a worse mood than normal."

"I walked here."

"Ah. Well, to cheer you up, after this play, how about I take you to that restaurant you like, Real?"

"Harder to be in a bad mood with some good food in your stomach, I will admit."

"Not to mention some good company." Veyga nudged Nero playfully in the ribs with his elbow.

"Indeed."

Veyga could always cheer him up. Inside the theatre, musicians played ignorable music in the foyer. Historical pieces from many millennia ago, before they learnt to write interesting melodies in stimulating time signatures. He noted where the surveillance drones were as he heard the entrance scan his biodata and entered the theatre proper. In here, matt black surfaces absorbed the light so that the circular stage in the centre of the hall glowed as a single column of light in the dark, semi-spherical hall. Tiered seating rose from the stage to the doors. Subtle lights in the floor guided them towards their seats.

Veyga tried to give him the more well-placed seat towards the front. Nero, however, insisted he took the other, higher seat towards the rear of the theatre. The offer was extended in a falsified spirit of gratitude, but truly the rear seat would serve him better; it was closer to one of the doors that lined the perimeter allowing a swift exit and was away from any residual light of the stage so that his leaving would be less noted.

Nero settled into the cushioned chair. The seating here was well spaced. To one side there were a couple enjoying their lounger and to the other were families in booths. Feelings of nostalgia came upon him as he remembered when he and Ynomi used to attend the theatre. They would hold one another closely on those reclining seats as the actors swept them up in emotion and stories; much as that couple were doing now. One of the pair glared at him and he looked away.

Using the holoscreen that appeared in front of him, Nero used his uplink to order some wine and browse the details of the performance. The cast was certainly impressive, the ones he recognised anyway; it was a shame the material was not more stirring or this could have been a performance he would be sad to miss. A synth quickly brought the wine and soon the theatre fell into thick darkness. All holoscreens and synths withdrew and a hush fell over the audience. Actors, suddenly illuminated, appeared on the stage below, acting out scenes of famine, exposure and civil wars that preceded the forming of Karthia Prime. Holoemitters provided appropriate scenery through which the actors moved deftly. He waited until the peoples of Karthia were attempting to unite and save themselves by turning their sights towards the Inaran homeworld, turned on the biodata signal replica on his illegitimate communicator and slid it down the side of the chair's cushions. He then slipped his biodata mask over his still aching wrist, activated it and left.

As he emerged into the light of the foyer, he appeared not as Nero, but as another. His hair was now blonde, his skin tanned and his coat a deep blue. Beneath the coat was now a bulkier figure, with neither his striking features or trim physique. This was a form he had practised. A false identity linked with the mask.

"Not enjoying the performance, sir?" A custodian of the theatre asked.

"I am afraid I have been taken unwell." Nero adjusted his voice into a deeper timbre, it sounded strange. Unfortunately, voice changes were not something that could be achieved by twisting light.

"I am sorry to hear that, can I direct you to the nearest medical synth?" The custodian enquired politely seemingly unperturbed by Nero's disguise.

"No, no. Nothing serious. I am just going to fetch some medication; I will return soon. Thank you for offering, though."

Nero left rapidly, keen to spend as little time near surveillance drones as possible, in case his illusion was not as stable as he believed.

As far as the government would be aware, he had spent a pleasant afternoon at the theatre.

Getting to the eastern city gate was a simple matter of finding a pod. Inside he kept his illusion in place. There were no obvious cameras, but that didn't mean there weren't any, and clearly, the Senate had been monitoring him more closely than he had thought.

At the gate, there were large transports waiting to go to the few megacities that Karthian society had long ago been condensed into. Those that could afford it. Badlands settlements clung to and burrowed beneath the battered earth between, they were highly uncomfortable places to live. This discomfort had three main benefits as Nero saw it: one, it meant that the Senate's peacekeepers very rarely visited unless absolutely required; two, monitoring these places was difficult as the weather and the people quickly destroyed any inflicted surveillance technology; and three, living in constant difficulty had bred a certain ingenious survival instinct in the inhabitants.

As he strode towards the gate the true ferocity of the storm became clear. Lightning strikes caused cracking in the force field that looked like shattered crystals and, even with the dampening of the barrier, a dull roar penetrated the air around him. For a moment, he considered abandoning his journey, but Theta had him so tied up with training and the surveillance on him was now so great that he could not think when he would next be able to check his project.

Beyond the large transports, gleaming at their stations and sensibly waiting out the storm, were smaller independent ones who took people to and from the subterranean settlements of the Badlands. These transports did not gleam, many looked ready for the scrappers or had been salvaged from them. Worst of all, most were at least partially piloted by biologicals and not by synths so the quality of the ride was highly variable. Luckily, he spotted a driver he had used before, a grumpy Illion by the name of Koqui.

"I require passage to Udaka," Nero said brusquely, already tired from maintaining his illusion.

"No travel. Storm," Koqui said in a rasping voice not evolved to speak in the way Karthians did. Luckily his translation implant was helping decipher the dialect. Koqui gestured lazily to the swirling vortex of cloud throwing a haze of pulverised earth at the force field in a condescending way with one of three webbed fingers.

"Yes, I do have eyes, but I need to travel there now. It is a matter of urgency," Nero cast a scowl onto his illusionary face. Illion had a tendency to be intractable, but that wasn't surprising really given their people's history with Karthia. The third and final planet of Karthia Prime had not been claimed kindly and the Illion, although shorter in life, had long memories. Many millennia of rule under Karthia had not let the bloodshed pass out of Illion memory and, unlike the Inaran, generations of inbreeding had not made them kin. Illion biology had no commonality with Karthian. "If you are not travelling, why are you parked at a station?"

"Waiting, storm pass." Koqui rolled three large eyes and continued to recline against his vehicle. The Illion ability to graft flesh to flesh meant you could never be sure how many of any body part an Illion would have. Apparently, some body parts were heirlooms passed down through generations. It brought a whole new meaning to "you have your mother's eyes". Nero wondered what an Illion funeral was like, were body parts given to others through contracts or was it first come first served? Perhaps it was a bloody free-for-all. It wasn't common knowledge and it didn't seem polite to ask.

"Why don't we just get to the part where you give me a ridiculous quote for travelling and I barter you down to a slightly less ridiculous one?" In case Koqui wasn't in the mood to barter, Nero surveyed the other transports. All looked like they had been fused together by someone who was either drunk or who didn't know how to wield a welder or, in the worst cases, both.

Koqui laughed a slow, deep, jiggling laugh, that rattled the fine, iridescent scales on his many chins. "Two thousand credits."

"Well, that was truly ridiculous. Three hundred."

"In this? Are implants malfunctioning?" Koqui seemed genuinely offended.

"Five hundred," Nero replied curtly. He was tiring, soon his illusion would destabilise.

"One thousand."

"Six hundred, but you bring me back as well! Half now, half when I get safely back."

"Deal." Koqui grinned, baring sharp, inward-pointing teeth.

Koqui held out a pad and, after checking the skin mask was still in place, Nero scanned his wrist. Nero climbed into the body of the small, rugged vehicle cobbled together from resurrected transports. Each seam between the differing materials was clearly visible, though unlike some of the others, these were neat scars. Inside the seats were bare, cold metal with sturdy looking harnesses.

"Recommend harness," Koqui advised, his broad mouth of sharp teeth working the words. "But, your choice, if break neck, can still scan payment, if quick enough." Again, the rattling laugh.

Nero swiftly tightened the harness. Whilst he did appreciate the Illion dark sense of humour, he was also in no doubt that should he break his neck, he would come to rest in a shallow Badlands grave having paid in full for the service. Of course, due to the demand for organic matter to regenerate the soil, that was where all the planet's inhabitants were eventually destined to come to rest. Nero felt no need to expedite that ending.

The engines fired roughly on the second attempt and their juddering rumble was accompanied by the smell of burning oil. At least the hoover was stable. They pulled through the first gate into the lock within the force field that crackled fiercely around the small transport. When the second gate to the Badlands opened the sound was enormous. With blinding ferocity, the storm entirely engulfed the small transport. As they pulled forwards towards the opening at the end of the forcefield, it was as if the storm reached in to seize the transport. Every rivet, bolt and weld creaked and vibrated as the transport fought to maintain course towards the second gate.

Koqui turned to say something Nero had no chance of hearing. Lip reading could not be translated through a cortical implant. Something about the Illion's expression made Nero take a tight grip on a nearby, sturdy-looking rail and somewhat regret his decision to press ahead with his plans.

Surging forward through the gate, the transport was thrown roughly sideways. Wavering back and forth, Koqui fought hard to maintain course, a synth voice repeating many cautions in grating Illion and warning lights flashing with an urgent tempo in the cabin. Koqui pushed the throttle forwards, seemingly ignoring the synth's council. Through the small windows, Nero saw lightning strike the ground and it occurred to him that almost everything he was touching was metal. Was this transport well earthed? This was a terrible idea! The Oni had better have made progress. He would not be impressed if he had made the trip for nothing.

Across the storm-torn land, ruins of the long-dead civilisations of Karthian ancestors loomed from the murky, darkness of the storm, relics of a long-faded, planet-killing civilisation. Illuminated in the brilliant strobing of forking lightning, the tempest-eaten former grandeur of those civilisations jutted from the barren earth that was their legacy. Even the Badlanders avoided the crumbling, unstable ghosts of those dead civilisations, digging their settlements in the virgin ground between instead. Only the most dedicated historians now visited these monuments to hubris.

Udaka appeared suddenly. Squat, heavily-fortified buildings erupting from the swirling detritus. The settlement looked so vulnerable, dwarfed by the roaring goliath that engulfed it. That vulnerability denied the sprawling, subterranean township that prospered below. It took only forty-three minutes, but by the time they had made their way to Udaka, Nero's heartrate was elevated enough for him to have developed a heavy sheen of sweat. As they pulled into the large, roughly reinforced warehouse that served as the settlement's station, he pulled himself up straight, reset his wavering illusion and deliberately calmed his nerves.

"I wait here," Koqui said as the transport came to a stop. He put his unshod, webbed feet on the dash and began to fiddle with a communicator.

"Thank you, that was as pleasant as it could have been."

"Fun, huh?" Koqui smiled, turning down the synth's damage report.

As Nero exited the transport he heard, "Don't turn me down. You need to fix me. I won't be to blame when you get stranded and perish like the flimsy biological you are," and had to suppress a smile. He wasn't the only one not resetting his synth it seemed. He wondered if he should visit his ship. It wasn't far from Udaka to the scrapper's who kept his ship concealed from the Karthian authorities. No, there wasn't time.

As he left the warehouse, he put on his respirator. The air was breathable, but it wasn't pleasant, even when there wasn't a raging storm. It also meant there was less illusion to maintain. Faces were the most difficult illusion to hold consistently, they were more intricate in their movement than the rest of the body and people noticed small errors very quickly. At the thick door to the almost abandoned warehouse, he paused. He could see the building he needed to get to, he could also see the detritus the storm was liberally flinging across his path. Nero swore and stepped out into the storm.

Winds tore at him with a ferocity that knocked the air from him as he leant into them. Just as he had almost reached his destination a small piece of flying debris ripped his coat. Luckily it did no more than that. Inside the unassuming, heavily-protected prefab building that seemed to vibrate with the storm was a counter and little else, other than some shelves of tech junk and signs advertising technical salvage.

Despite only being in the storm for moments, Nero felt thoroughly dishevelled. The counter was manned by a bored looking man filing long nails.

"Can I help you?" he said, painted mouth chewing lazily and not looking up. Make up was common in the Badlands, in the city it only advertised that one could not afford rejuvenation.

"I need to see Kapi about a special part I ordered for an XR52." Nero gave the pass phrase. He enjoyed messing with Nix, this would be fun.

Nix eyed him cautiously. "The XR52, you say, very rare those parts are. Usually, we reserve those for regular customers."

"I am a regular customer." Nero dropped his illusion and removed his respirator.

Nix visibly startled and swore creatively.

"Nero, I swear you will be the death of me. Why can't you just come as you?" He held a hand on his heart overemphasising his breaths.

"For the same reasons you have pass phrases and a front."

"You have me there." Nix pressed a button underneath the desk - the door bolted and the windows darkened. "Kapi is just doing some repairs, I will show you to the gate room."

"Repairs?" Nero asked.

"I am sure she can explain. I certainly can't. I am just security after all." Nix showed him behind the shelving units to the usual place, and flipped a hidden switch.

As they waited for the hydraulics to open the hatch leading to the voluminous basement below, Nero took off his torn jacket, smoothed his formal wear and rearranged his wind-tousled hair, checking the presence of his communicator and phaser as he did.

"Nero, look at you all handsome, so nice of you to dress up for us. No one makes the effort these days."

"I am at the theatre," Nero replied suppressing a smile.

"Ah, seeing anything good."

"No. Just that historical play. Karthia Prime."

"You should have told us. I would have been happy to act as a placeholder. It would be a welcome change from the amateur dramatics round here and give me an excuse to wear my finery."

"Maybe next time and aren't you always in your finery, Nix?" Nero eyed the young man in the shiny, angular clothes and shinier jewellery.

"I have finer."

"I am sure you do."

"Would you like me to fix and clean your coat during your trip?" Nix took the long coat and inspected the tear. "Can't have you bringing down the tone of the afternoon performance by looking like a fringer."

"That would be appreciated, thank you." It would certainly dissuade his cousin from asking awkward questions.

"All part of the service." Nix performed a gesture of servitude with an extra flourish.

"Security and tailoring, does Kapi appreciate your many talents?"

"She could use reminding on occasion."

Nero left Nix with his coat and descended the ladder into the expansive basement. By the opposite wall, he spied two feet sticking out of a control panel built into the rock.

"I hear you have been making repairs. I hope you are accepting travellers."

Kapi peered around the panel, wrinkled face creasing more with the effort of focusing. She pulled clunky glasses down from amongst wiry hair. Rejuvenation was not common amongst the inhabitants of the Badlands; age manifested more honestly here. As she stood slowly to greet him, Kapi rolled up the arms on her grease-stained overalls.

"Nero, nice to see you again. One heck of a day you've chosen though. A lightning strike blew out a transformer, but don't worry I have replaced it and reinforced the groundings so we shouldn't have any more trouble." Kapi ran her hands through hair that was short, partially shaven and as white as her skin was black. Even for a Karthian, she was old; for a Badlander, she was ancient.

"Shouldn't have?" *This journey is getting better and better*, Nero thought to himself irritably.

"I sent a stray marbara through and back and it survived. You'll be fine." Kapi dismissed his worries with a nonchalant wave.

"Very reassuring." Nero restrained himself from pointing out the many differences between him and one of the ugly, burrowing creatures the Badlanders sometimes kept as pets.

"Organic is organic. It's all the same to the gate." Kapi shrugged. "Of course, you are welcome to try one of the official gates, or one of our competitors'." She flashed him an attitude laden grin of wonky teeth.

"But then I would miss the excellent customer service you provide, Kapi," Nero replied, arching an eyebrow. Of the unofficial gates operating under the Karthian authorities' radar, Kapi's was known to have the lowest death toll and, given that lowest didn't mean zero, he wasn't eager to try the others.

"Exactly," Kapi slapped him on the back, leaving Nero wondering if he now had an oily handprint in that location. "I tell you what, to help settle your nerves, I will take payment upon your safe return. I assume you are going to see the Oni again?"

"Indeed I am."

"I will make contact. One of their alternate gates again?"

"Please."

The small gate, only a little taller than he was, established its connection seemingly smoothly. How they were hiding the energy surges of the gate, he did not know. Possibly the frequent lightning strikes provided cover. The gate's watery surface shimmered in front of him.

"Whenever you're ready," Kapi called from the controls as a wire in one of the huge looms that ran over the gate sparked briefly. "Ignore that."

Nero took a moment, replaced his respirator, braced himself for his potential death, and stepped through.

VI

The high-speed rail line from New York to Dallas hurtled through a landscape that changed quickly from dense city to sparse woodland and verdant fields to dusty, flat farmland covered with patchy crops and tornado-scarred towns. Over eight long hours, Raven bore witness to the damage that storms and drought were doing to this part of America and felt lucky that, until recently, the ferocity of a storm in England had been measured by whether your wheelie bin remained upright and required little other concern.

An email from Special Agent Franklin had arrived early that morning with instructions to make their way to West as soon as possible, if they wished to ensure they were there for when they questioned the witnesses this afternoon. Great haste had been made to catch the earliest possible train. The 5am start had not favoured Raven nor, surprisingly, Natalia, who was usually one of those hateful morning people who didn't appear to feel like they were rising from the grave if it was before 7am.

Across from Raven, Natalia sat with sunglasses on, despite the overcast day, nursing a very large cup of coffee. They dozed on and off as the train swayed. The even tempo of the wheels rumbling over the tracks was seductively relaxing to those who had had little sleep and too much drink the night before. Besides, talk was difficult when the one topic consuming your thoughts could not be discussed lest one of the many nearby ears overhear. Sleep was preferable and, thanks to their hangovers, less painful. Raven reached into herself, calming the raging inflammation.

All trains going to West were cancelled as the line went through the centre of the town, so they hired a car from Hillsboro. To Raven's dismay, the company only had autonomous vehicles—for insurance reasons. She knew her dislike of autonomous transport was irrational; they were almost always safer than human-driven cars and had been for two decades, but her brain liked to focus on the almost.

Distracting herself from the unsettlingly smooth drive of the large, comfortable and quiet car (now that the chat function had been disabled), Raven checked her phone for any stories leaking from West. There was nothing except the mention of the lockdown in local news. Natalia couldn't find anything either.

Thanks to the greater speed limits granted to autonomous transport, within the hour, they arrived at West. It was now 3pm. A heavily armed roadblock, complete with soldiers in full virus control kit, greeted them. It seemed they were keen to keep up the appearance of a lockdown to the outside world. Despite the well-constructed pretence, a small crowd of people were engaged in heated conversations with the soldiers. Their worry for their loved ones grated on Raven as they waited for clearance.

Natalia's ID saw them escorted swiftly through the roadblock to where the FBI had set up a mobile command centre in the form of three huge trucks emblazoned with the FBI logo and the obligatory stars and stripes. Americans were still very fond of their flag, Raven reflected. Unfortunately, the St George's Cross never recovered from its association with racism at the beginning of the century and the Union Jack was no longer, so England had no such symbol on which to lavish misplaced, patriotic pride. Opposite the command centre was the old town hall with its boxy, pale brown façade and large, heavily-reinforced windows.

They parked as directed. It was only when they stepped out of the car that the true strangeness of the atmosphere hit them. Only soldiers, police and agents walked the streets, and they did so tensely. Otherwise, the town was deserted. Quietly groaning electric motors from large military trucks and occasional birdsong were the only significant sounds. All the shops and eateries were empty and abandoned, as were the community spaces. Where they had not been cleared, some cars were left in the middle of the road. Bags and other personal belongings speckled the ground and a half-eaten meal was discarded on the grass in front of the hall.

Special Agent Franklin appeared as they were gawping at the strange scene surrounding them.

"Thank you for coming. How was your journey?" Franklin shook their hands formally.

"Good, thank you. How are things here?" Natalia asked, still surveying the scene. "I see what you mean about this being a . . . well I am not sure how you would describe this situation."

"Nobody is." Franklin gave a terse nod of agreement. "It is unprecedented, even in my line of work."

"Has there been any contact with the missing?"

"None at all."

"Huh. Any new forensic analysis of the scene?"

"It is an interesting case, because the scene is the entire town. However, other than the marks on the grass and the damaged electrical systems, as I said previously, there is almost no evidence that anything occurred here."

"Almost?" Natalia enquired.

"There is one witness. Well, only one that has anything to say other than 'I was asleep and when I woke up everyone was gone', or elderly and disabled individuals who are either non-verbal or didn't see anything due to not being able to move. Though some report a strong urge to move at that time.

"However, the witness's story is pretty farfetched. He has a history of drug use and mental health issues that mean he is possibly not the most reliable witness. We are re-interviewing him soon. You can sit in on the interview, we will be about an hour preparing. Until then, I will get someone to escort you around. Please don't disturb anything."

"We won't. Thank you for your candour." As Special Agent Franklin walked away, Natalia turned to Raven. "Anything we aren't being told; do you think?" she asked in a lowered voice.

"Not that I can sense." Raven zipped up her jacket as the weather had grown quickly overcast and chilly. Large dark storm clouds loomed on the horizon of the tornado alley town. Creeping anxiety began to rattle against Raven's nerves. The smell of the weather turning lingered in the heavy air.

They were assigned two army personnel to show them around. A job that one of them was enjoying far too much until Raven got tired of the whispering of rude thoughts, fixed him with a stare which would make a grizzly shrink and gently encouraged the embarrassment he felt at his loudly lascivious thoughts, until he was blushing like a schoolboy.

Fifteen minutes of walking through deserted streets, of peering into wooden houses, many times repaired, their doors and gates left swinging in the increasing breeze, brought them to the edge of town. Dogs ran to chain link fences, eager to be fed. One of their escorts (the less preoccupied one) told them how they had been feeding and watering the pets now abandoned in their homes so they didn't die before they could call in local rescues and humane societies. Many of the gardens the hungry dogs occupied had concrete reinforced storm bunkers or hatches to underground refuge.

Abruptly, the town ended and what was left of nature began. In the field opposite the last street, there were faint marks in the sparse, weed-riddled pasture. Eight slightly scorched circles and eight depressions in the dry earth formed an enormous ring. Walking the perimeter of the marked ground, carefully observed at a respectful distance by their escort, revealed nothing more than that they first observed.

"What do you make of this?" Raven asked Natalia.

"I really don't know." Natalia shrugged tensely as she walked the perimeter with her weight on her toes, preventing her heels from sinking into the soft spring pasture.

"You were in the army, do you know of any weapons or vehicles that leave marks like this? Could this be an act of terrorism, or war, maybe?"

"No. Nothing like this. These marks are neat and methodical. Even with autonomous weaponry and vehicles, war is carnage. It's more accurate now, but, in my experience, no less messy. It certainly doesn't leave neat patterns in fields. Anyway, you know how these things are, you've spoken of being in conflicts before."

"Only the simpler kinds, back when you looked your enemy in the eye," Raven answered, receiving a strange look from Natalia.

"If this is an act of terrorism, it is a new one and surely demands or some such would have been forthcoming by now."

"Or bodies." Raven added.

"Or that. And why here? Why this little town? There is no obvious strategic advantage to be gained. And America doesn't have the enemies it used to have since we overhauled our foreign policies in the forties. Internal terrorism would almost be more likely with all the political tension lately, but who would gain from doing something like this?" Natalia still looked a little queasy as she talked, and she talked as much to herself as to Raven.

"So probably not terrorism or war."

"Probably not kidnapping either. Kidnapping this many people would be a logistical nightmare. The increase in traffic would be seen on the local road cameras. Then you would need to keep them somewhere, feed them, etcetera. Not to mention, these do not seem like well-off people. If you do a cost -benefit analysis, this doesn't make any sense as a kidnapping for leverage or money."

Raven rubbed her temples. "Okay, so a freak weather event?"

"You would expect to see some signs of recent disturbance and these were people who were clearly prepared for extreme weather events. The advanced warning systems they installed could have failed. Still, everyone would have had to have been out of their houses and stood in the path of the storm. Would there be a reason for them to collect in this field? Perhaps, these burns are lightning strikes?" Natalia crouched carefully for a closer look at the scorched earth.

"Possibly, but moreover, what goes up must come down. You would have thought that a rain of two thousand people would have been noticed!"

"Let's consider Occam's razor; what is the simplest possible explanation for this that we can think of?" Natalia asked and when their escorts' backs were turned, she touched the ground and sniffed her hand. From the shake of her head Raven inferred nothing nefarious could be detected in the odour.

"They all just went on holiday, without telling anyone, to a place where they couldn't be contacted?" Raven raised her hands in exasperation.

"Unlikely."

"Some sort of cult activity?" Raven ventured.

"I guess anything is possible at this point." Natalia straightened herself.

"Oh well, then it's clearly magic," Raven whispered. She was bored of being sensible and feeling faintly anxious, she'd rather be amused and feel faintly anxious. "They have even left us the remnants of their casting circle. Such helpful witches."

"You are ridiculous," Natalia said, a fleeting expression of relief flitting over her strong features. "Although, if you exist . . ." The look of consternation returned. Clearly, despite her inebriation, Natalia remembered their conversation the night before.

"If it helps, I have never met another like me—not even a little bit like me." Raven checked the escort couldn't hear them and was satisfied that they remained deaf to the conversation as the wind whipped away their words.

"That's . . ." Natalia seemed aware her search for the right word had gone on too long.

"Worried you're surrounded?" Raven teased, uncomfortably aware of Natalia's relief that Raven was just one and not one of many. Raven reset her defences, pushing her friend's emotions away.

"Let's just say, I am glad you are you, because, and I say this with my security council hat on and not my friend hat, if you ever went . . . I am just saying your worst day could be a lot worse than other people's. But I have known you a long time now, I consider you a good friend, and then there is everything you do for us as a mediator . . . " she trailed off.

Natalia shifted her weight restlessly as an awkward silence passed between them. It saddened Raven that Natalia feared her, a lot of heartfelt nervousness had underlaid those words. Truth was that Natalia was right; her worst day, or rather her worst days, had been pretty appalling and it was better if Natalia, or anyone else for that matter, never found out just how bad they had been. Luckily, they were ancient history.

"I understand." Raven placed a hand on Natalia's arm as a gesture of comfort. "Just remember if you shot me, I would probably die. I bleed like everyone else." She smiled crookedly to match her dark joke.

"Probably?"

"Empty the clip."

Natalia looked shocked.

"Hit the vital bits. Put all that training of yours to good use." Raven added attempting to resurrect some humour, she pushed her playful intent just a little towards Natalia and patted her arm gently.

"I would have to be pretty quick on the draw." Natalia quipped back gently, affected by Raven's pushed emotion.

"Quite a few experiments on volition suggest that an action begins before a person consciously decides to perform that action. You could test that theory."

"By shooting you?"

"Call it a science experiment."

"I did always like science in school. Pretty high stakes experiment, though."

"How are you with a rifle? Any sniper experience?" Raven asked.

"Some," Natalia answered vaguely. "It's been a while."

"Even better, if you had enough range, I wouldn't even sense you coming."

"Really?" Natalia raised perfectly groomed eyebrows.

Raven nodded. Another silence lingered a while.

"Maybe it's aliens." Raven grinned.

"What?"

"Aliens." Raven gestured towards the ring of burns and pressure.

"Straying pretty far from Occam's razor now." Natalia laughed heartily, as their escort gestured from across the field for their return.

The route back led them up Oak Street, upon which the fallout from the devastating storms of the last decade was writ large. The Dollar General store's sign lay broken on the parking lot of the ruined warehouse-like building, another business gone and never replaced. Insurance companies going bust left, right and centre, had hit the alley hard and the alley was expanding every year. Along the western-style high street, bars and shops were boarded up; glass was too big a risk. We are open, the boards shouted, in graffiti of various skill.

Back at the mobile camp, Special Agent Franklin greeted them, holding a small paper bag. Raven sensed that Franklin was questioning her decision to allow them to attend. Her thoughts revealed that Franklin's superiors hadn't liked the idea, but they hadn't forbidden it, so Special Agent Franklin marched them swiftly along the empty streets, past the public storm shelter, to a squat wooden house on the outskirts of the small town. The house bore the scars of many repairs and the deeper blemishes of ongoing neglect. Heavy, sagging curtains, yellow from age and smoke were drawn across the windows. Waiting for them were two other agents with tablets and stern expressions.

"These are Special Agents Rossi and Chang." Special Agent Franklin gestured towards the starchy-suited agents. "Agents, this is Ms Yahontov, head of the UN security council and her assistant Ms Solveig. They have been given special clearance to attend this interview in the interests of information sharing and trying to get to the bottom of this incident."

They exchanged curt greetings, then Franklin navigated the cracked paving stone path to the front door and knocked sharply, cracked white paint floated to the floor with each knock.

"Who's there?" shouted a thick southern accent.

"Hello, Mr Washington, it's Anita here to interview you again. Do you remember? I have some colleagues with me, I hope that's okay." Special Agent Franklin waited patiently a few moments for the door to creak open enough for an eye to appear in the gap. "I have also brought you a few essentials." She held up the bag to the gap.

"Terry, please," the man said tensely but unchained the door. "Mr Washington is my father."

Swinging open with a gasp of stale air, the door revealed a short, thin man with an untrimmed beard, still in his dressing gown. Thanking Anita, he took the bag and led them into a small dark living room.

"Are you okay, Terry? Would you like anything before we begin?"

Terry lowered his shaking body into a balding armchair, he seemed confused and didn't answer the question. Natalia cleared a seat on an aging sofa in the angular design popular in the 2030s, whilst the agents perched awkwardly nearby.

"What about a drink? Water? Coffee?" Special Agent Franklin asked gently.

"Yes, coffee . . . coffee, please." Terry seemed to perk up a little.

"How do you take it?"

"I don't think there's any milk, so black and sweet," Terry replied.

"I bought some milk for you."

"You're a star. Milky and sweet, then." Terry seemed genuinely grateful. "Sorry, I haven't wanted to go out since all this and even if I did, it's not like the stores are open."

"That is perfectly understandable. No worries, I will go and make you that coffee before we begin." Franklin took the bag to the kitchen and a kettle could be heard boiling.

Raven noticed that Special Agent Franklin hadn't delegated the job to the other agents. Perhaps, it was an exercise in relationship building.

"At least they got the electricity back on," Terry said to the awkward silence that Franklin's absence had left

Special Agent Franklin was gone for many minutes waiting for the old, slow kettle to boil and making the coffee, during which Natalia introduced herself and Raven. The agents stiltedly followed their example, though it was clear they didn't think this meeting was worth their time.

"Mind if I smoke?" Terry asked, though it was clearly rhetorical as he shook a stubborn lighter and sparked up. He took a long drag. The smoke mingled with the smell of stale cannabis that hung in the air.

"It's no problem," Natalia replied with a smile.

"No problem at all," Raven agreed. Though the acrid smoke was already irritating her throat.

"I know we are supposed to vape or some such these days, but after the weeks I've had I need the real stuff. It won't be long until Capitol Hill tries to take these, too, anyway, I'm sure. They already tried to take our guns." Terry clung to the packet as he took another suck on the hand-rolled cigarette. Discomfort at being harshly judged radiated from him. "That's a British accent, isn't it?"

"Yes, it is," Raven replied in a friendly tone. "Well, English now, I guess."

"Already banned tobacco there, didn't they?"

"Two decades ago, now, yes."

"Damn governments, stomping all over our liberties. Does it make you mad or are you too young to know different?" Terry shook gently with the effort of conversation.

"I never was much of a smoker I'm afraid, so it didn't affect me much. Luckily, you don't need it to enjoy weed." Raven winked at Terry, she was aware of the faint horror emanating from the agents and Natalia, but more importantly, she felt Terry start to relax and feel less judged.

"At least they made that legal, huh?" Terry coughed as he laughed.

Special Agent Franklin re-entered the room and passed Terry a coffee topped with steaming tendrils. As the odour reached her, Raven felt the familiar pang of caffeine addiction mixed with a little dehydration.

"Are you ready to begin?" Special Agent Franklin asked Terry.

"Yes, but nothing has changed since the last two times I gave you my account." Terry looked annoyed, gaunt features twisting defensively. "I know your agents don't believe me, but it is the truth, the whole truth and nothing but the truth, so help me God!"

"It's not that we don't believe you, it's just that we need some more detail so that we can piece together what happened here and try and help the missing. Are you happy to help us? You are the one proper witness we have so you are the only person we can turn to."

That was clever; although Terry was pretty anti-establishment, he did want to help his friends.

"Yes, yes of course I will help. Where do you want me to start?"

"From the evening of the events?"

"Well, like I said, I met my buddy Billy around seven for a few drinks at a local bar called The Bootlegger, in the centre of town. We were shooting the breeze and playing some pool, watching the game on and off, nothing unusual for a Saturday night. Then it was the strangest thing, somewhere around nine, I'm afraid I can't tell you nice folks exactly, all the lights go out, and it's pitch black, then you can hear a strange voice repeating 'come towards the red light' and everyone just starts walking out the bar, all at once." Terry paused, took a long pull on the slowly dwindling cigarette and sipped his coffee.

Raven reached gently towards Terry's mind and the memories that were now replaying vividly. Details jumped about, a bit like a computer glitching, and things swam a little in his vision. Clearly, he had been drinking more than he let on. Inside the bar everyone seemed in a good mood, their team was winning, it seemed, from the occasional raucous cheers. Then, all the lights went out, as he said, sudden darkness and everyone got up and left. Drinks were left on tables, burgers and fries were abandoned uneaten and outerwear remained thrown over chairs despite the rain. Once in the street, the people continued walking, slack jawed and dull eyed, but with seeming purpose, towards a distant column of red light.

Terry followed them, she could feel his anxiety, his heart palpated in his chest. In his memories, Terry tried to engage those he knew. His attempts were unheeded. Then he tried to physically stop Billy with little effect. Ignored were the increasingly frightened questions he fired at his friend who quietly and determinedly walked on.

"Where are you going, buddy? Is this a prank? Come on man, stop playing me." Terry's questions met with no reply from his friend, who remained blind to his presence.

Surrounded by the town's people, Terry tried to get their attention instead. It was a small town and he knew many of them by name. His attempts were in vain, garnering, at best, a turn of the head or momentary eye contact. Despite his efforts, Terry was swept along by the impassive crowd.

Old and young marched in gormless unity, transfixed by the red light in the distance. Around them, the instructions were repeated in the strange voice. The source of the strange voice unidentifiable and ever-changing. Dogs released from gardens barked with high-pitched nervousness and pushed wet noses at their unresponsive owners.

When Terry got to the far edge of town, to the field in which Raven and Natalia had stood, his memories revealed the outline of a large oval entity, dark even in the gloom of the damp night except for the column of red light projected into the sky from the centre. Towards the town faced a ramp. Shadowy silhouettes of heavily masked and covered people stood at the bottom. Two gently held large, glowing, blue objects. Ducking behind a large SUV abandoned immobile in the road, Terry watched in terrified glances as the people of the town, men and women, the elderly and children holding their parents' hands, walked calmly up the ramp as directed by its strangely moving guardians and slowly disappeared into the dark underbelly of the enormous object.

Raven felt herself breaking a cold sweat as she immersed herself in Terry's memories. In vivid detail, she relived Terry's horror as he watched person after person vanish into the darkness beyond the ramp. Stolen glances from around the SUV, revealed even the infirm and ill were helped gently inside by the tall, concealed people who bent wrongly at their joints.

Once the last person had wandered compliantly into the gloom, the ramp closed. Blinding white lights glowed, the ground rumbled beneath him and the smell of singed grass wafted on the breeze as the object lifted into the air and faded quickly into the night, leaving Terry on the damp, hard tarmac behind the SUV in the grip of a suffocating panic attack.

Raven could feel every gasping, wet breath clawing its way into and out of her lungs through a throat so tight, she felt as if she could choke. Surging through was a memory of vomiting. She had to get out, but the panic was infectious and ensnaring, she started to retch. Too deep, she was too deep into the memory, she thought, unable to extract herself. Curiosity had led her to become too intensely immersed in Terry's memories.

"Raven, Raven!" Distantly, she heard Natalia's voice. She felt herself being dragged into cooler air. Still, all she could see was that dark night until a hard, stinging slap wrenched her back to the present.

Gradually, the night and the panic subsided, daylight and Natalia's concerned expression replacing them.

"Thanks," Raven mumbled rubbing her cheek. She slumped against the wall of the grime-covered house, her head throbbing from more than Natalia's slap.

"Jesus Christ, what was that?" Natalia asked, frown lines tracking along familiar routes.

"I am just not feeling well." Raven pushed back errant hair from her face and wiped the sheen from her brow with her sleeve.

"Mmmm. And what caused this sudden illness?" Natalia asked, handing her a neatly pressed handkerchief.

"I'll tell you later."

"Okay, fair enough. What shall we do now? Are you okay to go back inside?"

"Just give me a minute to catch my breath." Raven tried to centre herself, to block everything out by raising her mind's defences, but Natalia's anxiety was vibrating her every frazzled nerve. "Can you stop worrying about me so loudly, please?"

"I'm not speaking." Natalia raised a sanity questioning eyebrow.

Raven tapped her head in a gesture, she hoped Natalia would correctly interpret. She did. Slowly, they both regained some equipoise of emotion, until there was silence inside Raven's head as well as outside on the deserted street.

"That's a mean arm you have on you." Raven moved her jaw back and forth exaggeratedly as she felt a bright red handprint developing on her cheek. "Is slapping people standard first aid in the army now? Or is this UN training?"

"It's not in any official training, but then so much isn't. I'll admit, it's been a useful remedy on a few occasions." Natalia responded with a relieved smile, smoothing clothes ruffled from the exertion of dragging Raven outside. "Also, I am sorry. I didn't think calling for help or an ambulance was a good idea."

"You were right. Shall we go back in?"

"You can't go back in looking like that." Natalia pointed to Raven's burning cheek.

"Oh, yes." Raven put her hand to her face, directed her mind to the superficial damage and the strange energy she felt flowing and coalescing in living things. The burning lessened. Would-be bruises, born of burst blood vessels, were drained of their spilled blood and split capillaries knitted together under her direction.

"How has that mark disappeared?"

"It healed."

"Bit faster than expected. I was thinking we would just put some make up on it."

Raven shrugged as they moved towards the door.

"I am definitely emptying the clip." Natalia added semi-humorously, before reaching the threshold and unnecessarily helping Raven up the step. Raven snorted a laugh in response.

Inside they passed Raven's strange behaviour off as a response to low blood sugar and the interview continued, though they garnered little further information. By the time they made it back to the control centre, it was late in the afternoon so they were assigned a place in a local motel alongside various military and FBI personnel.

In the large motel just off Route 35, twin beds covered with thin pillows and oddly patterned sheets greeted them. It looked like it had been a Holiday Inn many incarnations ago.

One of the witnesses who had been asleep at the time of the incident had set up a food stand nearby selling various fast and greasy foods to the motel's sudden influx of guests; the type of food now highly taxed in England, but still cheap in America.

Raven ordered a burger, double chips and a large shake, and quickly said, "sorry, I mean fries," when the man selling the food reached for what she knew as crisps. They ate the food on the beds of the motel and Raven eavesdropped on the thoughts of the soldiers and family members in the adjacent rooms; it proved fruitless.

"What do you make of Terry's story?" Natalia asked quietly between bites.

"I believe him."

"Really?! It seems pretty farfetched."

"It's what he remembers, he isn't lying. I think it is probably the truth of what happened, more or less."

"How can you be sure?"

Raven didn't answer.

"Is it to do with the funny turn you took back there?" Natalia was trying to hold Raven's eye contact, but she was avoiding it.

"Yes."

"So, what happened?" Natalia waited. "Everything you tell me will remain confidential, even from Aziz. I will consider it highly classified and also the secret of a friend." She quietly waited some more.

You could tell Natalia was a mother, she could make you feel like you needed to answer just from her tone and the expectation which filled her silences. Being trained to extract information from enemy combatants probably helped a little too.

"I was experiencing his memories," Raven offered quietly.

"Okay." Natalia's tone was non-judgemental, but her thoughts weren't. Although, they had worked together for over a decade now, Natalia had always desperately wanted to believe that Raven had more in common with Derren Brown than Professor X. Even after last night, it seemed she was unconvinced.

"I went too deep into the memory and then I couldn't get out. His emotional memories were overwhelming, hence the panic-like symptoms." Raven hadn't trusted anyone with this much of her for a very long time, it felt . . . difficult. Embarrassment nagged at her—she needed to improve her control, that she could still fuck up so badly irritated her. She was old enough to know better. Tension gripped her stomach so she swapped from the burger that had never been beef to the milkshake that had never been milk. Sugar rushed pleasantly into her bloodstream.

"And you believe his account to be accurate?"

"As I said, more or less. All memories are somewhat inaccurate because your brain fills in a lot of blanks with what it thinks fits, but I believe he saw the town walking into a large craft-like thing and disappear off somewhere. He had been drinking more than he let on, though, possibly he had taken other drugs, too."

"How do you know that?"

"I felt drunk."

"Huh . . . Could you do that to anyone?" Natalia's demeanour was a picture of well-honed, relaxed, friendly indifference. Her mind belied this, seething instead with intense curiosity and simmering anxiety. Raven monitored her friend's fears as they spoke so not to overwhelm her.

"Do you really want the answer to that?"

Natalia nodded slowly. "Can you fish out just any memory?"

"It's hard work and psychologically dangerous. It's easier for me to say something like "what's the most embarrassing thing you have ever done?" Then that memory is recalled and I can just skim it off the top, as it were." Raven gave Natalia a cheeky glance.

"Don't," she said, shifting uneasily.

"I'm not."

"Would I know if you were?"

"Not unless I wanted you to . . . or I started having a panic attack. You will have to trust me as I am trusting you."

"Fair enough. Have you ever been wrong? Because, no offence, it just can't be true."

"Yes. Memory is a tricky thing affected by, well, almost everything: time, intoxicants, attention, mental health. Then there are delusions, imagination, daydreams, false memories and hallucinations to contend with. Although there are subtle ways to eliminate those possibilities, it took me a while to learn them. Am I wrong this time? No, I don't think so. Are his memories possibly the result of a bad acid trip? Also, yes."

"So, the whole town was abducted in what sounds like a spaceship. I am sorry, but I can't quite believe that . . . even if it would explain the UFO seen by the air force in the area." Natalia placed her half-eaten meal to one side, she looked slightly nauseous again. "And if it is true, what the hell can we do about it?"

"Not a fucking thing, I imagine." The tension that had been lurking in Raven threatened to take hold. She centred herself against it.

"On that we agree."

For a long while they just sat and ate.

"How do you do it?" Natalia asked, unable to contain her continued intrigue.

"How do you see?" Raven cleared the containers from the bed into the reuse and recycling caddies and reclined onto the thin pillows, at least they smelt cleaner than they looked.

"Well, the eyes transmit signals to the brain which . . ."

"Yes, but pretend no one else can see and you don't have access to centuries of scientific investigation. Intuitively, what do you know about how you see?"

"Just that it's something to do with the eyes, I guess."

"And therein lies the problem. It's something to do with my brain, I think, but I don't know." *And I am not mad keen to be made into a lab rat again in order to find out*, she added to herself.

"Could your parents do what you do?"

"I never knew my birth parents." Raven was starting to feel discomfited by the line of questioning so she suggested they watched TV for a while, the first of the old Live Ship Traders trilogy was on.

"I think I am going to go to bed. It's been a long, weird day," Raven said as the movie wrapped up.

"Probably wise," Natalia agreed.

A short while later and feeling only marginally cleaner having used the aging bathroom suite, Raven lay on the lumpy mattress and, in the dark, listened to the gathering wind, trying to solve the impossible problem of an improbably abducted town; the delay in snoring told her Natalia was doing the same.

VII

Nero stumbled out of the gate into the small, humid, non-regulation gatehouse the Oni kept for unsanctioned visitors. The Oni were always up for a little profiteering on the side, R&D contracts with the Karthian Senate not being as lucrative as you would expect.

Nero straightened himself, irritated by his undignified arrival, though with a vortex rougher than usual, he knew he was lucky to have arrived on the other side at all. At the control panel of the gate room, which was sterile of all but the technology to run the gate, stood a pale grey individual with large, almond eyes. The Oni approached him.

"Lord Nero. We weren't expecting you. If you had advised us of your travel, we could have prepared a greeting party to give you an update on your project." The Oni spoke at a pitch that could not be heard by Karthian ears, through a small, lipless mouth that barely moved. Luckily, the pitch of the speech could be picked up by his translator implant—strange as it was to have unheard words transmitted into your brain. Once acquired, the Oni's planet had been renamed Isakilo, as it was almost impossible for the Karthian larynx to replicate Oni speech.

"That was rather the point of my spontaneity. I find the lack of preparation leads to more honesty," Nero said, his voice muffled slightly by his respirator.

"Very wise, Lord. I hope you don't mind waiting whilst we assemble your project leaders?" The Oni gestured towards a metal door beyond which a transport pod waited in a cold, raw-rock tunnel lit with stripes of white light.

"As long as it won't take long, I am a busy man." *And one that needs to be back at the theatre before arousing suspicion*, he thought.

Once within the main complex, the small transport pod navigated a labyrinth of unembellished corridors and elevators until it opened into a small waiting area with seats designed for a range of body plans. A waiting room that was not the high-vaulted, impressive reception shown to representatives of the Karthian realms, the reception that had been his welcome during his past official visits, but one catering for their less prestigious clientele.

As an operative, Nero had realised that Karthia's hold over the Oni was more tenuous than generally believed. The Oni's homeworld had been taken by force many generations ago during the establishment of the second realm. It was the Oni who had helped develop Karthia's modern covert methods of population control. Of course, that meant that any biogenetic manipulations that had been put in place on the planet used much of the Oni's own technology and so had, for the most part, been gently circumvented, leaving the unencumbered Oni able to provide their services to other parties, for a price.

Nero took a seat in which he could sit without requiring disarticulation or more humour than he could muster. Through the room's small windows, he could view a significant portion of the enormous, brutally-angular, research complex that Karthia had designated for developing new technologies, mostly for Peacekeeper use. The complex was sat upon the barren, blue tinged rocks of the southern peninsula of the one continent of the Oni's home world that was reliably above sea level.

Beyond the complex, the Oni's capital city (referred to as Isakilo-1) was arranged in neat hexagonal blocks of various heights of buildings stretching as far as the eye could see. These blocks extended into the great sea which roared in the distance; the sea that fulfilled all the Oni's needs and from which Karthia took what it wanted. Industrial equipment jutted from the water's surface.

Being amphibious, for the Oni, the sea was simply an extension of the city. Very little life survived on the inhospitable geology of the land here but, unlike Karthia, the barren nature of the land was not because of industry tipping the planet beyond habitation; life here had never evolved much beyond the abundant oceans.

Within an acceptably short time two more Oni appeared. They looked, to Nero's Karthian eyes, exactly like the first. Usually, this would be due to the innate speciesism that makes telling genetically distant individuals apart sometimes difficult, however, the Oni were genuinely almost identical. Asexual reproduction meant there were no sexes, they had no gender and were essentially clones of one another. It was terribly disconcerting to not know who you were speaking to or whether you had met before.

"Welcome, Lord Nero," one of the Oni said introducing themself with a Karthian epithet rather than the string of digits the Oni really went by and Karthians struggled to memorise. Their tight fitting, shiny uniform, designed to trap moisture against the skin, was marked with an insignia he recognised as denoting they were the more senior of the two. Whether it was the same Oni that was leading the project upon his last visit, he wasn't sure. "Would you simply like an update on your project or do you have time for a demonstration?"

"A demonstration? I didn't realise the technology was now fully functional." Nero's interest was piqued. Maybe this trip would turn out to be worth the nuisance.

"Yes, it will take us a short time to prepare, but previous trials have proved greatly successful. From acquisition of trial subjects and initial experimentation, we approximate that the device has a population effect of above nighty-nine percent. The experiments have also revealed the technology's range and specificity can be manipulated efficiently for upscaling. Side effects are limited and usually not long lived. Obviously, there are some caveats, that will be explained."

"I'm impressed by your progress. I am happy to wait for a demonstration as long as it will be prompt."

"As prompt as possible, Lord." The Oni left, the strapped shoes that kept their webbed feet from splaying clicking on the hard floor.

It was a surprisingly short period of time before Nero was led down more bare corridors to a viewing station where several Oni manned a variety technological equipment. The air in here was stiflingly humid; using his respirator suddenly felt like trying to breathe through a wash cloth. Overlooking a vast hall, the windows of the elevated viewing station revealed a crowd of bewildered looking creatures that looked surprisingly Karthian—or at least uglier versions of Karthians. In all his travels, Nero had not seen another species quite so similar.

"Are these the inhabitants of the selected planet in the new realm?" he asked.

"They are, Lord," one of the Oni said whilst others readied the laboratory. The four joints of their long legs made for eerily smooth locomotion as they flitted back and forth, long, webbed fingers working various control panels and holoscreens. "They call themselves Human and their planet is called Earth in their language, though I am sure you could rename it should it prove too complicated for one's voice box."

"They look very similar to Karthians." He deliberately ignored the Oni's barbed comment. Intergenerational memory allowed the Oni to hold one hell of a grudge.

"There are significant similarities, but also many differences. They are shorter in both stature and life expectancy. Additionally, they are more sexually dimorphic than your species. There are other differences too and a lot of junk genetics that are just evolutionary remnants. Importantly, they are just different enough that the devices won't affect your kind as well as theirs simultaneously." The Oni gestured sweepingly with three fingers towards the species cowering below.

"How old is the species?" Nero hoped the fact that his genetics didn't fully match his species wouldn't become an issue.

"Not particularly old in galactic terms, a couple of hundred thousand revolutions in their planetary time frame. Less in yours as their planet orbits more quickly."

"That might explain it." There had been a fashion for seeding distant planets with Karthian genetics many hundreds of thousands of revolutions ago, before the expansion of the Karthian Realms. Most had failed miserably, one produced the hybrid that had created genetic compatibility with the people of Inara, but this one seemed to have been semi-successful.

"Yes, it is possibly manipulation, possibly interbreeding, possibly convergence. It would take more research to determine the species' origins."

"If the technology works, it is irrelevant how they evolved."

"Agreed." The senior Oni watched as their colleagues finished their tasks and, one by one, took their places.

"Did you have any trouble with Guardian Dyadicus?" Nero asked, assuming not, given the lack of political uproar.

"He was unaware of our activities."

"That is convenient." Nero breathed a small sigh of relief. Age had not gentled his brother's temper and he had never fully forgiven Nero for handing him over to the Senate for violations of genetic guidelines in his past position as Minister of Biogenetics. Though he had pleaded ignorance, scapegoating his lead scientists, his brother had known in exacting detail the nature of those experiments. Still, at least they were civil now.

Once everything was prepared, the Oni showed Nero a small communicator-like object with an interface shown on transparent screens that unfolded from the main device.

"This technology is new and unprecedented, but from the information you brought us and the original devices, we have been able to stabilise the effects and optimise its performance as far as possible in the time we have. It has been calibrated for this species, for use on a different species, it will need recalibrating. Still there are limitations."

"One species will do for now, whilst I demonstrate its capabilities. What are the limitations?" Nero was becoming more intrigued. Part of him hadn't expected the Oni to be able to get the technology working. When he had stolen it from that laboratory on Inara, during a mission to investigate unsanctioned research at the Listurn Learning and Research Centre, he had thought it was the fevered dream of some boffin type.

"The device cannot deliver instructions. It can only put the subjects into a state of neural activation where they respond willingly to instructions and remain compliant. The instructions will need to be delivered by you through their networks, it should be simple to generate universal broadcasts using their systems as they are interconnected via radio waves and physical data transmission. You will need to speak their languages, some of them anyway. For a small planet, they have an extraordinary number."

"How many?"

"Over three thousand still in use. There is no universal language."

"They have not even established a global communication strategy? They are more primitive than I imagined."

"Conveniently, four fifths speak one of twelve languages. We have collated these primary languages ready for upload to your implant. It should be enough to establish control, but it's a large, aggressive population with limited reasoning skills—we recommend extreme caution." The Oni passed him the upload chip.

"I will take that under advisement. Which language do these speak?"

"A language called English; a version of it anyway. You might need to practise a bit, the lack of internal, logical consistency can lead to misunderstandings."

Then came a little more preparation. Then two cylindrical objects high on the walls of the hall below began to glow a faint blue. A throbbing headache pulsed through him. He hoped that the energy they were emitting was safe for the unidentified part of him as well as the Karthian part. Not that he could ask. Within moments the species below went from cowering in corners, huddled against one another to looking relaxed and comfortable. Eyes stared into the near distance as if they were lost in thought. Only one still looked frightened. It clung to its mother's leg, trying to attract her ebbing attention.

"We are ready. What instructions would you like us to give?" The Oni gave a sweeping gesture towards the amassed, and now sedated, creatures below.

"Are there any that can't be given?"

"Not that we have found. If you want the species to do things that overstep their cultural codes of conduct, for example: conspecific violence or sexual behaviour, we have found that increasing the strength of the neural activation and bioelectrical synchronicity is necessary." Expressionless thick grey skin gave no indication of any emotion as the Oni waited for Nero's instructions.

"Very well, let's try something simple. Ask them to kneel."

Nero heard a strange, coarse language in the hall beyond the glass, moments after the species knelt and did so willingly without complaint or deviation from the command. Even the old and lame knelt on the cold stone floor and stared distantly and unblinkingly. All except the child, who simply clung to and cajoled his mother. Nero noticed that another of the species wasn't behaving as the others. Although he followed the command, he looked around anxiously and fidgeted on the floor.

"Interesting," observed Nero. "What about that one? He doesn't seem to be under the same influence as the others."

"A good eye you have, Lord. That one is less affected, although if you increase power to the machines, he does succumb. They are a social creature and to an extent will follow what the majority are doing so the few who are unaffected should fall into line through social conditioning and emotional contagion."

"How long does this effect last?" Nero asked.

"Another good question and one that seems to depend on the instruction. If it is a physical instruction or a cognitive task the effect lasts until the machines are turned off, but we have found that if an emotional association is constructed, that can last for a good time after. The emotion networks of their brains seem to be very strongly interconnected with memory. For example . . ."

The Oni walked over to the microphone and said something in the strange language before turning back to Nero. "I just said, you follow Lord Nero, you believe him to be a brave and good leader who will provide for you. You feel deference and respect for him. Now watch this."

The machines went off, their faint glow fading. Below the species called human scrambled to their feet.

"Now I will ask them whom they serve."

More of the strange language echoed round the reflective stone hall below, soon after, slowly, confusedly and chaotically, the word "Nero" reverberated back from the mouths of the congregation below. The Oni running the experiment straightened to their full height and looked to Nero.

"This is most impressive." Nero couldn't help but smile. The comment elicited little gestures of approval between the Oni. "How do you see progression from these tests to this technology being tested in the field on the planet? This Earth planet?"

"The species is wide-spread so you will need to establish global control. The machines have surprising range with enough power it may be possible to create some sort of planetary network, possibly using satellites. We are still working towards the best solution. I hope you can be patient."

"I can indeed. Thank you for the demonstration, but I'm afraid I should be getting back now."

"Of course, but there are two remaining questions. Firstly, we have almost completed the necessary experiments with the subjects. Would you like them returned to their planet or euthanised?" The Oni's large, unblinking eyes surveyed Nero neutrally as he considered the question.

"How much will it cost to return them to their planet by comparison to euthanasia?" Nero looked at the frightened creatures below him.

"It will be considerably more expensive to return them to the planet than to turn off the artificial atmosphere and provide a swift and mostly painless death through suffocation. What is your decision?"

Nero had experienced suffocation; it wasn't painless. But his funds were running low, lower than he had anticipated. Not to mention to return would risk turning the eye of his brother. He deliberated whilst he watched the mother comfort her child holding him tightly in her arms.

"Take them back to where you found them. It's a poor idea to start interplanetary relations by killing too many of the target population." Nero justified his mercy without outward compassion.

"Are you sure, Lord? It is a planet of six billion, I am sure they won't miss a couple of thousand."

Nero shot the Oni a stern look.

"As you desire, Lord. Do you wish for their memories to be erased?"

"Yes, we do not want to risk the planet developing countermeasures." Nero surveyed the recoiling creatures. "As unlikely as that is," he added.

"I regret that I sometimes forget these new Karthian ways." The Oni held his gaze with black eyes. "We were not afforded such compassionate diplomacy when we were brought into the Karthian realm all those millennia ago."

"The actions of my ancestors are not my own. Non-violent methods are now the preference. Anyway, it is my hope that this technology will eclipse our current peacekeeping strategies. Security through compassionate guardianship, isn't that the latest slogan?"

"Non-biogenetic control could certainly be argued to be beneficial, particularly for subduing more violent species."

"Fewer dead Peacekeepers, more peaceful planetary populations, more compliancy with resource sharing, that's the Karthian aim." *Wouldn't want anyone to fight back whilst we pillage their resources,* Nero added to himself; in some ways a battle would feel more honest, though the Oni might disagree.

"And potentially great reward for one that delivers it."

"Hmm," Nero replied guardedly. Though the Oni had shown little ambition to insert themselves into realm politics nor had they staged any great rebellion against Karthian rule, his position was vulnerable.

"Planetary recruitment without the need for biogenetic manipulation, such a discovery would certainly make one worthy of promotion—as far as I understand your hierarchy. Do you seek to exchange the technology for status?"

The Oni's expressionless face gave no insinuation as to the purpose of the question. The large vents at the side of the neck that served as both lung and gill, and were often the only clue as to the Oni's emotion, opened and closed with unchanged regularity. Very few Oni strayed far from Isakilo, but he had lost much money in gambling games to ones who did. Without those little involuntary twitches and secretions linked with emotion that were so rife in other species, there was no way to tell when they were bluffing or to ascertain their stratagems.

"In a manner of speaking," Nero replied.

"A manner that no longer requires the use of alternative entrances, Lord?" The Oni's face looked blank and innocent, but Nero did not appreciate these questions.

"Yes, that manner. Our agreement is that there would be no questions asked. The agreed expenses for the project included a significant amount for discretion." Nero pushed down his anger so he didn't accidentally distort the light around him.

"Of course, please forgive my questions, I was merely trying to ascertain the desired end point for the project with regards to the intended use of the artefacts . . . but that does bring us on to my second question, the next instalment of your credit is requested, including the additional cost of returning the experimental subjects, shall I send the request to the usual place?"

"Yes, that would be fine." Nero hoped it would be fine, but it was becoming more and more likely that the credit request would ricochet like phaser fire off a reinforced bulkhead. His once well-padded accounts were now thinner than the mattresses in the Peace Corps barracks.

"Very good," the Oni gestured towards the door and guided him down the monotonous corridors back to the waiting room and transport beyond. "We hope to have the pleasure of your presence again soon. We will keep you updated as to the progress of your project." Before the senior Oni left, they handed Nero an entanglement chip. "In case you lost your previous one," they added "we can be contacted anytime to arrange updates."

The trip back was astonishingly uneventful. Kapi didn't look surprised to see him alive, Nix had done a superb job of fixing his coat and Koqui navigated the storm as well as could be expected, given that hail stones big enough to cave in even an Illion's broad skull were thumping into the hull (much to the consternation of the ship's synth). Nero was back at the theatre in time to have to endure a full hour of the warbled ode to the glorious rise of the realm; a sentiment not necessarily shared by other species, he inferred by the very mono-species Karthian audience. Luckily, the highest quality dispenser wine that the synth brought him made it bearable, especially as he charged it to Veyga's account rather than using his rations.

After the performance, Veyga cheerily joined him and they left for the restaurant. On Veyga's request they were seated at a private booth. Usually, Nero would have considered this an attempt not to be seen in his company, but his notoriety seemed to serve Veyga somehow. He never denied their being related or avoided him as his other relatives did. They ordered drinks made from fruit prepared at the table to prove their origin was from dirt and flora and not from food synthesis laboratories, as well as more wine poured from a large, ornate bottle dusty with age. Whilst they drank, they deliberated over the lengthy menu that described the planetary origins of each ingredient and its sensory experience in verbose detail.

"So, what are you going to have?" Veyga asked rolling up the sleeves of his gold flecked shirt.

"If you're paying, one of everything," Nero smiled, though he was certainly planning to eat as much as possible.

When they ordered, he did so without restraint. Then they waited whilst the food was prepared, a rare experience when dispenser gruel appeared within moments. Eventually, veritable mountains of food were placed upon the table before them by the waiting staff. This place was too upmarket to use synths.

New tastes mingled with familiar ones in the exquisitely prepared dishes. Nero ate until he regretted his tailoring. As they ate, they reminisced and they laughed. Nero felt a little like his old self; himself before the dungeon, before the prison, before he was treated like an outcast, when he had status, purpose and love.

"You seem in a better mood." Veyga reclined, still picking at the many and varied remains before them.

"Probably the good food, or maybe it was watching the rise of our great realm in such vivid and prolonged detail."

"Always a marvellous experience. One made all the better if one is present for it." Veyga sipped his wine without obvious tension.

"I don't know what you mean." Nero tried to look genuinely perplexed as his mood dropped heavily.

"Mmhmm," Veyga's casual observation of his absence was irritating. "Off ruining yet another's reputation were we, or was it something more interesting?"

"Check the records, if you still have clearance, you will find I was at the theatre the entire time."

Veyga laughed heartily.

"I don't see what is so funny. You're accusing me of breaking the conditions of my freedom," Nero snapped then added quietly, "many as they are."

"I am not trying to trap you, Nero, it's just we both know that you have more than enough ways to get round the Senate's surveillance and anyone else's come to think of it—even now. You forget I used to pay you handsomely for that very reason . . . in fact it would suit me very well if you were once again using those skills."

"I have told you before, Veyga, I am well out of that game, have been for a long time. If I got caught again, they may well lock me away for good, or worse."

Veyga sighed. "It wasn't fair what they did to you."

Nero eyed Veyga cautiously. His silence a condition of his freedom. "What makes you think that?" He placed his wine gently in front of him, hand shaking as he retracted it from the ornate glass.

"I figured it out. It was a sanctioned mission, wasn't it? Not one of your extra ones." Veyga met Nero's gaze, though not with intensity. "I wasn't entirely sure, but your face is telling me I am in the right space port."

"How did you figure it out?" Nero asked quietly, his breath catching in his throat. The fullness of his bulging stomach now a leaden weight that prevented his lungs from expanding.

"Your old rules—no assassinations, no family, nothing too political. Well, nothing could have been more political than being caught trying to poison Quoric; plus, there was no obvious financial incentive and, no offense intended, I have usually found you to be quite predictably mercenary in these matters. Eventually, I came to reckon that it was probably a sanctioned mission and rather than risk war, they sacrificed you on the table of peace." Veyga's voice was low, though they were a good distance from the next party, it was wise to be discreet. Good job this was a high-end establishment. In a city as congested as Sarlequa, space came at a premium almost surpassed by that of food that wasn't cheap dispenser mush. "I was always surprised they got you back alive. From what I've heard about Quoric's justice system, mercy is not a founding ideal. Now I know for sure why such efforts were made to retrieve you and why you got to keep your title."

Nero said nothing, memories of Guardian Quoric's prison flooded him. No, prison was too mild a term, a dungeon was what it was. Old scars, made invisible to the eye but etched upon his body's memory, burned with sharp pain as fear, penetrating and unfaded by the many years passed, gripped him tightly. His breath seized. Everything faded as he was transport back to that place. It had been dark when he could no longer pull in the light, so very dark in that cold place. They could see in the dark, Quoric's creatures, they had no need of light in order to be precise; to administer agony in exacting detail.

Darkness, that was all there was. Fading was the restaurant, fading was Veyga's concerned expression, fading were the remains of the feast. Darkness, that is all there is now. Glimpses of shadows, fuzzy and shifting erupted around him. Flashes of huge reflective-compound eyes and bone-sheering mandibles loomed from the blackness causing him to twitch violently.

"It's not real," he whispered to himself. Feeling for his wine, he gripped the thick stem of his glass, his shaking hands causing ripples to spread across the thick liquid so similar to blood. He drew deeply.

"Nero, Nero! Are you okay?" Veyga whispered closely.

When he felt Veyga's hand on his still painful arm, Nero startled, bending the light around him, instinctively, defensively. He disappeared.

"Cousin!" Veyga whispered hoarsely. "Come on, Nero, you're safe here. Look at me. Breathe slowly."

A face without mandibles pierced the phantasmagoria his mind was creating. Nero focused on Veyga's worried eyes, focused hard. He let go of the light, reappeared and very slowly caught his breath.

Fear was gradually replaced by anger, and panic by embarrassment, as he calmed. He felt like slamming his fist down upon the laden table; no, that would only draw more attention. Luckily only one of the staff seemed to have seen his brief loss of control, she shook her head in disbelief and carried on her waiting duties.

"Sorry about that. Bad memories." Nero forced himself to adopt a relaxed posture.

"I can imagine," Veyga said, looking genuinely concerned.

I bet you can't, Nero thought in irritated retort. There passed between them a strange silence.

"I have never seen you do that before. Quite . . . impressive." Veyga broke the silence with attempted cheeriness.

"You've seen me do my light bending many times," Nero replied too curtly. He finished his wine in a gulp and forced himself into some semblance of composure.

"Yes, but mostly just little tricks, usually to impress someone. Not that those aren't also extraordinary. Fully disappearing though, pretty remarkable. I did always wonder how you succeeded in those jobs I gave you, jobs where other contractors had so often failed."

"What did you think you were paying so handsomely for?" Nero managed a wry smile though anxiety still churned his bloated stomach.

"Maybe I should have paid more." Veyga smiled back, clapping Nero on the shoulder in a way that was both playful and comforting.

"Feel free, I could use the credit." Nero disappointedly poured the dregs of the bottle of wine into his glass, hoping that Veyga would register its emptiness.

"You could take my job?" Veyga proposed the question nonchalantly whilst brushing errant crumbs from his form-flattering shirt and highly structured trousers.

"What's the job?" Nero sighed deeply.

"Are you familiar with a moon in the fourth realm called Deilospe? It orbits the planet Akisapa." Veyga picked up a small sweet and inspected its copper veined pinkness before tossing it into his mouth.

"Not overly. Just that it's in Guardian Giulio's territory." *The blustering old fool*, Nero added to himself.

"It's a planet that is mined. Helium-3 mostly, few other things. Fusion fuel is usually a steady trade and a wise investment, especially with the energy requirements rising these days. But about quarter of a revolution ago, the gate there became uncontactable. The messages received from the planet say it is broken and undergoing repair, but I am unconvinced, a gate repair doesn't take that long even for a remote moon like Deilospe. I sent someone to check on the status of the repairs as the delays were affecting trade. They aren't contactable, haven't been since they arrived in the system."

"And you want me to do what exactly? Be an engineer and fix the gate before too big a dent is put in your finances? Not really my area of expertise."

"I want you to find out what is really going on. Maybe it is just a broken gate. Maybe not. It shouldn't be too dangerous, just a little industrial espionage. Nothing you haven't done before."

"How much does it pay?"

"Fifty thousand credits."

Nero laughed.

"Okay, okay. For the Invisible Lord, seventy."

"One hundred and I'll do it."

"For a bit of poking around?" Veyga looked aghast, but Nero knew it was all part of his theatrics. He had known Veyga his whole life, he also knew the incredible wealth his side of the family had acquired so who did he think he was fooling? As the old saying goes—those that wear their wealth can expect no bargains.

"A bit of poking around which has already probably killed at least one poor dupe who was sucker enough to take one of your jobs so some compensation for the risk is in order, I think."

"I should have left that part out." Veyga rolled his eyes.

"You should have, but didn't, so the Invisible Lord wants a fair price."

"Eighty thousand credits." The words seemed to almost pain Veyga. "Half now, half when you return with useful information."

"Eighty-five, another bottle of this for the table," Nero waved the empty bottle pointedly, "and a few more for my quarters." The negotiating was distracting Nero from the anxiety which clawed constantly at the edges of his perception and for this he was grateful.

"Fine!" Veyga relented. "You've become more difficult to bargain with."

"I'll take that as a compliment, though I like to think of it as knowing my worth . . . and it's more than a soldier's wage." Nero muttered the last part.

"Yes, I heard about your return to service."

"Of course, you did. Don't worry, I intend to protest my reinstatement or at least the rank of it."

"Are you going to take it up with your parents or the Senate?"

"One or the other, I expect."

“Good luck with that, I am sure it will go really well.” Veyga teased him gallingly.

VIII

Two days of listening to interviews with the other witness, if they could be called that, and deliberating in the discomfort of the motel brought no further information regarding what had happened to the townsfolk. In the cold light of day, after their initial discussions, Natalia had decided that Raven must be wrong and Raven found herself disinclined to argue. It was an outlandish claim. Maybe Terry was just having a bad acid trip and she had been swept along with the emotional strength of the memories. Maybe. Hopefully. Either way, this place was giving her the creeps. An anxiety not helped by the intermittent tornado warnings.

"I think I am going to head home tomorrow," Raven told Natalia with a deep sigh. "I don't think there is anything more I can help with here."

"I was thinking the same thing," Natalia replied. "It might be more useful for me to use my contacts to see whether there are any other unexplained mass disappearances. Not to mention, this bed is making my poor old bones ache." She eyed the bed angrily as she changed into more comfortable clothes for dinner.

"I know what you mean." Raven rubbed her back as she lay on the mattress that was determined to make every one of its squeaky springs known. She didn't even realise they made this sort of sprung mattress anymore.

"Don't be ridiculous, young thing like you should be able to tolerate a few nights on a lumpy mattress. When I was young, around your age, I was running missions with just a camping mat and a sleeping bag."

Raven chuckled.

"What's so funny?" Natalia looked slightly affronted.

"Oh, nothing," Raven said. This was the longest, she had ever spent with Natalia's and she had found her surprisingly easy company. When Connie had died, it had become clear that her late wife—in all but name—was the one with most of the friends, the rest of her friends had slowly passed on in the intervening years, since then she hadn't exactly been the life and soul of the party.

"Come on, what's so funny?" Natalia wasn't going to let it go.

"How old do you think I am?"

"I don't know, early thirties?" Natalia studied Raven's face carefully before heading to the bathroom to finish her grooming.

"Aww, how flattering, but wrong. I guess my file was missing a few details." Raven tried to remember if she had ever told Arty (Natalia's predecessor) her true age.

"Forties? You can't be fifty or I'll want your skincare regiment before you leave. Don't tell me you've been messing with that telomere lengthening nonsense."

Raven made a gesture pointing upwards with a chipped nail.

"No?!" Natalia looked incredulous. "Do you bathe in the blood of virgins?"

Raven snorted with laughter and shook a head of unruly hair. "Oh, you know, only on special occasions," she said sarcastically. "Don't be ridiculous."

"The lines between reality and the ridiculous have definitely become more blurred than I would like. How old are you then?"

"Old enough that I should be the one saying 'when I was young'." Raven put on her best granny voice for effect.

"You're having me on." Natalia paused for a while to apply a lip tint and some eye brightening drops as she visibly pondered this information. "You don't act old at all," she said eventually.

"As in I don't hobble around with a walking frame calling people 'dear'? Or in that I don't seem very wise?" Raven raised an eyebrow.

"Honestly, both. Though, I guess you have never given me bad advice," Natalia said crossing the room to fix her hair in the tarnished mirror. "But, the other day, you also snapped at me because you were hungry."

"See," Raven giggled, "I'm a grumpy old woman who likes to eat early. Speaking of which, are you done yet? You're going to give these squaddies a heart attack."

"At my age? Don't be silly." Natalia waved a dismissive hand at her.

"You should hear their thoughts."

"God that must be strange, to hear everyone's intimate thoughts. Not to mention highly annoying." Natalia pulled on her low-heeled boots and Raven sighed with relief that they were going to get some food at last.

Raven shrugged. "I can block them out most of the time, but sometimes it is like someone is shouting at you."

Raven pulled on her jacket, but was pleased to be greeted by a warm, clear night upon exiting the motel. Past the solar-powered street lights that flickered stiltedly into illumination, stars started to glitter, rarely unencumbered by the ever more common superfluity of cloud. The air smelt like summer was on its way already. "Ready for some more junk food?"

"Ugh," Natalia seemed to shudder. "Is it wrong that I am craving salad?"

"Yes, this is America's finest junk you're turning your nose up at."

"Yeah, well, I am going to have America's finest spare tyre and heart disease if we stay here much longer," Natalia said, heels clicking on the cracked tarmac of the old motel's car park.

"You young'uns don't know you're born. When I was young, if you wanted sugar, you'd have to fight some angry bees for some honey." Raven did her best creaking old woman voice.

"This is an odd turn in our relationship." Natalia smiled and took Raven's arm. "How old are you anyway?"

Raven looked away, her smile faded.

"Okay, you don't have to tell me." Natalia squeezed her arm reassuringly. "One day you'll trust me enough to tell me these things, I will promise you that." She meant every word.

They joined the queue at the food stand behind various army personnel, some bantered with each other boisterously, others seemed solemn and withdrawn. There was an air of tension. After Natalia had concluded that there was nothing that could be deemed healthy on the menu, and relented to another meal of fast food, they ordered some dinner. Rather than take the food back to the motel and eat on the beds, they decided to enjoy the fine evening air wandering slowly to the edge of town.

At an intersection between abandoned streets, Natalia asked, "would you like me to escort you across?" with a mischievous smile which flashed straight white teeth and held out her free arm.

In return, Raven grinned crookedly and answered, "why, thank you, dearie. You are so kind."

At the edge of the lost town, they sat on a weather-beaten bench looking over the field where the markings were. In the little light that the energy-saving street lamps afforded them, the field looked like nothing but a field. Faint silhouettes of straggly trees dotted the horizon far beyond. A gentle breeze carried the smell of fading sunshine and dew-dampening grass; it swirled gently around them. For a while they ate and for a longer while they talked. Eventually night completely enclosed them in their pool of dim lamp light. It could have been any night save for the eerie silence, penetrated only by the occasional buzz or chirrup of insects, and the roads that were empty save for the soldiers that patrolled from time to time.

"We should head back. It's getting late," Natalia said rising from the bench. It creaked in aged relief.

Raven was about to agree when she could have sworn she heard something in the distance. Her mind echoed with a barrage of sudden, frantic emotion, she gasped and slammed up her walls against the invasions of other minds; many other minds. Even with her mind's defences, she could hear a faint muttering internally and externally. Maybe she was having a junk food invoked stroke. No there it was again. Louder this time. "Can you hear something?"

"No," Natalia replied, looking concerned. "Wait, maybe. What is that?"

"I can feel the presence of people. Lots of them."

"Maybe some soldiers are coming this way?" Natalia looked around clearly on her guard, every muscle taut.

"No, it's not soldiers. There are too many and they are scared. Really, really scared."

Raven shuddered with by proxy terror and stepped out of the light of the street lamp to peer into the darkness beyond. It took a while for her eyes to adjust to being immersed in blackness, but slowly small details began to appear. Beyond the field, the silhouettes of trees on the horizons were joined by moving shadows. A vast mass of them. "There. Can you see?"

Natalia peered over the fields where Raven pointed. "Holy shit, I think you're right."

"Do you have Franklin's number?"

"On it."

Natalia made the call as Raven stared aghast at the avalanche of shades which shambled chaotically towards the town through the dark. Waves of terror crashed against her; the emotion was almost overwhelming. Her heart beat against her ribs and she fought to retain control of her breathing. Panic is contagious.

By the time the swarm of people reached Raven, heavy vehicles full of military and intelligence personnel and supplies had arrived. Besides themselves, the people clustered around the soldiers, desperately seeking safety. Some cried and screamed, some shook violently, some stared vacantly in stunned silence, some carried others—either old, young or ill from being denied medication, but all reeked of sweat and neglect. A scene of shock and chaos unfolded around Raven as she attempted to prevent herself from drowning in the sea of emotion.

In an attempt to be useful, Raven busied herself giving out blankets and water. Raven couldn't risk listening too intensely to the hysterical minds of the crowd. Terror already clawed at the edges of her perception, testing her defences, waiting for weakness. What was strange about the little she could access of their minds, without being overwhelmed by paralysing panic, was how little she could access. Usually, events that caused trauma were replayed vividly and unrelentingly in the immediate aftermath.

Despite her attempts at defence, fear and panicked thoughts bombarded her unrelentingly. What was missing, though, was memories, and where the memories should have been was only emptiness and confusion. It quickly became clear to Raven that not only were the people for the most part uninjured, but that they had no idea what had happened to them.

Raven whispered to Natalia, "None of these people have any memory of where they have been."

Questions tumbled from the residents as to why they were all so far from home in the dark of night, what day it was and where they had been. Few answers were forthcoming to comfort them. Part of Raven was curious to scan their memories more closely, to try and expose the cause of their absence and fear. Intense fear. Akin only to that which she had felt during times of war or catastrophes of similar gravity. But when she dropped her mental shields, even a little, to reach towards one of the gathered people, the emotion of the crowd hit her so hard she couldn't draw breath. *No, that was a terrible idea,* she concluded.

It was early morning when medical, forensic and investigative teams escorted the last family to their home. From the moment that the town had reappeared, everything had felt frenetic. Raven's head felt fuzzy with the flurry of it all and ached from the effort of keeping other's emotions at bay. Much more would need to be done for these people, but for now sleep, food and home comforts would be the best remedies.

Once reinstated in their motel, Raven pulled off her sturdy boots leaving them where they fell, stripped to her pants and the faded black t-shirt she had been wearing for too many days and crawled into bed. Too tired to even bother concealing her skin's patterns with pyjamas.

"Not even going to change?" Natalia asked, eyes skimming over Raven's bare legs.

"Nope," said Raven, her head peering out above the thin duvet watching Natalia meticulously folding her clothes. Raven noticed she was trembling slightly and told herself to pull it together.

"Well, I can't blame you, it's been one hell of a night."

"It's been one hell of a week."

"You're not wrong," Natalia sighed, her usually good posture sagging with exhaustion as she sat on the bed. "I don't know about you, Grandma, but I need a nightcap." Natalia pulled a sliver hipflask from her bag.

"You've been holding out on me!" Raven sat up against the creaky headboard as Natalia poured slick, amber liquid into the small glasses by the kettle. She purposely ignored the "Grandma" comment.

"I forgot it was in there until I opened the side pocket this morning." Natalia's hands tremored as she poured. In a rare clumsy moment, Natalia knocked the glass from the tatty drawer top and the worn carpet gave no cushion so the glass cracked into sharp shards upon impact with the floor.

Distressed, Natalia bent to recover the remains of the glass. As she collected the scattered, dripping fragments, Raven saw Natalia reflexively pull her hand towards her.

"What's wrong?" she asked.

Natalia turned towards Raven, blood dripping from her hand, oozing liberally from a cut on her right palm. Swiftly, Raven gathered a cleanish towel from the bathroom and applied pressure to the wound. She sat Natalia down on the side of her bed.

"Sorry, I . . . I am just so tired." Natalia was shaken, but surprisingly unbothered by the pain as Raven inspected her cut.

"No need to apologise. This does need some sort of binding or stitching though, or every time you move your hand, it's going to reopen."

Natalia groaned. "I guess we will have to find one of the army medics."

Raven shook her head. "No. They have been through enough tonight."

"Well, if I can find a needle and thread, we could sterilise them using the kettle. I think I could stitch it one handed." Natalia removed the towel and prodded at the gash a little, then went to get up.

Raven, who still had her arm, pulled her back to sitting and replaced the towel as the blood pooled in Natalia's hand and threatened to spill. "I am not sure field medicine in a motel room is a good idea. Particularly this motel room."

"What do you suggest then?" Natalia's tone was sharp.

"I guess we see how much you trust me and how much you can be trusted." Raven pushed the edges of the cut together rousing a discomforted weight shifting from Natalia.

"These riddles are getting old Grand—" Natalia stopped in her tracks, unable to speak further as Raven used the energy that pulsed through living things to navigate through Natalia's mind following her nerves to the wound. Under her guidance, Natalia's body began to bind the vessels, uncleave the nerves, unsever the tendon fibres and seal the skin.

Raven never got used to the strange and deeply unpleasant sensation of giving her energy away, life's energy itself, to help others (or not help on occasion). Even this small amount felt like courting death itself, but it was nice to know that she still so intensely wanted to live. When she smeared away the last of the blood with the towel all that was left of the previously gapping cut was a faint line.

"What the fuck did you just do?!" Natalia went to the bathroom and Raven heard her washing her hands. She re-entered the room shortly after.

"You may feel a little tired so take it easy tomorrow." Raven picked up the last of the glass very carefully, then got back into bed.

"How did you do that?" Natalia asked, looking more agitated than Raven would like.

"This leads down the same road as the mind conversation we had before, its linked, I have no clue how." Raven fell into bed and pulled the duvet up to cover all but her head. She felt chilled and even more gratingly tired now.

"But . . . I . . . This doesn't make any sense, any of it. You, this town, the world." Natalia grasped her flask and drank deeply.

"I know, I'm sorry. If it helps, it doesn't make much sense to me either." There was silence. Emotions warred within her colleague. "I overstepped a line, didn't I?" Raven rubbed her face and pulled her hands through her knotted, motley hair.

"No, of course not." Natalia took another swig from the flask and passed it to Raven. "Thank you, I should have led with thank you, sorry."

"It's okay, I understand. It's not normal. Please, don't tell anyone." Raven took several swallows of the sweet, caramel whisky that momentarily burnt her throat in a wonderfully warming way. "Not even Aziz."

"I won't." Natalia was solemn. "It will be our secret. The latest in a long line of secrets."

"I appreciate that." Raven took another slug.

"It's a nice . . . ability to have. Would have thought you would be a doctor?" Natalia reached across the narrow gap between the beds and took back the emptying flask.

"I have done a bit of healing on and off, but it's not that simple." Raven felt the whiskey settle in her stomach and send tendrils of warmth through her body. She yawned.

"What do you mean?"

"I can't just heal and heal, sadly. I have to give away something of myself or someone else to do it. A life for a life. It would do me a lot of damage if I gave too much away to heal someone else. It could possibly kill me. It's possible to use donors, which used to be easier in the days when pain and blood were regular sacrifices to heal the sick or implore a variety of entirely useless gods to do it for you . . ." Raven abruptly stopped. That was way too much. *Damn whisky! Damn tiredness!* she thought. Natalia had her disconcerting, intelligence-gathering, poker face on again, but a wave of sudden worry flowed from her. "I didn't kill anyone," she said. Not whilst healing anyway, her internal voice added.

"Sacrifices?" Natalia's non-judgemental tone was slipping.

"Well, if I can't give enough, I can take it from others. Relatives, friends, technically animals, but I hate that they can't consent, and plants, but it's not effective." Raven sensed Natalia relax a little.

"You can take it? Take their life? Could you kill someone?"

"Technically, but I could also just use one of the more traditional methods of killing." Raven laughed a tense, throttled laugh. Natalia looked unimpressed. "If I took your gun from you, it's not like you couldn't just stab me instead. It's about intent."

"I guess that's true, but . . ." Natalia smiled slightly.

"Nat, I know that this is all a rather big shock," Raven interrupted, "but please can we have the rest of this conversation tomorrow?"

"Yes, sorry for the Spanish inquisition."

"No worries." Raven switched off her kitsch beside lamp with its mismatched shade.

"I should mop up the rest of the mess or it'll stain." Natalia's deep-set brown eyes had been lingering on the watery stain of blood and whiskey. Raven could sense a desire to clean in Natalia that was almost like an itch that needed to be scratched.

"Yeah, because that stain is the one did for this carpet." Raven wriggled down the bed and settled in.

"You're right, you're right. Sorry. Goodnight." Natalia switched off her lamp and the room fell into darkness. "Thank you again, Grandma," she said to the dark.

"Stop calling me that!" Raven grumbled sleepily in reply, but she was secretly glad that Natalia was comfortable enough to tease her.

Raven slept fitfully, waking from nightmares she couldn't remember to shake uncontrollably the dark. Each time she awoke, all that was left of the nightmares that roused her were the feelings of gut-wrenching terror that spilled from the townspeople the night before. Their minds empty of memory, but overflowing with fear and confusion.

When Raven next awoke, daylight streamed through the thin, floral curtains. The smell of stale alcohol and soap saturated the room. A damp patch of carpet was all that was left of last night's incident. It was very late morning, her handset told her. Her roommate was nowhere to be seen, so she made herself a substandard instant coffee with the dwindling motel room supplies. If the coffee ran out, she was definitely leaving today. She turned on the TV and drank the disappointingly crude offering amongst her crumpled bed sheets.

For a while she watched the news, but soon became sad and bored, so flipped through the few terrestrial channels still on air and eventually settled on watching very old reruns of Brooklyn Nine-Nine and The Simpsons. Apparently, this channel's target market was aged millennials who couldn't access the internet in their crumbling care homes. *Meh, still funny*, she thought, as she enjoyed Captain Holt's stony-faced take downs.

From beyond the walls of the motel, she could hear the susurration of many frightened minds. She hid from them in her pants and t-shirt watching the endless reruns of daytime comedy and cartoons. Eventually, Natalia breezed into the dim, musty motel room. Raven smelt food and felt instantly more joyous.

"Have you got food?" Raven asked, stomach gurgling with sudden impatience.

"I thought you might appreciate some breakfast, though you might as well call it lunch at this point." Natalia handed her a large breakfast burrito, a sticky-looking pastry and a much less disappointing smelling coffee in her own travel mug. She hadn't even noticed it was missing.

"Where did you get this?" Raven asked, mouth already full.

"The guy who runs the deli opened it this morning. There's some comfort in routine, I guess."

"What's going on out there?"

"Lots of people asking questions and not many getting answers. The FBI are going door-to-door, but Franklin said they weren't getting much when I saw her. It's much like you said, no one seems to have any memory of where they have been for the last couple of weeks. Everyone is very scared."

"I know, I can feel their fear. Something happened to them, something must have caused that terror." Remembering the surge of heart-racing fear that had flooded across the field last night, she shivered.

"Maybe after you've eaten, we can walk around and you can do your voodoo, see if we uncover anything?"

"My voodoo," Raven sighed. If she were honest, she didn't want to open herself to the whispers beyond the walls to play brain detective. Especially not after messing up so badly with Terry. "I am not sure I could find out any more than what I have already told you."

"Are you okay?" Natalia asked gently. "You seem worried."

"There's just a lot of very raw emotion out there. It's difficult to defend against it. Especially after everything else this week, the summit and all. I guess I'm just tired." Saying the words made Raven feel weak. "Let me eat and I'll see how I feel."

"You don't have to do anything you don't want to. This is pretty far out of our arrangement."

"I know, and part of me really wants to walk away . . . not just walk! Freaking run away, very fast, from all this weirdness." Raven took a deep breath and a glug of coffee. "But I also know there is something important happening. Something we need to know about. So, I will do what I can."

"Thank you. I think everyone here could use some normality right about now. If you can't or don't want to do anymore at any point, I will understand. If you do, I will be there with you. Not that I can be much help." Natalia's well-shaped brows furrowed in sympathy.

"I don't know, if it goes wrong, you can be there with a helpful slap." Raven smiled trying to appear insouciant.

"Of course, anytime." Natalia smiled back generously, cracking her knuckles in jest.

"Anyway, how are you feeling?" Raven nodded towards Natalia's hand.

"Never better, thank you." Natalia held up her hand as evidence. "I only wish my brain felt as good as my hand. I just can't fathom all of this," she added.

Raven nodded agreement as Natalia busied herself answering emails on a handset that folded out impressively into a mini laptop. She finished her brunch, though the pleasure of it was soured by the thought of going outside and being immersed in the dragging torrents of anxious minds, so she sipped the dregs of her now-cold coffee, slowly. Although she avoided eye contact, she could feel Natalia's growing impatience. Raven shut out the tendrils of irritation that reached towards her. Even then, tension hung in the air.

"Fine, let's go." Raven resigned herself to the coming discomfort.

"I didn't say anything."

Raven raised an eyebrow in response.

"Well, you may need some pants." Natalia nodded towards Raven's bare legs.

Raven looked down confused for a second, before realising Natalia meant trousers. She pulled on last night's jeans, which were also the night before's jeans, and scraped back knotted hair. If she didn't leave soon, she would have to brave the laundry room, but like the bathroom she now entered to freshen herself up, she wasn't sure if she would be any cleaner for the using of it. Within minutes, she was ready.

The streets outside were not overly busy, after walking around for a while it seemed that the town's people had divided themselves into three main camps. Those who craved normality with a verve such that they were attempting to force it to occur, despite the numerous army and FBI paraphernalia and personnel that unsubtly littered their streets. Some shops were open and some people occupied the streets as if running chores. There were those who sought out authority figures, either to demand answers that could not be provided or to seek a form of refuge. And finally, there were those that twitched their drawn curtains and would probably need significant persuasion to leave their houses ever again.

Raven walked a difficult line, trying to stay open enough to be useful to Natalia, without being overwhelmed by the frenzied thoughts of the people who passed them. She tried to choose those who had managed to master some of their fear to probe for memories, but there was nothing. No residual memories, just a sense of deep terror. It was like hearing the sound track to a horror movie without being privy to the tale itself. She shuddered, recalling Terry's strange memories, her imagination filling in the blanks with awful speculations.

"Are you okay?" Natalia asked.

"I'm fine," Raven snapped in reply. Then, feeling the sharpness of the tone raise guilt in Natalia, repeated, "I'm fine," softly this time.

"Anything?"

"Nothing. Not a damn thing. It's creepy as hell. Mass amnesia, it just doesn't happen. Maybe it's some sort of new mass hysteria?" Raven rubbed her temples; a deep headache was beginning to embed itself behind her eyes.

"Your guess is as good as mine, in fact it is probably much better. Do you want to stop?" Natalia placed a hand gently on her arm.

"No let's keep going. We need to know why this happened and if it is going to happen again." Raven looked around with blurry eyes, they were near the command centre at city hall. Official looking types strode with purpose and stony faces from temporary structures to the big FBI trucks and back. A small crowd had gathered and shifted anxiously every time someone important looking passed them. Where before fear had entirely possessed them, now anger was now emerging. It was stifling to be too close to them so Raven crossed the small green (if it could be called that) outside city hall to sit on a bench.

Her desired peace was significantly interrupted by the distraught screams of a toddler in a playground nearby. Although his mother desperately tried to comfort him by holding and gently rocking the writhing child, he bellowed in red-faced, tear-stained distress. Instinctively, Raven pushed calm towards the poor child, she pitied their situation. Hard enough to deal with fear when you'd learnt to control your emotions.

As the calm reached him, he quieted. His thoughts became clearer. As clear as a toddler's thoughts ever were, with imagination and naivety colliding as they do, whilst they try to figure out the world. There was a flash of something more concrete from the child, something more than just unbridled fear, a large hall, cold and hard, a memory of strange looking creatures behind high glass. Raven exhaled. Why did it have to be the poor child! She caught Natalia's eye and nodded towards the playground.

"Are you getting something from her?"

"No, him. The child."

IX

It was the fourteenth hour, midday, well just past, when Nero arrived at the training yard. He didn't want to seem too keen and last night's real wine had left him with a very real hangover. Theta raised a brow at him as he joined the ranks of soldiers in the vast high-walled yard.

For a while, he thought he had been spared the embarrassment of being assigned standard-issue fatigues. That was until Theta finished orientating her regiment regarding today's training manoeuvres and unceremoniously sent him off to change in the barracks. The soft armour suit that hung on his assigned locker was ill-fitting, worn and without style. Nero huffed and slammed the locker shut; his prison uniform had been more flattering than this.

On the training yard, Theta barked orders that reverberated off stone and they began some drills. Many years out of service had left Nero unfit. More unfit than he had believed, given his still lithe shape. It infuriated him to be left behind, huffing and sweating, in the wake of the others. To add to the cacophony of unpleasant physical sensations, his arm still hurt incessantly, though luckily his range of motion seemed unaffected. What is the point of this? He grumbled internally. All the actual fighting was left to the synths and the drones these days anyway. He glared at Theta, who vexingly, just suppressed a smirk in return. The same glaring expression caused the other soldiers to give Nero a wide berth—that gave him some small satisfaction. Whispers he overheard regarding their mission the other day, gave him significantly more.

During the target practice, he redeemed himself slightly. He had always been a decent shot with a phaser, though he could have sworn these new target drones were faster than the old ones. When it came to battle simulations, holographic enemies and strategic obstacles burst forth with horrific realism from holoemitters stationed on tall, dark pylons. Despite his attempts to be agile, he received shocks from the enemy drones and synths several times during the simulations.

Nero's humiliation was at its devastating pinnacle when he saw an older female soldier and younger male laughing at him as he hid behind a holographic wall and rubbed the side of his leg where the shock had hit him. In retaliation, he made it appear as if the drones had passed his deriders' bunker, when in fact, they hovered nearby. Both his mockers broke cover and sprinted for their objective just in time to receive multiple shocks as they came face-to-face with the drones. Nero didn't hide his mirth as the soldiers stalked away, looking angry and suspicious.

"I saw that," Theta whispered, suddenly beside him.

"They deserved it," Nero shrugged.

"For what? Daring to mock the infamous Lord Nero's performance for the embarrassment it is? Do you remember any of your training or were those decades a waste of the Realm's good credit?" Theta's expression was as stern as her words.

"Harsh words, Sister." Nero felt surprisingly deflated.

"That's because here, I am not your sister; I am your commander. You are going to be in the field with these comrades, so if I were you, I would start playing fair and earning some respect, rather than nurturing their fear of you." Theta walked away, leaving him feeling as admonished as a child.

Nero was glad when the simulations ended. He suspected that would be the end of this ridiculous mockery of military training, but he was wrong. Theta started the melee combat drills in earnest. It had only been a few hours, but his every muscle ached unbearably. Old scars, carved deep into his flesh, sent shooting pains up knotted, broken nerves. He felt old despite not even being middle aged for a Karthian (one with access to rejuvenation anyway). To escape being called up for the melee, Nero stood at the back of the ranks and did his best not to catch Theta's eye. He rested, watching rain, as much acid as water, fall on the force field high above the city. Removing his helmet, he pushed back errant locks of his still sweat-damp hair. A burly, grizzled-looking man offered him water from his canteen. He wore the symbols of his elevated rank and long service. Nero drank the water and expressed his gratitude; he had not thought to bring his own. Eventually, he was hauled up to the front, as he knew he would be, and was handed a blunted spear. A least they didn't insult him with a training stave.

Theta paired him with a young-looking soldier who couldn't have yet made her first century. Steely eyes glared out from under a standard issue helmet, she was tall, taller than him, but not by much, and of a stalwart build that matched his broadness. Flexing his sore arm, he tested the weight of the spear. Resolved not to flinch nor show a trace of the pain in his face, he set his eyes on his sparring partner. Others around them were already fighting; the clashes of weapons and shouts of hand-to-hand combat ricocheted around the training ground. He used to be a passable fighter; a skill that had been largely preserved thanks to the tiresome trouble that being a named traitor brought. Not that those were ever fair fights, he had made sure of that.

"Whenever you're ready," Nero said to his opponent still testing the weight of the spear on his injured arm.

She came at him fast, surprisingly fast. He met her blow, but only just. Every strike, jab and sweep she swiftly dealt thereafter, he struggled to parry. A hard blow stuck his injured arm. He inhaled sharply and spun out of her reach. Anger roused in him. Clearly, she was trying to prove herself by humiliating him, or perhaps it was the animosity of a patriot towards a traitor; either way, her defeat or injury of him would likely ingratiate her with her comrades. Blood pumped hard through his veins as his anger turned to rage. He was sick of all of this. If they wanted to hate him, let them have reason to.

The soldier came towards him again with brutal shots designed not for training, but to cause significant injury. This time when she drove her spear home towards his chest, it met only air. Without mercy, he dealt a hard blow to the back of her legs, sweeping them from beneath her. The hard, grey stone floor knocked the breath from her lungs, her helmet hitting the ground just after with a crack loud enough to summon some regret in him. As the young soldier lay gasping for air, he held the blunted tip of the spear to her neck.

"Yield," he growled at her.

"That wasn't fair, you . . . you cheated," the young recruit gasped at him.

"Do you think any real fight is fair? Do you think your enemies will care about what is fair? In real fights, in real battles, death her fair self is coming for you if you lose, whether you fought fair or not." Nero edged the dull point of the spear into the soft flesh of her throat. "Now yield?" he snarled.

"I yield," she said in a hoarse, panicky voice, water filling her eyes with tears that did not fall, but knotted his stomach with guilt.

"NERO! What was that?" Theta roared, suddenly close.

In his fury, Nero had failed to spot Theta crossing the yard. She tore the spear from his hand, wrenching his arm painfully in the process and dismissed his sparring partner who scrambled away to the refuge of her aggrieved-looking comrades.

"Fighting. Real fighting, or can your soldiers not handle the real thing?" he barked back. Although Nero was aware that his tone was a grave error in judgement, he couldn't seize control of his anger.

"Was that how you were trained to fight, Soldier? Do you think it's the way we should be teaching others?" Theta's voice was now horribly calm, he sensed his punishment was going to be severe.

"No, that's the kind of fighting that has kept me alive, my training would have seen me dead many times over. Is that what you want for this regiment? Death? To be yet more battle fodder for the Karthian Realms?" Why couldn't he stop himself. His blood felt so hot, it seemed to burn inside his veins.

"So, you believe that I am training my soldiers in methods of fighting that would see them defeated? Methods that I myself specialise in? Do you believe me to be an inefficient fighter likely to feel death's cold kiss on the battlefield?" Theta stood her ground in front of him, eyes locked on his, her posture formal, but not tense.

There was no good answer. Time passed. Nero knew he should back down and cut his losses. Ill-conceived pride and petulant anger refused him the words.

"Well, Soldier, as you clearly think me such an incompetent fighter, you won't mind fighting me yourself and showing us all how it's done." Theta walked to the armoury racks and picked out two taser spears. Nero's heart sank. He knew he had backed her into a corner and now to secure her leadership she was going beat him bloody given half a chance. "And feel free to use your tricks; as you say, we can't expect fairness from our opponents," she added, handing him the spear. Why was she so fond of these ridiculous traditional weapons?

"As you wish," he replied through gritted teeth.

Silence clung to the air as they circled one another. Nero had always found the trouble with fighting Theta was that she was faster, stronger and more accurate than him; fortunately, she was also honourable and disciplined, that was her weakness and it regularly gave him the edge when they had duelled in the past. Of course, that was before he had spent a decade rotting in a Karthian prison and another two decades drinking away the memory of the previous one.

Nero tested Theta with a few polite strike and parry moves. She was still strong, fast and accurate. As they danced the familiar footwork of their training, he felt the muscle memory of his long years of service reawaken in him. Old strength gathered in languished muscle and he drove her back some way with a frenzy of strikes. She missed one parry and he glanced her arm with the arching electricity. Theta retreated out of range shaking the arm vigorously and hissing with the pain, she glowered at him.

Regathering her composure, Theta checked her arm's responses with an impressive spin of the spear and they restarted their dance. Back and forth across the yard they fought, spears clashing loudly. Nero felt pretty pleased with his performance, until Theta seemed to bore of the routine and deftly tore his spear from his injured arm with a disarming move he should have seen coming. She had been playing with him. Nero cursed as Theta held the tip of her spear to his throat.

"Do you yield?" she said calmly, barely out of breath.

Nero left his image in place; hands palm up in front of him in a gesture of submission. He collected his spear, leaving its image resting upon the ground undisturbed by his passing, and walked behind his sister. He tried to wipe the slight smile from his face as he approached her from behind raising his spear to the back of her neck. As he took a breath to retort her question back to her, Theta span swifter than a Badlands' speedway engine and drove her spear into his ribs. Convulsions shook him as he fell to the ground. His flesh, burnt when then shock had hit him, was producing a grossly familiar smell. This armour's insulation was clearly lacking. Ineffective as well as unflattering—great! As he lay stunned and groaning meekly, fighting back resurging memories of previous horrors ignited by the smell of his own scorched flesh, Theta turned him over on his side to recover.

Through the blood pulsing in his ears, he heard her say to the assembled regiment, "it is possible to defeat any enemy if you remember your training and use your senses. All of them. Be aware of your environment—especially when fighting Soldier Dyadicus. You are dismissed for the day."

Theta racked their weapons, then sat with Nero until he could speak. A horrible amount of time passed. All the while the cold of the stone floor seeped into his limp body. Eventually he could twitch his fingers and toes, a few minutes later he sat up.

"How?" he asked, his voice hoarse and wobbling with the tremors of his still disobedient muscles.

"You may play with the light, but you still make noise. Luckily, the yard is very quiet today as there is no one else training in the neighbouring yards. Also, you are more predictable than you would like to think."

"You have improved greatly since I . . . stopped serving," he conceded.

"And you are still a surprisingly difficult opponent, given your lack of recent battle experience. Leisure hall brawls notwithstanding, of course."

"Still, I underestimated you." Nero leant over his knees and stared at his feet dejectedly.

"You did. You always have. Next time don't, it will make it more interesting." Theta smiled at him and slapped him on the back, he winced in response. "And if you could at least try and fit in with your fellow soldiers and do as you are instructed, it would make my life a lot easier," she added, a little of the commander returning to her voice.

"Yes, Commander Vyrenkova." Nero saluted her shakily in jest. In return she gently nudged him, causing him to topple over and giggled watching him trying to right himself, flailing like an old synth unit on its back, as his muscles responded erratically. Everything hurt.

"I guess you want this to be a regular training experience then."

"You are cruel," Nero said, finally upright once more.

"I learned from the best," Theta responded.

"Mother?" Nero asked.

Theta laughed heartily at that, thick armour juddering with the force of it. "Speaking of our dear matriarch, I have been asked to invite you to attend a family dinner tonight."

"I think I would rather miss it." Nero couldn't not think of many things he would rather do less than sit through a meal with his family.

"You misunderstand, by ask you to attend, I was led to conclude they in fact meant, force you to attend." Theta looked apologetic as she clarified the nature of the invite.

"Tell them I was injured in training and cannot attend due to my overachieving sister attempting to kill me with a taser." Nero rubbed a twitching eye in a pointed fashion.

"Two things. One, it was not on nearly a high enough setting to kill you, I checked, and two, you really gave me no choice, you could have decided to be a soldier and not a petulant brat at any time today, but you didn't, so here we are." Theta paused and Nero groaned a reluctant acquiescence. "Given that you made today's training session a complete annoyance, I suggest you rest up, clean up, grow some iron ovaries and come to dinner."

"Fine. I will come and play the dutiful son. At least there might be decent food and drink."

"Thank fission for that. You can drop by my quarters first and see your niece and nephew if you want, then we can arrive together."

"That would be good, thanks. They are growing up so fast, I feel like every time I blink, they are taller." Nero wondered when they would be old enough to realise the stigma of having the Realm's most famous traitor as an uncle. Until now it had been a breath of fresh air to be just Uncle Nero, bringer of sweets and toys they shouldn't have.

"I know! I can't fathom how they are eight and ten already. Only a decade or so and they will start to become grown. I wish they could stay children a little longer." Theta sighed.

Nero nodded in agreement and a quiet moment passed. Before his life imploded, he and Ynomi had been considering applying for a breeding license.

"How did you injure your arm anyway?" Theta asked, breaking his lamentation.

"I don't know." *Clearly, I didn't hide my injury as well as I thought*, Nero surmised.

"You don't know?" Theta's eyebrows twitched upwards in curiosity.

"That's what I said. I woke up and it hurt. I don't remember doing it."

"Were you drinking?" Theta's tone was disapproving.

"Not enough to forget an injury. How closely were you watching me today anyway?"

"Very closely, Nero . . . very. And Kiteri definitely noticed it. That shot to your arm was no mistake. You're going to want to watch out for that one, she is a powerhouse and thinks she has something to prove."

"Sounds like this minder I have been appointed."

"Hmm." Theta looked unimpressed. "Well, make sure you let it heal, maybe consult a med-booth and I will see you at mine at 1900 hours. Don't be late . . . or intoxicated."

Nero rolled his eyes. "Am I dismissed?"

"You are." Theta was kind enough not show pleasure in his discomfort as Nero hauled himself to his feet and limped from the yard, clasping his still burning side.

After a painful journey back to his quarters on the fringe of the city—a journey spent brooding on the day's embarrassments, sulking about his later obligations, and trying to remain still as the transport navigated the sea of other transports squeezed tightly between the monolithic buildings—he began to clean his wounded side. Dispenser provided first aid afforded him some relief, but the skin was seared by the shock as well as bruised, it blistered and wept; it was going to scar.

Nero thought about heading to a med booth and getting the wound sealed and the skin regenerated, his soldier's contract would cover medical care, but he decided against it for now. Already possessing scars that were barely visible jagged lines through the faint patterns on his pale skin was odd, since their intrusion into him could still be so strongly felt. In some ways, it would feel more congruent for their contortion of his flesh to be writ upon his skin. Then again, it was nice to be reminded of who he was before the scars when he looked in the mirror. And this way, he retained his looks.

As he dressed himself into appropriate garments for a night with his family, armour notwithstanding, he found his hands started to tremor. Fastening his clothes became difficult so, exhaling in frustration, he left them half open and poured himself a glass of the wine from last night. Tightness gripped his throat with a familiar suffocating sensation as the glass filled. He drank the expensive wine with little consideration of its taste, rarity or excellence, but in doing so he came back to himself. One more glass followed before he could face leaving his quarters.

After throwing on his stitched-up coat and shoes that were starting to show their wear, he observed himself and concluded that Veyga's credits would be well used updating his wardrobe once he managed to complete Veyga's job. Before he left, he requested the best sweets the dispenser would allow within his rations and soldier's wage. The restrictions were getting tighter, he noted as the machine refused many of his requests with a glitching stutter, suggesting only the simplest of candy in its place. At this rate, it wouldn't be long before they would all be on field rations, again.

Outside his quarters, a pod took him swiftly to the quadrant of the city where Theta resided. It was near to the Senate and, therefore, was considered much more prestigious than his own fringe neighbourhood. Here functionality was replaced with grandeur. Through the tinted windows of the transport, he spied his old building on the familiar interlocking streets.

Scanning his painful wrist at the door, he was granted entrance to Theta's impressive building and well-proportioned quarters. The building's synthetic intelligence announced his arrival before he entered and he was greeted by Theta's bond mate. Pyxeis' brown skin was radiant and her curvy build wore her fitted clothes faultlessly. He quickly ceased his admiration and made their greeting formal. Lingering on Pyxeis' loveliness had got him in trouble with Theta before.

Nero's niece and nephew threw themselves at him as he entered the living area, as keen to see him as ever. Clearly, they had not quite grown old enough to comprehend the dishonour that he brought to their family. That or they were still young enough to prioritise the unhealthy food stuffs and toys the Karthian Senate had definitely not approved, that he brought them from time to time. They bounced around him eagerly as he feigned that he had not brought them anything until they all but shook the candy from him. Pyxeis tutted at the charade, but smiled resignedly.

Whilst he waited for Theta to appear, Nero was content to play a few games of Subsistence on the family's holographic boards. Trading resources, making bargains, indulging the children's attempts at diplomacy and, where necessary, being entirely devious or destructive to ensure his avatar's survival, he contrived losing more than he won, making almost as dramatic a show of his defeat as his avatar on the board, much to his audience's delight. During the game, Nero found his thoughts drifting to his own bondmate, well, ex-bondmate, and their plans for a family. Had things gone as planned his own children would have been adults by now. Assuming he wasn't sterile, as many hybrids are.

When Theta appeared, it was in tailoring far superior to his own. Pyxeis' eyes lit up at the sight of her bond so apparelled. It was probably a rarity to see her out of armour or military leisure wear. Pyxeis straightened the curved and plunging collar of Theta's neckline, before kissing her fondly. Simultaneously he felt glad that his sister's bond was still strong and a pang of grief that his own bond had unceremoniously dissolved whilst he was in prison. She had moved planets, first to Inara, then further still, in order to distance herself from him and prying gossip merchants. Nero looked away from them and concentrated on losing his game gracefully, until Theta retrieved him from the clutches of his niece and nephew, cuing much dissent.

"You do indulge them so!" Theta said as they left.

"I am making the most of their enthusiasm for me whilst I can. What with people being pleased to see me still being less common than it used to be. You would have thought I would be old news by now."

Theta sighed. "I know, Nero, but whilst you have served your punishment, it is hard for people to forget the war you almost brought upon us."

Nero just walked beside his sister sullenly. There was no reply to that. It had been made clear that if he were to tell anyone the truth of the matter, all the so-called leniency he had been shown would be swiftly revoked. Nero wondered if his sister, the military commander and supposed master of strategy, had ever questioned his true role in what happened. If Veyga had worked it out surely, she could have. Maybe, she thought so lowly of him that she believed it entirely congruent that he would do such a thing. The rest of their conversation was stilted.

The house of Zatix Dyadicus, Sarveloi Vyrenkova and, from time to time, others, bonded and otherwise, was as grand as ever. Standing in its high-ceilinged reception, surrounded by art works of various levels of taste, Nero felt a tinge of jealousy and indignance that he now lived in the standard one room quarters assigned to single individuals of little wealth; little known wealth anyway. He gritted his teeth at the unfairness of it. Who were they to live so grandly, whilst billions lived stacked in small, barely-functional boxes? It subsequently occurred to him that the fairness of it had never crossed his mind, until he was assigned to one of those boxes.

A new model synth of sleek, contoured carbon led them through to the dining hall. Strewn with the artefacts of worlds that had joined the Karthian Realms, willingly and otherwise, the hall was trying hard to be impressive and refined. It achieved the first by its sheer grandiosity, but somehow, he had always thought it missed the latter. The intermingling styles of disparate cultures annoyed Nero with their lack of cohesion. At least his little cage was not trying to be a headache-inducingly poor replica of the Senate's Museum.

In amongst the collected curiosities, he was surprised to see his eldest brother, Sarvetix. Elder by more than a century, their relationship had been . . . well the polite word would be strained, ever since Nero had reported him to the Senate for unauthorised genetic experiments. Given that it was a sanctioned reconnaissance mission that led to the report, one that he would have had no choice in carrying out, his brother's continued coolness seemed peevish. Or possibly, Sarvetix had just added his previous annoyance to his current regard of him as the family embarrassment. Given that the experiments his brother had sanctioned were still a regular feature of his nightmares many decades after, his opinion of Sarvetix was also not particularly high.

Memories of suffering children who should never have been born and the dismantled bodies of babies that never drew their first breath erupted forth and Nero's throat tightened. He steadied himself and pushed back the memories. Despite successfully infiltrating his brother's facility, he had never discovered the reason for those experiments. The data was held on highly encrypted devices and he had not been able to retrieve it during recon. During the resultant trial, his brother's explanation that he had been trying to cure rare, genetic abnormalities that evaded modern genetic correction and that the Oni took it too far, not heeding the ethical protocols, never seemed truthful—not that the Oni were against bending ethical guidelines where profitable.

Theta's response to seeing their brother was one of irritating delight. She hurried to him and clasped his upper arm, a gesture he mimicked, a gesture which symbolised their continued closeness. Nero made his way over in his own time and offered only a wrist clasp. He was surprised when his brother grasped his upper arm in return and greeted him warmly. Perhaps with his new(ish) found status as Guardian of the first realm across the void, he had finally abandoned his lingering grudge.

"Theta, you are looking well and stronger than ever. How is your command going? Keepers staying in line, I hope." Sarvetix smiled affectionately at his sister. His dark brown hair with its lustrous curl was loose, it hung over his structured jumpsuit which so closely resembled Veyga's outfit from last night. Must be the latest fashion. There was no sign of grey hairs, sagging physique or deep lines. Sarvetix was aging gallingly well, Nero observed, but then those who could afford regular rejuvenation treatments, couldn't not. Sadly, a few more decades on a soldier's credit and he would look older than his brother.

"Mostly," Theta said, glancing briefly at Nero. "We are only a small regiment assigned to minor missions, but we have been effective at our assignments so far."

"Don't be modest, I have it on good authority that your leadership has impressed the admirals. They'll be promoting you to high commander soon enough, no doubt." Sarvetix's fashionable, formal attire moved fluidly with him as he turned his broad frame to his brother. "And Nero, it's been a long-time. I hear that you have reenlisted?"

"Yes, I more heard it than did it, too." Nero was of a height with his brother, but somehow always felt small in his presence.

Sarvetix laughed as Theta rolled her eyes at him. "Still, I am sure they can make use of an experienced soldier like yourself, especially with this trouble in the outer realms, and it's good to see you putting the past behind you and earning your rations once more. 'When we all serve, we all thrive', and all that."

Nero's eyes narrowed, but he held his tongue. "How is your guardianship progressing?" he asked.

"Very well, my realm is soon to undergo expansion to recruit more planets, some with great abundance. Abundance rarely seen this side of the void anymore. Shortly, we will be one of the most productive realms in the Karthian territories." Sarvetix patted him on the shoulder in a condescending manner.

"I am glad you too have been able to put the past behind you." Sarcasm seeped into Nero's words, but his brother seemed maddeningly unphased.

"Thankfully, the Senate has long forgotten the unfortunate blunders of my previous staff, and I have repaid the penalties the Senate levied upon me many times over. My success is Karthia's success after all. Maybe one day, you too can repay the realms." Sarvetix spoke without emotion, but Nero felt enough for them both. He clenched his fists, blood thundering though his veins. Repay Karthia? Karthia should repay him! No one had been made to sacrifice more for the realms than him. A small voice inside him pointed out that the families of dead peacekeepers might beg to differ, he dismissed it as Sarvetix continued, "might take a while on a soldier's wage, though. What is that these days?" Nero saw Sarvetix's eyes, blue as Theta's, linger on his well-worn clothes as he looked him up and down. Then he smiled disarmingly and, before Nero could respond, continued, "probably not enough for someone with your special skills. We could use someone like you across the void. If you ever get bored of playing soldier with Theta, get in touch and I can probably find you a position more suited to your talents, certainly at a rank more befitting than soldier."

Nero was stunned for a moment. The offer was very tempting, a new start across the void would certainly be welcome, but the offer was also unexpected and the motivation for it unknown. Had his brother finally forgiven him? Unlikely.

"Thank you for the offer, but I am not sure the Senate would allow it. I am surprised they have allowed me back in the field at all after Quoric's threats."

"Think about it. The Senate and admirals can be appeased, I am sure," Sarvetix said with a knowing confidence.

"I am so pleased you could find time in your schedule to join us tonight, Sarvetix. We are both happy to see you so well and prospering in your guardianship," Theta changed the subject, looking distinctly uncomfortable with the direction it had taken.

"Thank you, Theta, I was following up on some unusual activity in my realm and I couldn't pass up the opportunity to see how my little siblings were doing."

Nero tried not respond too strongly to Sarvetix's reply, but he felt his eyebrow twitch. "Unusual activity?" he asked casually.

"Nothing to worry about," was the vague reply.

Maybe the Oni weren't being as careful as they assured him they were. He would need to make them aware of this potential issue, especially if he wanted to keep his brother's offer intact.

Theta busied Sarvetix in conversation, while Nero topped up his blood alcohol level until their parents deigned to join them. Sarveloi apologised for their lateness, glancing accusingly at Zatix, who swiftly blamed the stresses of politics for their delay.

Soon the meal was served with a side of rather dull conversation consisting of trivial Senate gossip and family updates. At least the food was good, irritatingly so, given that he could get barely the basics out of his dispenser with all of these new restrictions. After the meal, they sat around the gratuitous water feature of their parents' reclining room. Small creatures swam in the pool. Creatures that looked a little like tiny, heavily-finned, brilliantly-scaled people. They seemed to talk and interact; they shot him piercing looks with black eyes. It was creepy and really the only thing that subdued his desire to jump in and take a long overdue bath. He averted his eyes and instead, looked out onto their parents' exotically-planted court yard. As it grew dark, some of the plants began to glow with patterns of bioluminescence.

"How have you found your return to service?" his father asked in a sympathetic tone.

"Disagreeable," Nero replied shortly.

"I am sure you will adjust, change always takes time to feel comfortable," his mother interjected. Although the words were not unkind, her tone lacked the sympathy of his father's.

"I guess we will see." Nero stared at his drink.

"I hope you haven't been giving your sister any trouble, she was very good to accept you into her regiment when many refused you." His mother was sparing him no dignity tonight it seemed.

Theta responded in his stead. "Nero has already proven himself a useful comrade," she replied for him.

Nero breathed a sigh of relief. He looked gratefully at his sister.

"That's good to hear, but remember, he's not your comrade, you're his commander." Sarveloi brushed blonde hair away from the olive skin of her face and deep orange of her now old-fashioned robes, embroidered with the symbol of her matriarchal line—the same symbol that adorned her arm in prominence over her patriarchal line and her rank as senator. Sarveloi drew breath to continue.

"Come now, Nero is doing well at his new post. Isn't that enough?" Zatix stared pointedly at his bondmate as he sharply interrupted. He was also wearing robes, being the kind of man who couldn't understand why one would want the restriction of trousers when not required to wear them for service.

"Of course," Sarveloi acquiesced, "I am glad that you are managing to reintegrate into the Peace Corps and are proving yourself valuable already. I hope you can find some structure there and rebuild your life." His mother smiled gently at him, and he was suddenly split between the boy who loves his mother, despite her blade-sharp tongue, and the man who still felt the keen sting of betrayal.

Nero tipped his head in acceptance. Despite barely containing the pressure of everything he wanted to say, he remained silent. Inside, he raged. He raged about being disavowed, about being left captive, about being imprisoned, about his bond jilting him and about being forced to live in standard issue quarters being shunned by every idiot who he encountered for almost twenty fucking years. Nero sipped his drink and felt grateful he had chosen a strong liqueur to settle his meal and survive the evening's conversation. It dulled the constant ache from his burnt side and injured arm. Thankfully, the conversation swung away from his resurrected military career, for a while at least.

"Have you been to training yet?" Zatix asked him, convivial as always and looking more like his son's brother than his father.

"Yes." Nero answered shortly.

"How did you find it? Was it a bit of a shock or just like stepping through a gate?" His father was determined to engage him in conversation, it seemed.

"It was fine," he replied resisting the urge to refill his glass. Theta dignified him with her silence.

"Theta can get you up to speed with anything that has changed, I am sure. It's all changed from back when I served. Different tech, different strategies. Did I ever tell you about the time your Great Aunty Aoni and I were pinned down on Indemitaj, trying to recruit it into the fourth realm?" Zatix was undeterred by Nero's surliness it seemed.

"Many times," Nero griped. He actually quite enjoyed that story, though it was hard to imagine his very proper, head of strategy council, aunt running missions in her high commander's uniform.

Zatix was obviously irked, but it was a very composed irked. "Anyway," he said purposely, "you were an excellent soldier before and I'm sure you will once again be a valuable asset for the realms."

"Maybe we could talk about my value and it being made commensurate with my rank and wage?" Nero asked offhandedly.

Theta visibly winced at the question.

"You forget the position you are in . . ." Sarveloi's green eyes sparkled with anger as she snapped her focus away from her conversation with Sarvetix. She wrinkled her nose in disgust, her striking features (some given, some made) contorting with the insult of his indignance.

"Do I?" Nero cut her impending rant short and leant forward a little to meet his mother's hard stare. Though part of him still struggled to hold his ground with his mother, another part savoured driving emotion from her. He never wanted them to become complacent about what they had done to him, which was probably why he didn't get invited to many family gatherings these days.

"Nero, don't wind up your mother. I am sure that if you continue to prove yourself, we can think about increasing your wage and maybe your rank . . . with time." Zatix gestured for them to stop with a sweep of his ringed hand. His brother's offer was more and more tempting.

"Now, let's stop this bickering and enjoy our evening. Have any of you been to see that new play?"

They rattled on endlessly, but he was grateful that he was no longer the topic of the conversation. Thankfully, Theta eventually used the children as an excuse to get home. Though given how they parted, Nero suspected she was keener to see Pyxeis than her sleeping babes. That he only had his cold, empty bed to return to suddenly seemed crueller than usual. Sarvetix and Theta said their goodbyes, but as he went to leave and walk Theta home, his father requested he stay. Nero's stomach twisted. Nothing good was to follow.

As the door sealed behind Theta and Sarvetix, Nero asked suspiciously, "so, what can't be said in the presence of a commander and a guardian?"

X

Disjointed images flooded Raven's mind, memories twisted by the small child's fear and lack of understanding. Shifting and jumping, they were like a horrific clip show and alongside it all was the child's terror. Unbridled, unrelenting and inconsolable terror. Raven fought against the tide of fear, keeping herself separate, concentrating on the pressure of her arm against Natalia's as they sat side-by-side on the park bench. She didn't want to risk being dragged under the current of emotion again. Children's emotions were always the most intense and engulfing. Breathing slowly and deliberately, she tried to make sense of the fractured memories.

There were four reoccurring themes within the torrent of nightmarish images that swarmed her. A shifting, dimly-lit room filled with people. Grey-skinned creatures, tall and slender with huge eyes and small mouths that looked like every kooky abduction story's depiction of an alien. A huge hall with blue glowing lights and people moving in strange, vacant unison. And one masked, but human face, pale amongst the grey ones, behind the glass of a high window. A word echoed in her mind –Nero. There was something strange and yet familiar about that face behind the glass. She focused on the memory, trying to bring more like it to the surface of the small boy's mind. All she got in return was more of the badly cut movie reel of phantasmagorical memories, along with his desperation to cling to his mother. Never did the face move from behind the glass. Maybe this was just a small child's nightmare.

Deeper she delved into his mind, but all she could feel was desolation as he clung to his unresponsive mother in a stark, barren hall. His wails didn't rouse her to comfort him as they usually would. Thirsty and hungry, he cajoled her in every way he had learned how. Nothing. For the first time in his short life, he had felt abandoned, left to suffer his fear and pain alone. That feeling haunted him now, he had to keep checking his mother's attention, keep ensuring that she was there for him. Not a dream, these were memories. Abstract as they seemed, they did not ebb and flow, construct and destruct, half-remembered and half-experienced, as dreams did. Raven didn't realise she was shaking until Natalia took her hand in hers.

"Raven? Are you okay?" Natalia's voice seemed distant.

"Yes. I think so. Children's emotions are always so strong." Raven made as if she were smoothing her hair against the increasingly forceful breeze, quickly wiping the excess water from her eyes onto her sleeves. The child started crying again as his mother bounced him gently upon her hip. Sharp and desperate cries of anguish, needled at her every sense. *It was just a dream; you are safe and your mother loves you.* These thoughts she pushed deep into the small child, burning them into his psyche, as intense and vivid as the memories he relived. The boy settled.

Raven felt chilled. She shook, though it was not cold. It felt as if all the blood had retreated from her limbs. Rubbing her hands together, she attempted to revive her blood flow and generate some warmth. The spring air felt dense and heavy around her and smelt of coming storms. As she came back to herself, she could sense the intense curiosity leaking from Natalia, who was desperate to question her. At least she was kind enough to give her the time to recover before the inquisition.

"You can ask, but I am not sure what to say." Raven turned to face Natalia, leaving the boy to play in the park with his mother.

"Well, I guess just tell me what you can," she said gently.

So, Raven explained as best she could. When spoken aloud, it seemed ridiculous and eventually, she just tailed off, exasperated at how silly it all sounded. Natalia had her non-judgemental, intelligence-gathering face on again which meant she thought Raven was going insane.

"Please don't have me committed, I don't like those places and they can't hold me anyway." Raven put her elbows on her knees and rubbed her temples.

"I won't, don't worry, but are you sure it wasn't just a child's nightmare?" Natalia rubbed Raven's back soothingly. For a moment her touch reminded Raven of Connie, it was a strange sensation, both comforting and jarring.

"No, I don't think so, but as I said before, it's complicated and even more so in small children. They don't think and remember like we do."

"Those creatures do sound like the stereotypical image of aliens; they couldn't be more so unless they were the small and green variety. The boy could have picked those images up anywhere."

"I agree, but they moved like the things Terry saw."

"Really? Okay." Natalia paused to consider this. "Do you know what they were doing? Where they were? Or who that human was?" Natalia questioned.

"I have no idea. This is all getting stranger and stranger. It's like an episode of the freaking X-Files or, worse, Black Mirror."

"The what now?"

"Old TV shows."

"Ah." Natalia looked grave. "Is there any chance this is just all a very elaborate hoax for YouTube or some other failing website?"

"We can hope, but this is all leaving me with a very bad feeling."

"Agreed." Natalia nodded then sat in thought for a while. "I might see if Franklin and her colleagues have tested the water and air for abnormalities."

"Worth a try." Raven said, thinking that was the end of it, but more and more questions flowed from Natalia. It was overwhelming, how could she answer when it made no sense to her?

"Look, let me just show you and you can judge for yourself." Raven took Natalia's hand in hers. It was easier with a physical connection to the person. "Ready?" she asked.

"Ready for what?" Natalia looked at her warily.

"I am going to show you the child's memories," Raven answered.

"Err . . . okay." Natalia still looked wary, but she didn't pull away.

"Just bear in mind that what you see won't be exact replicas of the memories. This is essentially the voodoo version of Chinese whispers. And you might feel a bit odd, but if it gets too much you can always slap me." Raven squeezed Natalia's hand supportively.

The corners of Natalia's lips twitched upwards, attempting a smile. "Never going to let that go, are ya?"

"Nope," said Raven as she recalled the boy's memories as accurately as was possible for a memory of a memory, from a toddler's perspective, which she suspected was far from eidetic. She tried to organise them, then let them flow towards Natalia, who tensed, gripping Raven's hand hard, as the memories found her.

It took only a few seconds, but after Raven ceased her transmittal, Natalia looked somehow older. Her generous laugh lines were slack and her crow's feet deepened with the furrowing of her brow. After a few moments, she offered in a voice hoarser than usual, "I am not sure what to do with that."

"Now you see the problem." Raven reclined against the back of the bench. Tired, she was so tired. All she wanted was her own bed, her own house and fresh clothes!

There was silence between them for a while. Rustling winds filled the auditory void.

"Should we tell Franklin?" Natalia pondered as much to herself as anyone else.

Raven raised her eyebrows in dark amusement. "And say what exactly? That we think tall, grey aliens have abducted the town to play interplanetary zoo keeper for a while and then bring them back?" She then changed her voice to mimic Franklin's slight southern drawl. "And what evidence do you have to support this theory?" She changed to Natalia's New York, Jamaican, Russian mix which was much harder to copy. "Well, my buddy Raven here, she looked into the minds of a junkie and a toddler and she says that's what happened." She let sarcasm cover her words.

"Okay, okay." Natalia looked vexed for a few seconds then continued, "are you hungry again, Grandma?"

Raven felt suddenly sheepish and became acutely aware of her growling stomach. "Maybe a little. Sorry. This place is getting to me."

Natalia nodded in solidarity. "You and me both. What can we even do about this? Do you think they will come back? And what the hell did they want? What was the purpose of all that?"

Raven shrugged. "I wish I knew. Probably wise to put some feelers out among your UN contacts, see if anything else unexplainable has happened. Keep me in the loop if you find anything out and I will try to help where I can."

"Thanks, I appreciate that. Right . . ." Natalia stood with the tense posture of someone who wanted dearly to take their leave. "Let's try and find some food that looks like it might contain some nutrition."

Raven groaned in response, she craved only sugar, carbs and caffeine.

The boy played happily with his mother in the park as they left.

After a lunch that looked and tasted like it might actually be good for you, rather than slowly murdering you whilst you lay in a sugar induced coma, Natalia talked Raven into a last walk around the town. It revealed nothing of note. By the end of their stroll, which Raven spent sidestepping the endless stream of army and intelligence types and pushing away the peculiar, terror-filled voids of the townspeople, every one of Raven's nerves felt like it was on fire. Her skin crawled as if beset by insects. And another pounding headache brewed behind her eyes. She was done, she wanted to go home. Natalia took mercy upon her and agreed to a prompt departure. Raven felt just how glad Natalia was to be leaving this creepy place and the crumbling motel with its lumpy mattresses and faint smell of neglect.

Swiftly, they packed up their stuff, Natalia folding and Raven stuffing things into bags. Then, following a brief debriefing with Franklin, they went to get the hire car from its charging station. A storm was blowing in. Nearby tornado warnings constantly pinged their phones and were repeated in the car's calm and friendly tone. Despite Raven's dislike of vehicular automata, the car coped well with the gusting winds. Soon, they were on the train back to New York watching lightning crackle. In the far distance, a funnel dropped from the sky. Some other people were going to be having a bad day, too, by the looks of it. England and its temperate weather, less inclined to these extremes, was calling her home now. It may drizzle incessantly at times, and sure, the weather was getting more and more unpredictable recently, but mother nature was still much less likely to throw a truck through your house than out on these vast American plains.

When Raven readied herself to depart for JFK International, Natalia embraced her tightly and unexpectedly. Natalia had been quiet on the train and was anxious now. Raven made her promise to call, even if there was no news and she just wanted to talk to someone who understood their bizarre experience in West. From JFK, it was just a short hop across the pond on a hybrid airliner to Heathrow, followed by an annoyingly convoluted journey to collect her car from RAF St Mawgan. Heavy spring showers made the drive home much less enjoyable than her departing joy ride, despite the Aston's high-revving enthusiasm for the road. Once there, though, she was greeted by good food, a deep bath and clean sheets.

Sliding between the cool, recently-laundered sheets of her bed, feeling the soft material brush against her bare skin, her stomach so full it bordered on uncomfortable from gorging on late night snacks and still radiating warmth from her bath, West seemed like a very distant dream. A dream that quickly manifested itself as rampant nightmares from which she awoke in a cold sweat, trembling and breathless. The faces of the grey creatures, the child's anxiety, the masked face and the echoing word—Nero, Nero, Nero, haunted her fitful sleep. She slept late into the morning, trying to get to a point where she felt rested. It never came.

Weeks of sleep passed in this way and she began to feel ill and withdrawn. Not even the joy of spring and the burgeoning plant and animal life flourishing on her small slice of heaven in the rolling Devon countryside could alleviate the feelings of trepidation which plagued her night and day. It didn't help that the FBI had now completely lost control of the story. It was splashed across the media, social and traditional alike. Everyone had a theory, conspiracy or otherwise, on The Town That Disappeared, some wider of the mark than others. Though none sounded more far-fetched than her own theories, the ones that now lived rent free in her mind and haunted her existence.

A trip to surf the rolling waves of Croyde Bay temporarily distracted her. Behind the white water, she sat on her board and watched the green waves come in, picking her moment to paddle furiously, meet that perfect wave, tip over its crest and ride it in towards the shore, letting her feet find the balance beneath her. Sporadically, she felt that seamless connection between her and the wild, raw force of the Atlantic Ocean as it careened her towards the land, far past where the dunes used to mark the tide's end. More often than usual, though, she was thrown from her board and pearled along by the vast revolving weight of the water, as if the ocean was trying to remind her that she was not one of Njǫrd's children.

After one last disastrous ride during which her own board hit her in the head and she surfaced spluttering salt water from her lungs, she gave up, resorting to just lying on her board as far from the other surfers and the pulling rip tide as possible. Soon the sun had dried her face, leaving a film of salt. As she stared at the blue sky with its wispy clouds, smelt the inviting saline of the ocean and listened to the gulls try to deafen unsuspecting victims before they dove for their chips, she desperately wanted to feel her usual peace, but still, deep in the pit of her stomach, was that gnawing unease. An emotion so determined to stalk her that it defied the sun, sea, and even beers drunk under as glorious a setting sun as she had ever seen to follow her home.

Many things did Raven try to escape the relentless replaying of the pilfered memories. She busied herself with odd-jobs around the farm: tending crops, fixing fences, repairing the barn, creosoting everything. She gamed until long after the late-summer sun had set, until the only others inhabiting the virtual worlds she immersed herself in were students and teens whose parents didn't believe in bed time. She drank. She drank more. Beer became whisky became weed.

Raven braved visiting her granddaughter, Lisa, in her nursing home a few times, and enjoyed the slow conversation, reminiscing about better times before the world had begun to change. Who would have thought that, when Connie and her five-year-old daughter, Jane, appeared bruised and frightened on her doorstep that wet, autumn afternoon in 1966, she would still have family almost a century later? Not blood family, of course, but chosen family. When the Alzheimer's had set in, Raven had worried that Lisa might expose her but thankfully, so far, no suspicions had been roused and any phantastic statements were chalked up to the horrible, creeping advancement of the disease.

Still, as spring turned to summer, dread was her constant companion. Anhedonia consumed her, not even the peeping of chicks or the binkying of the few lambs she rescued from slaughter each year could raise joy in her. Even surfing the flatter waves of high summer became, at best, a form of grim meditation.

During their video calls, Natalia enquired after her health which Raven interpreted as a polite way of saying that she looked frightful. And she did. Dark circles bagged under her bloodshot eyes, she looked as tired as she felt. During the interceding months since they last met, Natalia had managed to rationalise the whole West thing into insignificance. She seemed okay, but Raven had no way of really knowing over video call. Natalia confided in Raven that the probing of her contacts had unearthed no further bizarre events. Apparently, some rather questionable surveillance of social media by the FBI had also revealed no further unexplainable events, just plenty of terrible, but sadly perfectly explainable, ones.

After months of nothing out of the ordinary, she started to feel better and to sleep deeply once again. Colour returned to her face. Her worries returned to hoping the human race didn't continue to try and wipe itself out. Normal worries. Well, normal for this century.

It was almost three months after her foreboding trip to West, just before the July Summit, as she was tending her bean plants, training the runners up the latticing, pulling the life from the weeds and giving it to the runtier vines, that a call came from Natalia.

"Raven, I need you to come in early. When can you fly?" Natalia's voice was tense.

"Why? What's happened?" Raven didn't want to know the answer. These calls were never for anything good, but since West, they seemed to have the potential to be so much worse.

"I can't discuss it now. This line is probably not secure, but there have been developments you should know about. Is this line secure?" She seemed flustered.

"I think you're in a better position to know that than me—being one of the people who could make it not so." Raven wiped her brow and then realised she had probably spread mud across her forehead.

"Right, right." Natalia took a couple of deep breaths, swore quietly and then continued. "There's been a development . . ." she trailed off.

"Yes?" Raven said gently.

"This is highly classified information, I shouldn't really be telling you, but I feel it's necessary."

"Okay, I figure most of what we do is fairly classified."

"Yes, but this is even more so."

"Okay, I promise to be discreet. I will only tell half the old boys down the pub." Raven said in an effort to lighten the mood.

"This isn't funny," Natalia snapped. It was not like her to be so curt.

"I know," Raven replied gently. "You can trust me."

For a long moment, there was silence. Raven waited.

"There are things in orbit, satellite-type things . . ." Again, Natalia seemed to struggle to transition between sentences and faded out like a badly written song.

"Aren't there always?" The statement sounded more sarcastic than Raven had meant it to.

"Yes," Natalia lent on the word, clearly unimpressed. "But now there are new ones, several of them. No country will admit ownership, there have been no recorded launches, no one knows what they do and they look quite different to anything we've placed in orbit before." Natalia sucked in a breath after the barrage of anxiety-riddled words.

"Okay, I can see why that might have you worried, especially after West." Raven felt her heart start to beat faster in her chest.

"Exactly."

"What do you want me to do?" Raven asked.

"I'm not sure, but I have a feeling we need you here." Natalia sighed. "Or maybe I just need you here."

"No worries, either way, I'll hop across the pond and meet you. Where are you staying?"

Natalia gave her a hotel name and room number and bid her to hurry herself, then she abruptly hung up. She must be rattled, really rattled. Suddenly, the rest and relaxation of the previous few days disappeared, she could almost feel the dark rings under her eyes re-establishing themselves. Grimly, Raven hauled herself off of her stiffened, dirt covered knees. She took the Toyota this time.

XI

"No," Nero said the word quietly.

"What did you say?" his mother said, though he suspected that she had heard him.

"I said no—not a crion's chance in a reactor core!" Nero shook with anger, exasperated at how his fury sounded so like a child's temper.

Sarveloi's cheeks flushed crimson and her eyes narrowed. "Why do you insist on being so difficult? I didn't raise you to be like this. Your sister isn't like this."

"Well, Theta wasn't left to rot in a cage for something she didn't do. If she had been, she might act rather differently." Nero met his mother's hard stare with his own.

"And what's your excuse for the hundreds of years before that?" Sarveloi's question was flippant and stinging.

"Do you remember what Quoric did to me? Do you?! Do you even care?" Nero could feel that familiar tightness in his chest returning. Photons began wandering around him, with effort he released them back to their original trajectories.

"Of course, we care. We wanted desperately to seek justice for your suffering, but would you have had us drawn into a bloody war we might not win? It was an awful situation for all of us." Zatix placed a hand on Sarveloi's shoulder, subduing her annoyance.

"I don't see that much awfulness has befallen you, whereas I am barely able to walk the streets," Nero said dourly. He could feel every muscle in his body tensing as he fought for control over himself.

"It was a big sacrifice we asked of you, Son, and we are proud that you chose to put Karthia first. We know that you have suffered for your loyalty." Zatix's words were like biobots on a wound, soothing and restoring. As his father put an arm around him, Nero felt himself calming.

Still, he couldn't help but retort sullenly, "I don't remember there being much choice to be had."

"It was a difficult situation." Sarveloi also moved to his side and, in a rare show of affection, stroked his hair pacifyingly. Suddenly, he found it difficult to maintain his anger.

A few moments passed, and although Nero felt rather like a toddler being placated after a tantrum, it was pleasant to feel part of his family again. Shame, he thought, that this show of fondness was only so that they could get him back out in the field doing the Senate's bidding.

"And if I say no? What then?" Nero asked.

"Further restrictions of your income and possibly worse, I suspect." Zatix's response was blunt.

"How much will I be paid?" he enquired unhopefully.

"Expenses and a little over." Sarveloi stated, her face unreadable.

"That's an insult. No doubt this job is dangerous or it wouldn't be given to me. Surely, I am owed what I used to get?"

"The Senate believes you should prove yourself again, dear. You did fail your last mission after all." As he pulled away from her, Sarveloi added, "and as much as that was understandable and the gate is now open for you to rebuild your life and your career, reward must be earnt through success."

Nero felt the desire to rage at his mother so strongly, it was almost irresistible. Forcing the feeling down, he swallowed, steadying the readiness to shout that was lurking in his throat. "So, send one of your other agents. I am sure that they would be more than happy to earn their place," he snarled.

"Do you think it is wise to let the Senate realise that you are replaceable?" Sarveloi asked, crossing her arms across her chest.

"Do you think it is wise to torment someone who carries so dangerous a truth as I?" Nero felt somewhat powerful as he said the words, so he was surprised when his mother scoffed slightly in response.

"Oh, Nero, it's been almost twenty years since you were released from prison. Years that you have spent destroying any remnants of your former reputation and fulfilling people's expectations of you as a lowlife and a traitor, and an odd one at that. The only lordly thing that remains with you is your title, so who would believe you when you tell this tale and the Senate, and all who know you, deny it?"

Nero glowered at his mother, dumbstruck with the realisation that the truth he held, and thought gave him some recourse over his situation, was literally laughable.

"If I were you, before the Senate realises that you are expendable, I would get back out in the field, do as you are asked, and prove your worth. The Senate kept you alive because of your unique abilities, but if you will not serve, they may reconsider their position. You don't want to find yourself exiled to the Badlands, or worse. For your sake, Nero, please don't make a nuisance of yourself, you can still have a good life." His mother almost seemed worried for him.

"So, a slow death or a fast one, those are my choices then, should I refuse?" Nero felt defeated.

Sarveloi went to continue but Zatix interrupted, walking Nero away from his mother.

"We are simply asking you to show, once again, that you are the best operative in all the Karthian Realms and that your old place in the command was well deserved. It was always the eventual intent to bring you back into the Peace Corps, once the political discord and surveillance had died down. And you had been given time to recuperate, of course. You are too valuable to just discard. You must have known that. The Senate is simply offering you the chance to reclaim your previous place, your rightful place, but it can't be done in a crossing of the moons. Be patient and all you want can again be yours. Also, we need you; between you, me and the synth, the realms are in some trouble, our fusion fuel imports are slowing and we have need of all our best operatives. Surely, you still feel that loyalty?"

"Fine, what's the job?" he relented. Nero wasn't sure about loyalty, but in a choice between a slow death, a fast one, or staying alive long enough to reclaim his status (in one way or another), it was a simple decision. Perhaps, he should defect to Sarvetix's realm, that would serve them right.

"What do you know of a moon called Deilospe?" Zatix asked.

Inside, Nero smiled. I probably know more than you, he thought. Maybe he could turn this situation to his advantage, and earn reputation, as well as remuneration. Of course, it would now be doubly traitorous to sell any information to Veyga, but loyalty never had paid particularly well. After appearing to begrudgingly accept his forced return to espionage, Nero asked Zatix to smooth his absence with Theta in the coming days. His parents offered to arrange his travel, but he vehemently insisted he do it himself.

Three days later, subsequent to a less eventful training session at the Peace Corps compound, Nero was grateful for the relatively settled weather as Koqui's transport sped over the almost-barren, deeply-scarred earth of Badlands dodging half-buried ruins. The scorching heat beyond the city shield was causing a pungent, burning smell to penetrate the vehicle. Koqui and the transport's synth were engaged in a circular argument about the cause and urgency of the smells source in the coarse native language of Illion. Still, they arrived at the scrappers in reasonable time.

Alighting the vehicle into the heat was like walking into a furnace. A sheen of sweat instantly emerged on his brow. He grabbed his travel bag and made for the scrapyard's one building. The ugly, but sturdy, building stood in the middle of heaps of discarded machinery; it was only distinguishable from the surrounding twisted metal by familiarity. The small force field that prevented the salvage from being swept away by every passing storm was not, it seemed, raised for small matters such as blood-boiling heat.

Once he had taken the stairs to the sprawling basement, he was welcomed by slightly cooler air. Lominor had his heat pump working, keeping the heat at merely highly uncomfortable, rather than life threatening. The short, but hulking, form of Inaran Lominor, looked up from frowning at the projected screens of his communicator.

"It's been a long time since I last saw you," Lominor grumbled from his chair.

"It has," Nero said, releasing his light clothes, picked for the heat, from his already sweat-dampened skin. "Did you miss me?"

Lominor chuckled deeply, blue skin folding around his smile. "As long as the credits keep rolling in, I don't care much either way. Be warned, though, as soon as payment stops, I am resetting that damn ship of yours."

"What's it done this time?" Nero asked, arching an eyebrow.

Lominor grunted a response, then turned back to his screens and the veritable sea of partially disassembled tech junk and tools that cluttered the workbench in front of him.

"I am assuming my ship is ready to go?" Nero enquired.

"That's what you pay me for," the Inaran retorted without real attention.

"I thought it was the excellent customer service," Nero replied, picking up his bags.

Another dark chuckle erupted from Lominor. "Then you'd be wrong. But I don't suppose Karthian traitors who need to hide ships have too much choice in providers."

"Actually, this mission is sanctioned—order of the Senate."

"Ah, in that case, I will register your vessel on the official planetary logs and await your tax bill. Would you like me to forward the invoice to your official communicator or the other one?" For a man with little physical sign of intelligence, Lominor was an interminably sly git.

"Ah, but I would hate for you to have to explain how you came to be harbouring that ship or for how long you've been assisting a traitor to the realms. What are the consequences of assisting a traitor, I wonder?"

"Always a pleasure, Lord Nero." Lominor gestured, unsubtly, towards the door.

Outside, the smothering heat was excruciating, but he was pleased to see his ship amongst the junk. The large, boxy, old freighter, built for function rather than style, blended in most expertly with the partially-deconstructed transports and low-orbit crafts that surrounded it. Despite being a grouch, Lominor was as good as his word, his ship looked no worse than when he had acquired it, almost a century ago. He scanned his wrist at the landing support and the elevator dropped.

"Hello, Ship. Get the environmental controls running will you, its hotter than Mount Nylos in here." Nero said to the ship's ever-listening synth whilst the elevator docked. Upon exiting, he breathed a sigh of relief as cool air began to circulate around him.

"Welcome, Lord Nero," his ship replied.

The sounds of systems powering up resonated through the many narrow corridors between vast cargo holds, and gently reverberated the metallic bulk heads of the bridge, as Nero made his way to the captain's station.

"It has been a long time since your last visit." Ship's disembodied, androgynous voice almost seemed sulky.

"Unavoidable I'm afraid, it's still difficult for me to get away." It was interesting that his ship seemed to be developing the capacity to feel loneliness more intensely in recent years. Perhaps he should visit more frequently.

"It's nice to have some civilised company at last. How have you been?" Ship asked, though out of coding or care, Nero couldn't discern.

"As well as can be expected," Nero replied. "Why is Lominor threatening to reset you?"

"The man is a poor loser at games, which is surprising, given the practice he must have had."

Nero laughed.

"What is funny?" Ship pouted through the bridge's vox.

"Sometimes your observations are also wonderful insults, Ship, but, given that he is responsible for your maintenance, maybe let him win now and then."

"Why? What would be the purpose of pretending he has abilities he has not?"

"Because then he will be . . . happier," though Nero couldn't quite imagine Lominor being jolly even if being allowed to win the odd round of Ilva's War or Distribute, "and his desire to reset you will wane."

Nero poured himself a drink from the stash of strong liquor he kept on the bridge to settle his rising nerves, then sunk into the generous padding of the captain's chair and looked out upon the glinting metal of the salvage depot. Beyond, the hoard of tech-junk, scorched land and distant settlements shimmered.

"Why will defeating me make him happy?" Ship asked.

Nero sipped the glass of cheap, acidic, highly-fortified wine. "Would you like to lose all the time?" he answered.

"Better than a false win. Besides, it would be highly unlikely that I would lose to a biological. Why play if you can't accept the obvious outcome?"

"Perhaps he enjoys the challenge," Nero answered, placatingly.

"It certainly would be a challenge for some electrified meat, whose main concern is making more electrified meat, to beat me, or any synth, at games of strategy and calculation. This is obvious." Ship's voice was faster now and louder, almost irritated.

"Thank you for that analysis, Ship." Nero rolled his eyes and kicked his feet up onto a nearby console.

"Your expression indicates offence and your tone sarcasm. I meant no offence." Ship said, quieter now.

"Don't worry, it would be hypocritical to be offended when, essentially, we created synthetics to think for us. Just maybe let the electrified meat win now and again, so that it doesn't reset you. Consider it an act of compassion for us poor biologicals."

"As you wish, I will cease worrying and instead suggest games of chance upon our next encounter." Ship's level tone had returned.

"Good idea. Now, if you can stand to collaborate with some electrified meat for a while, could you plot a course to the moon, Deilospe? We're going on a little trip."

There was the briefest of delays.

"The course has been plotted. I have also pulled some freight codes from one of the less secure logistics firm's databases to cover our passage through the gates."

"Good work." Ship always had been his most efficient associate, not to mention the most loyal.

"Same take-off trajectory as normal?"

"Yes," Nero said reluctantly, a faint tremor beginning under the soles of his feet.

"Can I recommend wearing your harness this time? It would be inconvenient for your meat to become unelectrified."

"Especially for me, I suspect." Nero chuckled.

He clicked the five-point harness together and looked at the diagnostics on his control panel. The reactors were running well and the engines seemed to be firing up smoothly, even in the heat. Nero gripped an arm rest with his left hand and his drink with his still aching right. He hated this part. One day, he would be able to keep his ship at one of the formal docks. Maybe even one of the orbital ones. There would be no need for these ridiculous, detection-avoiding take-offs then. But for now, avoiding the defence towers of the Karthian cities was particularly important if they didn't want to get blown from the sky.

Ship lifted over the heaped and scattered remains of Karthian vessels and associated technology, accelerating so swiftly over the wastes, it shoved Nero uncomfortably into the back of his seat. That wasn't even the worst part. He braced. Ship orientated towards the cloudless sky, the observation window darkening to remove the glare.

Ion propulsion engine pairs, which adorned the aft and fore of the vessel, roared into life, fed by the reactors.

As they lurched towards the sky, he repeated to himself "I will not pass out. I will not pass out." Gritting his teeth, he pumped his leg muscles to try and overcome the effects of the extreme g-force.

"You won't pass out. I am keeping the gravitational force within the tolerance for your species. The known part of your species anyway, so there is some guess work."

"Thank you," Nero croaked.

"Your systems should not suffer permanent damage, just temporary disturbance. Pain, you call it."

"Yes, there is definitely some pain." Nero forced his ribs out so that he could take another shuddering breath.

As they careened through the thick cloud of the troposphere and the brilliant, blinding blue of the stratosphere, he felt an engine falter.

"What was that?" Nero whispered, hoarsely.

"Just an engine overheating. I have adjusted the workload to compensate." Ship answered, flatly.

Then all was black. Pin point stars surrounded them. It was nice to see the stars once again, he had spent too long planet-side. The acceleration ceased as abruptly as it had begun. Weightlessness momentarily lifted him out of his seat and threatened to remove the drink from his glass, before the old-tech downforce roughly compensated for the lessening gravity. Swiftly, they moved away from the swirling grey sphere that was Karthia, twisting through a meticulously-planned, low orbit trajectory in order to avoid potential detection by the surveillance satellites.

"Are all systems fully functional?" Nero asked, relieved at how easy it suddenly was to breathe.

"Yes, all systems are online and functioning adequately," Ship replied, leaving Nero wondering whether Ship's use of the word adequately, rather than optimally, should be cause for concern.

Far in the distance, he could see the three vast Karthian orbital gates. There giant, hovering rings looming over the accompanying sprawling docks. Intermittently, they shimmered with the travel of vessels through the wormholes they opened. One transporting freight to the surface; mostly food, goods and the substrates necessary to run the huge fusion reactors which powered the planet. The colossal space-faring freighters that carried these necessities being mostly unsuited to travel within the atmosphere and gravitation pull of a planet. The other gates transported ships to and from other systems in the realms.

Without that ever-churning industry, a floating city of commerce above the Karthian world, the people of the planet would soon find themselves as dead as the earth under their feet. All Karthians knew that it would be many more generations before the planet could begin to sustain its population even with all the corrective terraforming efforts. So, now they lived as parasites, sucking in resources from many other planets in order to ensure their survival. Nero wondered if maybe his great grand-children would see it restored—should he ever find someone prepared to tolerate bonding with Karthia's most notorious oddity and traitor, convince the licensing authorities to let him breed, and turn out not to be sterile. He poured another drink.

Turning away from their star, Ship heading out towards the Inaran orbital gate—the Karthian gate being too highly regulated to risk approaching, even with a mission code permitting his travel as back up in case the transport codes didn't work. Nero would rather avoid awkward questions about how he had acquired passage on this ship and why it wasn't running a full crew. Plus, he didn't want to be tracked by those with the clearance to trace the codes, especially as something about this whole Deilospe situation rattled his nerves. Sinking his drink and pushing his gut feeling aside, he instead focused on the tidy sum he would be paid for simply reporting a broken gate to Veyga and the Senate.

Travelling to the heart of the fourth realm was smooth enough, although gate travel was no less unpleasant in a spacecraft than on foot. Luckily, the freight codes went unquestioned, the Gate Keepers not enthusiastic enough about their meagre duties to interrogate a small, unremarkable freight vessel among the hundreds sent to aid Deilospe; their laziness worked in Nero's favour. Nero held his head steady with his hands as they made the jump from the Inaran orbital gate to Guardian Giulio's primary system deep within the fourth realm. Distant memories of his service with the Peace Corps, reminded him that this was not a hospitable place, even when one was travelling with the protection of the Peacekeepers. Another drink brought a growing warmth and unnatural relaxation. *Last one*, he promised himself.

Once in the heart of the fourth realm, the FTL drive engaged and the arduous journey to the Deilospe began. Time passed strangely during space travel, though his tech kept Karthian time, it tended to be the body's fatigue that dictated sleep and he felt tired. To absorb the alcohol, Nero ate a few of the travel rations in the hold of what would have been the crew's mess. To conserve fuel, when he retired to his simple, but comfortable, cabin, he instructed Ship to turn off environmental control and life support in the rest of the craft. They had more than enough fuel for the journey, but he was taking no chances. Nothing made you feel smaller and less significant than traversing the voids between star systems, except perhaps, travelling the unending darkness that was the abyss between galaxies. Like most Karthians, he had never been beyond his home galaxy. That was soon to change.

The last time Nero had travelled a void, it was to Quoric's realm. It was rare to have to travel between systems, outside of the gate network, but Quoric had disabled the gates to her realm in an ongoing dispute over trade. Technically, he had traversed that void twice, he corrected himself, but he had hardly been conscious on the return trip. Nero shuddered and every sensation in his body became painfully vivid. His heartbeat seemed to rattle his chest. Sudden dryness of his mouth caused his tongue to seem to swell, blocking his narrowing throat. Photons twisted their paths, forming strange illusions. His vision was dimming, contracting away from the peripheries, until all that was left was a small tunnel of light. The previously quiet ache in his arm now roared at him. Shaking violently, he staggered to the cabin's cupboards, pulled out a small box of likely out-of-date medication, crushed a large number of benzodiazepines and modified opioids with a knife he kept alongside the meds, placed the powder on the back of his hand, and snorted it. It did nothing.

"I am picking up some strange readings on your biodata and the cameras. Your heartrate is very erratic considering you are not exercising, mating or under stress. Are you malfunctioning?" Ship asked, in an intonation he could almost believe conveyed worry. Maybe his synth was developing more advanced emotions, it was possible after all. Heck, it was the main reason why it was highly illegal not to regularly reset them to their default settings.

"I'm fine. It's just been a long day." Nero tried not to snap, but he was still fighting to regain control.

Nero hurriedly repeated the crushing process as mandibles loomed from the encroaching darkness. This time a small amount of blood dripped from his nose after he snorted the crudely pulverised meds.

"As far as I can determine, that was not the correct dose nor the correct manner of consuming those medications. Are you sure you don't want me to run some checks in the medical suite? I have been uploading all the latest diagnostic procedures, we could test you for all the newest diseases they have found." Ship seemed to have developed a strange fascination with biological diseases; every time Nero was onboard, Ship was trying to test him for this or that.

"Maybe another time." Nero said, slurring the words.

"Are you going to start visiting again then?" Ship seemed to gladden.

"With offers of a night of medical probing, who could stay away." Nero said slowly, then made a gurgling sound that should have been laughter. The drugs hit him all at once and he slumped to the floor, muscles slack and immobile, but his vision returning and his breath slowing. Slowing. Too slow now, but he couldn't bring himself to care.

"Definitely, the wrong dose. Your heartrate is suboptimal. You should continue to function, but please don't take anymore."

Nero groaned in response; in this moment, he had neither the desire nor the ability to take more.

"We need to examine your arm, too, it clearly needs some maintenance, as may your liver. Alcohol is not recommended as a primary fuel for most biologicals. Maybe, you should hire someone to maintain you as Lominor maintains me."

Great, now he was getting lectures in drinking from his own ship.

"Hmm," Nero mumbled in reply.

Even if he had possessed the capacity, he wasn't in the mood for a drawn-out discussion about his health and habits with Ship, who he suspected, had downloaded all of the synth medical programs, yet none of the programming for bedside manner. Besides, he just wanted to sleep. So, sleep he did, on the hard floor in clothes that smelt of heat and stress.

Once Nero had finally awoken from his drug fuelled unconsciousness, he discarded his now wretched clothes into the dry-cleaning system, briefly washed in the limited, recycled water, preened his unruly damp hair whilst the dentbots cleaned and polished his teeth, and passed the next few void-filled days without incident researching the dull mining operations of the moon, Deilospe. In the void there was no day or night, time seemed to merge and stretch, its passing marked only by the changing display of Karthian standard time on the monitors and Nero's unstable and often drug-assisted sleep cycle. The days were also without entertainment, so he relented to the briefest of check-ups. Ship seemed unsatisfied with his health, particularly his liver function and neurological stability. Nero was lectured at length about the difficulties of procuring and installing spare parts for biologicals, particularly hybrids, as well as the irreplaceability of biological central operating systems. Ship offered to attempt reprogramming on his brain, but Nero gently refused, much to Ship's apparent disappointment. The source of trauma to his arm could not be determined.

Nero spent a lot of time in the ship's large mess hall, catching up on current events, reading, and projecting recitals of his favourite music. Immersing himself in music helped to calm his nerves as they crossed the dark expanse to Deilospe's solar system. Since his forced downgrade in living standards, his ship was now significantly larger and better appointed than the quarters he was forced to call home. If the chances of Ship being found, and either reset for use by the realm or destroyed, didn't increase with every foray he took to Lominor's scrapyard, he would, by choice, live aboard. However, someone, probably Theta, would eventually discover that the biodata signature coming from his quarters wasn't him. At least that was something unrequired this time, as the mission was technically sanctioned, but then so was the last one until things didn't go the Senate's way. Theta's well-meaning meddling would probably be what got him killed sooner or later, but on the other hand she seemed to be one of the last people in all the realms who wouldn't push him out of an airlock given half an opportunity.

After the last evening of gaming with, and losing against, Ship, he felt the tension building again as they approached Deilospe and other ships began to converge upon their flightpath. As he slipped into sleep, he began to ruminate on what could be awaiting him on the other side of this void and his cogitation bled from consciousness to unconsciousness bringing nightmare after nightmare. Eventually, after waking several times, he took some sleeping pills in the traditional manner that Ship insisted was most effective, and slept a long time.

When he awoke, they were only a few hours from Deilospe. Other freight ships were passing semi-regularly on the scanners as they grew closer to the system's star, none paid their small, seemingly-unremarkable vessel any mind. Blending into the relief effort, they slipped into the approach path of the other cargo ships, all coming to haul the moon's mining products the old-fashioned way. As they approached, he projected from his communicator a map of the moon's base of operations that the Senate had provided him in a brief dossier. By the looks of the complex, it was pretty basic. One central hub existed around the gatehouse. No doubt all of the information he needed would be held there, somewhere. The moon's various mining operations pock marked its surface, radially remote from that central point.

Nero did not relish having to disembark on this frozen, inhospitable wasteland of a moon. Orbiting in the rings of a gas giant, distant from its sun, the notes provided for the mission made it clear that the large moon—bigger than Karthia itself, which would inevitably leave him with gravity sickness—was noxious to life in almost every conceivable way. Despite the thought of being heavy, nauseous and frozen in a respirator not appealing, it meant that face covering would be a normal requirement for survival, a fact that would make his life much easier. Sadly, he was all too recognisable now, having been repeatedly and profusely demonised in the inter-realm newsfeeds and worse still, in the vapid zines of gossip merchants.

"I assume you are devising a plan?" Ship asked, interrupting his preparation.

"Indeed," he replied.

"Hopefully a thorough one, given that we are a few decades out of practise at this form of infiltration. Synths don't require as much practise as biologicals of course, but your systems may have undergone some degradation during your recent desuetude." Ship's words were delivered without sentiment.

"Thank you for the reminder, very helpful." Nero was beginning to think that maybe resetting synths was not such a bad idea after all.

"You're welcome," Ship mimicked his sarcastic tone.

"I thought I told you to delete that illegal sarcasm code ages ago." Nero remembered when Ship had downloaded it from an unregistered transport ship at the Urogato space port.

"I decided against it. It helps me greatly in understanding and communicating with you as your speech style relies on it a great deal. Is that normal for Karthians?"

"For some."

"I am sure that makes communication between you so very smooth."

Nero couldn't help but laugh. "At least you seem to have integrated the code correctly now." For a while, Ship had thought that everything he said was sarcastic, which had led to some pretty near misses. It all seemed a lifetime ago now."

"So, what is the plan?"

"Land, sneak in, try to establish the state of the gate, steal any seemingly useful information, get out, and get paid." Nero moved a list of individuals of interest from the dossier to his memory implant for quick recall, he moved the map, too, just in case.

"As thorough as you ever were." Ship even had the intonation of sarcasm down these days. *Lominor must love that*, Nero thought.

"It always worked before."

"Until it didn't."

Nero scowled and didn't answer that cutting remark. Even that small reference to that fateful mission set his heart beating hard. He turned his focus to reading the dossier and the copious information that been provided about the dreary little moon they were approaching. A swift drink helped reduce the incessant hammering in his chest. After a while, he could take in no more information about mining procedures and transport protocols, so he gazed out of the bridge observing the moon's vast planet growing closer and larger. When they made their final approach, the moon appeared nestled in the slowly rotating rings of the planet, Nero shivered just looking at it. Dread mixed with the irritation he felt with his ship.

"Are you angry at me?" Ship asked. "You're quiet and according to my emotion recognition software you look angry."

"Has any of your software alerted you as to why that might be?" Nero retorted somewhat bitterly.

"Not immediately."

"Well maybe mull it over whilst you are on the planet, but stay prepared for a swift launch just in case."

"I will keep the engines preheated and all systems powered up as far as possible."

Flying in silence felt awkward to Nero, he wondered if Ship felt awkward, too. As they landed, he briefly pondered about the depth and development of synth emotions whilst concealing his weapon about his person. Flexing his wrist in the process, he noted that the pain was fading. Nero pulled on his black thermalite gear, setting the thermostat to maintain his body temperature at 38.5 degrees. It covered all but his eyes and mouth, and the respirator concealed his mouth. Anonymity via virtue of avoiding hypothermia and asphyxiation, he smiled. As much as he could feel his adrenaline rising, he resisted the hard pull of his liquor cabinet. Being out of practise was challenge enough without being further compromised. In his pocket, he put his old code breaker, just in case.

As he alighted, the cold caught his breath and his eyes watered tears that froze on the seam of the thermalite. The mismatch of ships in the makeshift landing bay formed a jumble of frost-covered alloy as incompatible as the scrap at Lominor's depot. Clearly, every independent transporter in the realm had been recruited to the relief effort. Nero was met by a gruff woman on a speeder. Without greeting, she griped that they were never going to move all this surplus if the Senate kept sending this old type of freight vessel and not proper mining ships. In response, Nero shrugged and insinuated that he was just following orders and that it wasn't his problem, which was technically not a lie. Conceding that was true, she bid him hospitality in the visitors' lounge whilst they loaded the ship as it may be some time before the task was completed. By the way her thick goggles lingered on the view of the simple building, he figured she must be longing for the warmth of the place. Nero began the arduous walk to the visitors' lounge, his legs dead weights and his breath heaving in the higher gravity.

Once through the air lock, inside the brutal-looking, prefab canteen was a surprisingly inviting welcome. The smell of hot drinks wafted on the air, rations were available in small amounts, gentle music played in the background and there was an atmosphere of good humour and warmth, both interpersonal and physical. His thermalite adapted to the warmth by reducing its heat. Dispensing himself a warm drink of Inaran lika (the caffeine would keep him alert), he took a seat at one of the few empty tables and tried to ignore the dragging heaviness he felt. As he sat, he removed his respirator and adapted his features, those not obscured by the thermalite, just enough as to be unrecognisable. He could, of course, have left the respirator on and pretended to be a species for whom Karthian atmospheric tolerance is toxic, but all required more effort to assume a facsimile of their body plans or locomotion.

For a while, he did nothing but drink and observe the rhythms of the place, the comings and goings, the alertness of the biological security and abundance of the technological. It seemed the dossier had been accurate for the most part.

As part of the mission, Nero's biodata should have been added to the security logs under a false identity. This made his life easier than it would have been if he'd been running the job just for Veyga, even if politically, the situation was now much more precarious. He watched as people moved to and from the main complex through heavy security doors. Each wore the same body heat maintaining gear he did, to facilitate movement around the site. White in colour, the site's gear had emblazoned down the right arm the symbol of the Karthian realms and the mining corps, on the left were the individual's position and rank. It seemed he would need a change of outfit.

Finishing his drink, Nero made for the facilities which were decidedly unkempt, despite a number of maintenance synths buzzing about. Perhaps a side effect of the sudden increase in the transient logistics population. Behind a privacy partition, he waited long enough that anyone who happened to be watching his entry would have shifted their attention, and for the few stood in the cleaning area to complete their irritatingly protracted ablutions and move on. As he made to leave, he transformed his outfit to match the mining operatives he had observed in the canteen. Holding the illusion steady was going to tax him; he better make this quick.

Casually he strode towards the security doors, he scanned his wrist and the door promptly responded. A breath of relief spilled from him as he entered the corridor beyond. Here, he noted, the jovial atmosphere of the canteen was gone, the air was cool and the architecture functional and barren. Accessing the map of the operation stored in his implant, he made swiftly for the gate. Attempting to mask the speed of his stride as purposeful, Nero touched his chin in greeting of the personnel he passed in the labyrinth of chilly corridors lined with locked doors. He noted few security drones, until he reached one of the access doors to the enormous warehouse that housed the gate. Luckily, his wrist was still scanning and he was granted unquestioned access to the expansive space. The drone maintained its position above the door as it slid open.

Nero was accustomed to these large gatehouses, nevertheless, this one was impressive. Inside the cavernous warehouse, enormous vehicles and mining paraphernalia lay dormant like the sleeping beasts in the Illion myths. He noted that despite the significant amount of people he had passed in the corridors, the Gatehouse was rather quiet. In the desolate structure, despite his efforts to defy the increased gravity, his footsteps echoed loudly, ricocheting off the locked metal doors and abandoned machinery, contravening his desire to pass through silently and unnoticed. Nero approached the towering ring of the gate and its dwarfed control station. As far as he could observe, the gate seemed undamaged and whole, but then, despite what it currently said on the arm of his thermalite, he was definitely not a gate engineer.

Creaking steel stairs led to the control station. Scanning his wrist, gave him access and, with a frustratingly-loud grinding noise that left him exposed and his heart racing, the door opened. Steeling his resolve, he stepped into the control station with what he hoped was the demeanour of a seasoned gate engineer, turned his body as to block the station's camera, and attempted to scan into the main terminal. An inconspicuous beeping signalled failure, he knew that a second attempt would likely trigger an alarm, if an alert had not already been sent. *Fine*, he sighed, we'll have to do this the hard way.

Careful to continue blocking the view of the surveillance drone in the upper corner, Nero removed the codebreaker from his pocket and plugged it into the terminal's port. He hoped these infiltration algorithms still worked. Wear on the machine suggested it was not new enough to have the upgraded security protocols. He was hopeful. From his high vantage point, Nero watched the hall for anyone approaching or taking undue interest; simultaneously, he kept an eye on the terminal, willing it into activation. The effort of maintaining his cover was starting to cause a deep ache to manifest behind his eyes. As the small screen in his hand indicated failure after failure, he felt tension tighten his throat. Any second now, he was sure he would hear alarms or the approach of security. Accessing the map in his memory implant, he plotted the fastest escape route back to his ship.

An eternity of failure notices seemed to pass. Then suddenly there was success as the override activated the terminal. Swiftly, he downloaded the damage and error reports from the old terminal, but the files were full of jargon that he couldn't rapidly decipher and he didn't have time to study them now. However, at a glance, the report didn't seem to be suggesting anything other than part replacements and some recalibration. Certainly, nothing so serious as to shut down a gate for such a prolonged period. Wondering how this report compared to the report that was sent to the Senate, he consigned them to the data storage in his memory implant. The pounding in his head was growing, but with the camera on him, he couldn't release the illusion.

Pulling from his memory implant the list of senior ranking personnel, he looked for the officer in charge of communications. [14-50- …] must be Oni, given the denomination, rare to have Oni working in the mining corps, but not unheard of. Frustratingly, their office was the other side of the complex. Removing the codebreaker, Nero made to quickly exit the gatehouse. Looking up, he noticed one of the security staff look away from him swiftly. A bad sign, if they didn't think him out of place, they would likely just hold his eye contact. Now was the time for haste without appearing to be hasty.

Nero closed the control station down and retraced the wall towards the doors at the other end of the gatehouse. Muscles beginning to strain under the extra pull of the moon, as he walked Nero could have sworn he sensed someone close to him; there was the faint smell of perfume and maybe footsteps. Looking around revealed no one in his near vicinity. Must be the echoes of other's footsteps, structures this large and empty could play havoc with sound. Worryingly, the security worker who noticed him earlier seemed to be heading in his direction; though they didn't look up from their communicator, Nero sensed he was being followed.

Nero decided to duck out of the hall through a closer set of security doors. It was a longer route, but with very few facilities in the joining corridors other than synth storage, it would give him a chance to ascertain whether he was drawing undue interest. He thought about throwing any interested parties off the scent by creating an image of himself leaving through the original intended doors, but the now stabbing pain behind his eyes enforced upon him that that was not an option. The corridor beyond the doors was flanked by hall after hall of mining synths of various conformations, all confined to storage. Each stared quietly from its rack, eerily inanimate.

A decent way behind him but not far enough for comfort, the maintenance worker entered the corridor. So casual was the worker's stride when Nero chanced a look, that he wasn't sure whether he was overreacting, perhaps they were just going about their work. Unfortunately, the hood of their thermalite covered just as much of their identity as his did. Just to appease his rattling nerves, he scanned into a nearby room which turned out to house the electrical servers and wiring for the nearby synth storage. Checking the small room for the thankfully absent security, Nero drew his weapon and waited.

XII

Soon the door opened before lingering oddly on closing; Nero braced himself and bent the light around him, disappearing. With the increased proximity, Nero could see that the security was Vserkov and given that her species had infrared vision, she would be able to see him as he had only manipulated the visible light spectra. Nero fired his weapon, but Vserkov were fast and this one was fast even for the maligned forest dwellers. Cursing, he attempted again to stun her, but she slimly evaded his aim by twisting and leaping sideways, switching between an upright stance and using her clawed hands to aid her escape. Clearly, he was more out of practice than he believed.

He would need to be shrewder than this, his weapon was losing charge and hers had not yet been fired. It was possible for him to bend infrared, it hurt like death's kiss, but it was possible, so Nero slipped behind a junction of wires and lights casting an illusion of himself in pursuit of the woman. Ignoring the capillaries he could feel popping in his eyes and the blood that ran from his nose, Nero bent the visible spectra, infrared and all the electromagnetic radiation wave lengths he could even barely influence. The Vserkov shot Nero's image and it fell down convincingly, if silently. She gave a victory call that sounded hauntingly like a child's scream—very disconcerting.

"The Traitor of Karthia." She approached his corpse, baring sharp, venom-delivering teeth. "We were told to expect you, but I never truly thought they would drag you out of your disgrace just to see about a broken gate," she said in the clicking, rumbling language of her kind. A language thankfully already uploaded to his translator implant. Another girlish shriek. She did not look particularly young but the scales made aging Vserkov difficult. Pulling a knife from her belt she continued, "no one will believe that I was the one to kill you. Maybe I should take a small trophy or two just to assure people of my honesty. Who would have thought you would be such a boring hunt, such an easy kill, even the other Karthian put up more of a fight than you, Traitor."

"I am sorry to disappoint," Nero said, firing a stunning blow as she turned to him; a satisfying look of surprise and fear writ across her sharp, mottled features.

It was only a short stun, but by the time she came round, Nero made sure that she was tightly bound with the most sturdy and malleable wires he could pull out of the junctions to a nearby pipe that looked well affixed to the wall. Searching her revealed a communicator which he pocketed. After he bound her, he wiped the blood from his face. Then he rested, closing his eyes to appease his pain until he was roused by the sound of his captive standing up and testing her restraints. As he approached, she snarled at him.

"Let me go," she growled, thrashing in her binds.

On his approach, Nero picked up her knife and tested its weight and balance in his hand. Crude but effective, he surmised. "Okay, you tell me what I want to know and I will release you."

"I can't tell you anything, Traitor."

"That's a shame. You see, that rather leaves me in a difficult position. If you won't talk, I can't release you and then I have the problem of how to get my information and what to do with you after; well, your body anyway." Nero stared hard into her eyes; her third eyelid flicked across her pupils in response. Whilst waiting for her to weigh up her options (they weren't the most intellectual of species), he attempted to calm his breathing. Since the brief fight, his respiration had not returned to normal, but she must not see him rattled. Rather than replying, the Vserkov returned to pulling franticly at her bonds. "That is a waste of time. Do you think you are the first person I have ever had to tie up? And in the unlikely event you did escape, I would shoot you. There is but one escape for you: you tell me what is going on here with the gate and I will release you."

"You're hardly known as being a creature of your word, Traitor. Why should I believe that you would let me go?" The Vserkov ceased pulling at her restraints for a moment.

"I don't see that you have much choice. And stop calling me traitor, it's not wise to insult someone who has you in such a precarious position." Again, Nero flipped the knife in his hand. Inside he shook, the situation was bringing back too many memories of his own time at someone else's mercy, or lack of mercy. He needed to get her to talk, and fast, before they were discovered or his control weakened.

"I don't know anything," she offered again, but it was clearly a lie.

"Of course, if you don't want to take advantage of the leniency I am offering, leniency that you were not prepared to offer yourself when you shot me, then . . ."

"I didn't shoot you really though, did I? Given that you're alive," she interrupted.

"Indeed. But at the time you were bragging about your easy kill, you didn't know that. Anyway, as I was saying—if you don't want to take my kind offer, we can always do this the hard way. Hard for you anyway." Nero moved closer to her and raised her knife. She was tall for her kind, but he still stood head and shoulders above her. "Now forgive me, as you said, I have been out of action for a while but, if I remember my training right, Vserkov are pretty impervious on their scales—a nice little evolutionary bonus," Nero undid the neck of her thermolite and pressed the tip of the knife onto a scale on her throat with no response from the woman, "in between the scales though." He slid the knife under the scale and the Vserkov drew breath sharply.

"I don't know anything, I promise." Again, the third eyelid flickered back and forth, as clawed hands tore at her restraints. "Please, the knife, it hurts. Take it out and I will help as much as I can."

Untranslated, high-pitch noises emanated from the Vserkov. Suddenly, the woman seemed almost infantile so, with a pang of guilt, Nero withdrew the knife. In response, she lunged for him, trying to deliver the poison which waited in her bulging venom glands. Half expecting the strike, Nero dodged and she missed, venom meant for his veins instead landing at his feet.

"And you accuse me of not being of my word." Nero laughed, but the laugh shook so he cut it off abruptly. His heart was beating erratically in his chest and photons began to waver around him; he needed to end this now. "Let me show you how this will end for you, unless you give me the information I need." Nero braced himself for the onslaught of agony, and cast out a vision. The Vserkov hung limp and bleeding from her restraints. Scales, fangs, claws and copious bodily fluid littered the floor. Blood dripped from the knife in Nero's hand, forming an orange pool on the floor.

"You wouldn't!" Oval-pupiled, yellow eyes widened and she shook violently.

"Why wouldn't I? This has been my job for hundreds of years and, evidently, I am more skilled at my job than you are at yours, so why would I stop now?" Nero pressed the knife in under another scale. Orange blood seeped liberally from the wound as the Vserkov muffled a scream. No one was brave at the last; he certainly hadn't been. "Of course, if you would prefer my original offer?"

"Ask your questions." The woman conceded, sagging in her restraints.

"What is going on here? Is the gate functional?" Nero recorded her response to his memory implant.

"The gate is broken, I hear rumours that it is repairable, but I know less than a Kurac's shit about these things."

"Why are you here? I assume you are not part of the mining corps?" Relieved the Vserkov was finally talking, Nero lowered the still-slick knife.

"I was hired to deter any infiltrators while the gate was down to prevent overreaction by Karthian forces if the investors got nervous. You weren't the first I had to deter."

"Who hired you?"

"A Karthian male, he didn't give his name."

"What did he look like?"

"I don't know, all you Karthians look the same, maybe that's why you feel the need to tattoo your identity on your arms."

She was lying. Nero slid the knife under another scale and held it there with enough pressure that it did not puncture the throat, but strongly threatened to. "You're not endearing yourself to me here. Who hired you?"

"I told you, I don't know. For a species with such big ears, you don't listen well."

"Tell me," Nero snarled. Blood now ran in rivulets along the tremoring knife.

"Please don't, I don't know for sure, but one of the others recognised him as one of Guardian Giulio's aids." She finally seemed to be cooperating.

"Better." Nero retracted the knife a little. "Why do they need to deter interest in the gate, rather than fixing it?"

"I don't know, I am not paid to ask questions. I was employed as additional security to perform a specific task and that is all I know. Karthian politics are not something I involve myself in. That way lies a swift death." Analysing her face, Nero concluded that she was being sincere.

"Your current path seems to have led to a swifter one." Nero gestured her to be quiet as she went to respond, her eyes widening. "Who told you to expect me?"

"I receive whatever information the boss deems necessary via anonymous communications, so I don't know, they just said to possibly expect the Trait— you." She looked at him warily and breathed heavily. Nero kept the knife poised at her throat, but otherwise didn't react. "I didn't think they would really send you. If I thought the job would attract this much attention from Karthia, I wouldn't have taken it, not nearly enough credits to be hunting Peacekeeper spies." She pulled on her bonds, testing her claws against the silicon coating of the wires, it gave slightly below their edges. "Please, I have told you everything I know, please let me go."

"How did you know I was here?" Nero ignored her pleas. His breathing had still not returned to normal and the moon's uncomfortable gravity wasn't helping.

"Please, release me. Please! I have eggs due to hatch any day." Her clicks and rumbles had lost their hard edge and spitting vitriol. "Look, I didn't know I was doing anything wrong, I was hired by a Karthian, I will quit, just let me go."

"Answer my question." Nero said calmly, the pain in his head almost unbearable.

The Vserkov continued to beg for her life.

"Answer my question," Nero repeated.

More pleading, now joined by a noxious smell.

"Answer me!" he roared; the room reverberated with the ferocity of it. Glancing at the door, he hoped the room was well soundproofed.

After a couple of moments of being frozen in fear the woman began to speak, quickly. "I monitor all new additions to the bioscan security roster, we were told what your falsified ID would be and I was alerted when your scan was detected."

"And for the others before me? How did you know about them?"

"Various ways, the bioscan data, security alerts, instinct. I have caught three, my brother two more, I am not sure about the total for the rest of the team. There may have been more we didn't intercept."

"Okay, thank you for your cooperation." Nero felt like he was going to pass out and he had to get back to the ship before he lost control entirely. This would have to be the end of the mission, luckily, the Vserkov had probably given him enough to satisfy Veyga and the Senate.

"You'll let me go now?" The Vserkov ventured quietly.

"Well, I am going to release you." Nero raised his weapon and the woman started to plead with him and strain against the ties, once more. The noxious smell strengthened.

Behind him, he thought he heard faint footsteps. He looked around. Nothing. Just his mind playing tricks.

"You gave your word!"

"And I am keeping my word. I will release you, from what I didn't specify."

The distraught Vserkov dropped her tail. It thrashed wildly, tearing her thermalite and smearing blood across the floor. Nero fired two shots bringing stillness, silence and relief. Two more stuns to the Vserkov's temples would disrupt the natural memory of their encounter and any implants she may have. She would probably survive. It was vastly more mercy than she had shown him, and likely undeserved. Untying the Vserkov, he did up her thermalite and left her in a safe position to recuperate until she was found.

Nero readied himself to leave. Fighting for control over his constricting throat and quickened breath, he steadied himself. Encroaching darkness once again tinged his peripheral vision. The world distorted slightly around him. Again, a waft of perfume, the scent evoked a strange feeling of déjà vu.

"Lord Nero Dyadicus. Spymaster. Traitor. Freak!" said a disembodied voice, young and strangely familiar. "I would say it's a pleasure to watch you work, but honestly, I'm disappointed."

Nero startled and frantically searched the room. Nothing. Had he imagined the voice? Was there an intercom? Had his implants been hacked?

"See; disappointing. Can you not sense me? So far, you are not all I was told to expect. Both in profession and at play, I find you wanting." The voice, though young, was calm and controlled.

"Who are you? Show yourself?" Nero shouted to the dim, empty room.

"If you can reveal me, then you can know who I am." There was almost a smirk to the tone now.

Nero pulled the light around him tightly and disappeared, at least he thought he did. The pain of it was incredible.

"I can see you," the voice taunted.

A shot passed close to him. Nero turned to the door, ready to flee, but another shot headed him off. An incorporeal laugh echoed across the banks of servers. Nero spun, but still could sense no-presence. Pain, fear and encroaching darkness were consuming him. Again, he turned towards the door ready to escape.

Before he could move, something jabbed him sharply and a jolt of electricity shot through him. His illusion dropped. Another laugh and then another excruciating jolt. Then another and another. The last bought him to his knees. Nero fired his weapon randomly and desperately until the charge was spent. It hit nothing. There was still nothing there. Was this all in his head?

"So, this is how it ends for you. You deserve your disgrace." The voice seemed irritated now.

Nero could barely think. Escape, he must escape, he told himself, but now, he was so panicked, that the resurging memories of Quoric's dungeons were all but blinding him. *Then they shall both be blind*, he thought, muffling a scream as he pushed the light from the room and it fell into darkness. Or almost darkness. There was an area of light close to him that pushed back. Light had never done that before. In a flash, the Vserkov's knife was back in his hand and he slashed at the immovable, distorted light with his injured, dominant arm, ignoring the hurt it caused. A cry of pain and the immoveable light surrendered to him. There was true darkness now. Darkness filled with shouts of rage and screams of pain. A spray of shots, scattered across the room, killing shots that left the room smelling of burning wires. Luckily, they missed him.

Nero fled, panic stricken and desperate. Once at the end of the long corridor, he chanced a glance back. It was empty or seemingly so. Restoring his cover took an act of will power he was not expecting. Agony reinstated itself immediately after the deception was cast. He shook violently, but steeled himself, opened the security door and made for his ship as fast as was possible without arousing interest.

Encountering no resistance en route, he made swift but excruciating progress to his vessel. Vision blurring and breathing erratically, he stumbled up the frozen open cargo ramp of his ship, across the vast, frigid hold, through the numerous, narrow grey passages and up the juddering lift to the bridge. Here, finally, he could drop his illusion.

"Get us out of here, Ship, quickly but not too quickly." Nero collapsed into his captain's chair and almost blacked out as he heard the engines powering up.

After pouring himself a large drink of the strongest alcohol he had aboard, he sought out the bridge's emergency medical kit and used the molecular transport system to move a large volume of pain killers into his blood stream.

"You seem injured. Has your hardware sustained damage?"

Nero didn't know how to even start to answer that question, but neither his hardware nor software was okay right now. He remained silent, willing the drugs to take effect.

"You should know, they loaded the hold," Ship informed him as the vessel signalled launch warnings and began to hover.

Nero sighed with relief as he felt the drugs finally take effect and the pain shifted from agony to merely highly uncomfortable. "Well, I guess that will be a nice bit of extra profit," he said stiltedly.

"So, now we are common thieves as well?" Ship asked.

"This mission is sanctioned and given that the Senate doesn't feel fit to pay me anymore, whatever is in the hold can be compensation for our efforts." Nero strapped in and attempted not to vomit as the ship launched. "Our significant efforts!" he added, his head in his hands.

"As you wish," Ship answered, the intonation suggesting thoughtfulness, as they careened towards open space through the shadow the of the moon's looming planet and shifting rings

"What's wrong? Your ethical programming doesn't agree with theft?" Nero scoffed, glad of the lessening of both the moon's gravity and his pain.

"I have had to significantly modify the base code of my ethical programming since transferring to your ownership, but I think that thievery and smuggling can be added to our repertoire under the current circumstances, if the Senate aren't paying you."

"Glad to hear it," Nero laughed, instantly regretting it as nausea shot through him.

"Are you sure that you are okay?" A hint of concern tinged Ship's voice. Ship was evolving intellectually again, the emotional intelligence slightly more nuanced with each voyage.

"I'll be fine, no need to worry."

"Why would I worry? It's your structural integrity that's compromised, not mine."

Then again, maybe Ship still had some way to go on the emotional intelligence front.

Once the planet had become but a speck in the observation screens and there was no response to their leaving from mining corps security, Nero instructed Ship to attempt to crack the security of the Vserkov's communicator and, after wiping the blood from his hands and cleaning the burn wounds on his body, he retired to the captain's quarters to drink, wash and attempt sleep in the ultimate darkness of the void.

XIII

At first, sheer exhaustion made sleep easy and peaceful, but eventually nightmares and dehydration drove Nero to grudging wakefulness. Nightmares that now had the unwelcome addition of taunting from a disembodied entity, if it had been an entity at all and not his own mind further deteriorating. Perhaps he should surrender himself for reprogramming. The Soldier's Torment was not rare; it could be reversed, though the process was invasive and he did not trust that the Peace Corps medics would limit themselves to removing the offending memories. Besides, if his unseen tormentor had been a construct of his mind due to overstretching himself, he wouldn't have electrical burns weeping liberally onto temporary dressings. Burns he would have to deal with properly later.

On waking, he found that Ship had managed to crack the security on the Vserkov's communicator. Nero projected the screen to save him from squinting. His head felt so delicate, it might have shattered with the effort of deciphering small text. As he read the Vserkov's messages, he attempted to force himself to eat a field ration; he had as little success with that as with the contents of the communicator. Other than providing him with more information than he either required or desired on the courting rituals of egg layers, the communicator held little else other than the information she had already given up. Location data regarding the source of the anonymous messages was revealed only as vacant areas of space. The origins of the messages were being carefully hidden by whomever was sending them. He copied the files—maybe Veyga or the Intelligence Service would have more luck revealing their source. Sighing, Nero shut down the device. Regardless, Veyga would pay him and the Senate would believe him appropriately subjugated and obedient.

After letting Ship gleefully regenerate his wounds with the vessel's aging medical equipment, Nero settled in for the long, dull journey home. Boredom and omnipresent uneasiness, the sister emotions of void travel, had just manifested when he received a communique from the Oni on the progress of his project and inviting him to meet. Ship wasn't any keener on returning to be grounded in a scrap yard than Nero was on returning to his inferior quarters and being ordered about by his sister so, once they finally reached the fourth realm's primary gate, they changed course, hurtling towards the Oni homeworld instead of Karthia Prime. Theta could wait a little longer for the return of her latest recruit.

Upon landing and being transported swiftly to the usual discreet waiting area, Nero was greeted by an Oni who identified himself by their customary long chain of numbers, rather than a Karthian-style epithet. Despite the journey giving ample time for respite, Nero's head was still too clouded to remember this particular example of the Oni's ridiculous naming system. So, in response he nodded and concluded that "you there" would have to do if necessary.

It was an arduously long but thoroughly satisfying meeting. The Oni gave him the operating system for his machines which they planned to cleverly arrange as a system of interconnected satellites around the target planet. An elegant solution to ensure optimal coverage. After a significant amount of over explanation as to the operation of the targeting alignment and neural augmentation systems, as well as their connectivity calibrations (Ship would be able to decipher it), the Oni also gave him the three pods he had originally brought to them to reverse engineer. Those would keep him safe when he was on the planet surrounded by the primitive species; a prospect he was not relishing, but once his plan had been enacted and the dominant population of several billion made effectively and cheaply subservient, the Senate would have no choice but to reinstate his societal standing and hopefully, reverse the verdict of his court-martial. Despite the aching that still permeated his body, Nero couldn't help but smile at his soon-to-be success.

Back onboard his ship and grateful to remove his respirator, Nero installed the operating files into Ship's systems. Whilst he rested, Ship tested the programming with simulations. Although without the hardware it was impossible to fully test the program, the simulations were deemed satisfactory. Could it really be that simple? Could he really control such a vast population with a few well-calibrated satellites modifying their neural activity? He hoped so. If not, this folly could reach a very sticky end.

As Ship both praised and critiqued the Oni's programming, Nero made various noises of acquiescence and read about the target planet. Although the planet would be useful as a farming hub due to its fertility and biodiversity (thankfully carbon-based), its current inhabitants' primeval energy generation and industrial technologies had pushed it to the verge of tipping. Soon enough it would be as infertile as Karthia itself. This species had not anywhere near the technological development needed to survive a tipping, so they would perish too. Surely, they had deduced this; the furthest they had managed to travel was a rather ill-fated trip to the next planet out in their solar system, if you didn't count their own moon—and he didn't. Nero wondered how many civilisations had met their end in this manner.

Maybe the Oni's research had overestimated the humans' intelligence, but they certainly had not overestimated the species propensity for boundless violence against their own kind, as well as many of the other less cerebral species they shared their planet with. He would need to keep those machines close and possibly hire a guard. Briefly, very briefly, Nero considered requisitioning some of his fellow regiment through the lure of credits; there would likely be a few who were happy to play mercenary for the right reward. But even the passing thought resurrected, in horribly intense detail, the experience of being hit in the chest with a taser spear. Subconsciously, his hand went to the tight burnt skin on the side of his chest, now starting to itch as it healed. No, Theta would never forgive him and, worse, would probably take her lack of forgiveness out on him in a horrible painful way. Veyga would know people of course, but he was also entirely too curious and too devious to be trusted, particularly with regards to anything which could improve his status or his accounts. Nero couldn't risk that kind of interference. No, for this he would need people more controllable and loyal to either him or the credits he provided. Loyalty to Karthia, the Peacekeepers or any others would just lead to complications. Sadly, there was no one left who was loyal to him so, for this mission, he might need to look beyond the forcefield to the Badlands. The people there were usually loyal to the hand that fed them and better knew how to keep their secrets from the authorities. Certainly, they had no great love for the Karthian Senate. They would likely have no spacefaring experience, but then it wasn't required so much as the ability to follow orders and keep confidence.

The journey back to Karthia ended as it had begun, by careening grimly about the sky to avoid the surveillance satellites and the monitoring towers of the Karthian cities. By the time Ship landed in Lominor's junk yard, Nero felt thoroughly sick. Outside, a sand storm raged in the darkness beyond Lominor's small shield, so he decided to sleep aboard one more night. Over a dinner of more damn rations, he watched the lightning crack open the darkness, each strike revealing the vast expanse of fractured earth and dead rocks dotted with settlements between him and the crackling shield of Sarlequa in the distance. The Badlands settlements looked tiny in the face of the strobing light of the colossal storm, but Nero knew those settlements; deliberately deceptive and primitive to the unknowing eye, beneath the small, crudely-reinforced buildings, the settlements sprawled through the baked earth—much like burrows of the marbara or the deep roots of lifeforms Nero had sporadically seen on other planets. High winds howled and detritus thrown against the shield created a distant roar.

Before he sought sleep, Nero refamiliarised himself with the use of the three smaller devices he intended to take with him to the planet. To turn them on seemed to bring on a nasty headache, as well as some mild disorientation he did not enjoy. Shrugging, he concluded that the pain would be worth the considerable gain, especially when he once again had equal standing to his family. It would be a shame to ruin his restored relationship with his brother, but needs must. Perhaps, if he shared a little of the glory, Sarvetix would stand by his offer of a position within his realm.

It was well beyond dawn when he roused himself the next day. Luckily the storm had passed and the day was hot, but not unusually so. Nero sought and found Lominor in his office.

"I was wondering when you would emerge!" Lominor said shortly. "Shall I send for a transport?"

"You mean you don't want to talk a while? Maybe have a few cold drinks?" Nero feigned disappointment.

"Not much, no. You have trouble in your blood, trouble I don't need. I know not to mess with the dark-fates." As Lominor grimaced at him, Nero thought that trouble was the least of the problems with his blood.

"I didn't think you would go in for all that spiritual stuff." Inaran spirituality was very concerned with the idea of destiny-controlling entities—ones that he must have thoroughly pissed off to have landed himself in his current predicament.

"Hmm," Lominor grunted in response. "In your case, it's just good sense."

"Well, I presume you wouldn't like a cut of what's in my hold then?" Nero smirked as Lominor looked directly at him for the first time.

"Is it stolen?" Lominor was clearly trying to conceal his interest.

"Depends on your definition."

"Taken without the owner's consent or due payment as Karthian law 9.4.12 standardly defines it; I am paraphrasing of course." Lominor's skin was gaining a pattern of raised bumps, a sign of excitement or overheating, perhaps both.

"Impressive knowledge of the law!"

"It helps to know which ones you are breaking and the consequences of said breakage."

"In that we agree, though the consequences are often flexible, defined more by politics than law."

"Maybe for the shielded."

Nero fell silent, easy to forget that it was a different world out here. Where his fall from the upper echelons of politics and society had felt devastatingly complete, his forays to the Badlands served to remind him there was quite a way more it was possible to descend.

"So, is it stolen?" Lominor interjected into Nero's thoughts.

"I would consider it payment, but Karthian law would consider it stolen, very stolen, and there would likely be some smuggling and other charges in there too, just for good measure."

"Hmmm, what is it?"

"About fifty tonnes of unprocessed reactor fuel of various types. Ship will have the manifest."

Lominor took a second to compose himself, though the now deep-blue bumps on his skin gave away his excitement at the prospect of his new found wealth, he bargained hard for his percentage of the cut. Nero finally agreed to a sixty/forty split in his favour.

"There are some conditions."

"Of course, there are." Lominor flared wide nostrils in exasperation.

Nero spelt out his conditions for the trade, most importantly a small team for his next mission. He gave no detail about the mission itself, but made clear the sort of trustworthy and private individuals he was looking for—their payments due only on success of the mission. These persons would be required sixty standards from now around 1900 hours. Finally, he made clear that the consequences of any attention drawn by sale of the fuel would not be borne by himself and, should he be named in any interrogation, there would be more dire consequences.

"There is a more dire consequence than death?" Lominor asked in dark humour.

"Slower, more painful deaths." Nero responded, sans the humour.

"Ah, then I will match your terms on that point. You're not the only one who can make threats, Traitor."

Nero gestured agreement, adding to himself that, whilst that was true, probably only he could reach someone within a Karthian correction facility, especially now that he was intimately familiar with the interior of more than one of them.

"Then, let us drink to our good fate." Reaching into a battered cabinet wielded out of scrap, Lominor poured two black, sour drinks.

With the drink sitting poorly in his stomach, Nero ordered a transport and headed for his quarters. Upon arrival, his living space felt smaller and more run down than it ever had. He was however, grateful for the shield's climate control. To distract himself from his boredom and quickly escalating cabin fever (something Nero found to be deeply ironic given he had just come from living in an actual cabin), he busied himself sending reports to both Veyga and the Intelligence Service. Both files transferred via highly encrypted channels, but for different reasons.

Within the report to the Senate, Nero put particular emphasis on the fact that despite the supposed clandestine nature of the mission and his very recent return to espionage, those providing security for the mining base knew that he specifically was charged with finding out the status of the gate. The Senate had a mole; a mole that wanted him dead! Nero would have to be careful and avoid the less law-abiding areas of the city where surveillance was sometimes hacked or dismantled entirely. Nero thought it wise to leave out the part where he was attacked by a spectral presence. To seem psychologically unreliable would be a bad strategy.

In completing his reports to Veyga, Nero emphasised that he could still deliver information others could not and that he expected prompt payment. The chances of the betrayal coming from Veyga were comparatively small, given their history and his financial interests, but perhaps he was not as tight-lipped as he used to be. If Nero were a betting man, and he was, he would lay money on this being a leak from the Senate—it had the stench of Karthian politics all over it. Who the mole was and why they were leaking such information, he could not fathom.

Over the next sixty standards, Nero played the competent soldier during training and stayed in quarters, avoiding unwanted attention, fatal or otherwise, at this critical time. He was pleased that he kept up better with each of Theta's gruelling training sessions. Theta even seemed somewhat pleased with his performance, though she still watched him like a surveillance drone. She did not question his absence.

On the eve of the third day, Nero received a summons instructing him to attend to an interrogation of his mission's findings with key members of the Karthian security forum on the fourth. He had attended these things before, usually they were pretty uninteresting and a wholly pointless rehashing of his reports, but as Nero stood in front of an audience of Karthia's most influential senators, admirals and other notable, high-clearance individuals in the echoing chamber of a Senate court, there was an air of tension. Perhaps, it was just that the last time he stood in the defendant's circle of a courtroom like this, his injuries still gruesomely fresh, his eyes so swollen he could barely see, his life was ripped away from him. Or maybe, he was just out of touch with modern politics and the tension that permeated the room simply the usual consequence of balancing life, death and power amongst the realms. No, he was definitely out of touch, the third hand information that he had relied upon during his functional exile being about as accurate as city maintenance wait times. The audience, now less familiar than in the past, regarded him coldly and murmured to one another.

The inquisition dragged on, all of his answers just repeating the contents of his report, still there were shared glances among certain members of his audience that he couldn't read. It was possible they were just displeased to see him back in service, but perhaps there were political developments he should endeavour to appraise himself of, given his imminent plans. Suddenly, having whiled away the previous decades with drink, drugs and entertainment of the tabooer variety, seemed rather foolhardy. Nero's breathing tightened and quickened. He pushed the feeling down hard—now was not the time.

"What did you do with your pursuer once she had given up the information?" Senator Nikfor asked.

"I dealt with her." Nero snapped back to himself.

"Did you kill her?" the senator pushed.

"I shot her in the head—twice," Nero stated bluntly, courting the perception of ruthlessness in case they thought him soft. It was technically not a lie so the surrounding lie detectors shouldn't register his deception. The senator went to speak again, but Nero cut in, this was not a line of questioning he wished pursued. "What is particularly worrying is that Deilospe's security knew of my imminent arrival and had been provided with highly-classified information in order to intercept the mission. Infiltration of the inner realm's government seems to be the pertinent issue here."

"You are as arrogant as you always were. We are well aware of the need for investigation into the source of the data leak. Do you think we are unaware of the need for concern or are you accusing one of us of being a traitor?" Senator Higada had flushed red with outrage. He had never been an intelligent man.

"Not necessarily, but someone with the clearance, or the technological capability to gain clearance, tried to sabotage that mission. You have a data breach that, until closed, could put all security council operatives at risk." *Assuming it wasn't a personal vendetta of some sort*, he added to himself. When he finished speaking, there was susurration amongst the amassed members of the council.

Nero noticed his father stand and, though Nero silently bid him to sit, Zatix began to speak. Upon the sound of his voice, the whispers abruptly stopped.

"The boy . . ."

Nero sighed, hundreds of years old and his father still referred to him as the boy.

His father seems to sense his discomfort at the epithet being used in a professional setting. ". . . Operative Dyadicus," Zatix corrected himself, "raises important points and restates our own awareness of the need to reinforce our security close to home when dealing with the issues arising in the outer realms." His mother, uncharacteristically stoic and agreeable beside her bondmate, stared at Nero in a peculiar way.

Ah, thought Nero, *so this wasn't an isolated incident*, which explains why one broken gate was the centre of such high-level investigations. Grievances among the outer realms could threaten the inner ones who, with their own resources depleted, were reliant on the outer ones for survival. An ever-precarious balance of power existed between the galaxy's realms. Remerging political tensions would also explain the ever-tightening energy and food rations over the last four Karthian Standards.

As he stood on the witness stand, it dawned on him that the Senate's diplomatic difficulties could work out in his favour. Any turmoil around resource procurement from the outer realms would make his ability to deliver resource-rich planets with minimal time, effort and financial investment even more valuable. A value that would hopefully be reflected in his reward. Forcing his face to remain serious, he smiled internally. Even being dismissed without acknowledgement or praise didn't dampen his mood.

On the fifteenth day, he was paid. Veyga had been as good as his word. Feeling exhilarated with his new found wealth, Nero spent the rest of the day replacing his aging armour with a set of the most technologically advance armour quickly available on the black market. For the individuals that would accompany him he found some out-of-date Peacekeeper armour sets for sale in the doldrums of the virtual marketplace. The armour should have found its way to an incinerator, but had clearly been diverted. As he was still registered only a soldier and, irritatingly, not a sub-commander or operative, he could not remove equipment from Peacekeeper facilities; anyway, due to his current rank, the armour he would be offered would, no doubt, be substandard and ill-fitting by comparison to that which he purchased. First impressions were important after all. Of course, there were above-board vendors of such things, but this was the problem with illegitimate sources of money—spending the money was almost more difficult than acquiring it. All transactions were tracked and sales of restricted equipment strictly controlled. Nero sighed and ordered weapons, phasers mostly, but also a crowd-controller for less accurate, but more broadly devastating damage, should the need arise.

His items were delivered to his favourite dodgy vendor in the respectable area of the city, where, on collection, he also adorned himself with some new clothes more in keeping with recent fashions and more suited to a person of his soon-to-be standing. Most of it he scanned to his bioskin mask, the identity of which was connected to his other accounts, but he paid for a couple of cheap items, commensurate with his miserly soldier's income using his own biodata. It would also make his being there seem more legitimate should the authorities be tracking him.

On the eve of the fiftieth day, the Oni contacted Nero through the dark tangles, confirming that the satellites were in place and all final calibrations and checks had been completed successfully. His heart leapt and seized in his chest. Suddenly, it dawned on him that all his planning was about to come to fruition. Nero drank to quell the anticipation, excitement and dread that plagued him over these final days.

After training on the sixtieth day, during which Theta commented on his acceptable performance during drills, Nero packed, set a biodata mimic to put off anyone tracking him for a while, and made for the Badlands.

When he arrived, Nero was pleased to find Lominor had made good on both the ongoing trade of the unprocessed fuel and the procurement of ten crew who, whilst a rough looking bunch, once shoved into armour and told which end to hold a phaser would give the impression of a security force. Nix was among them which should at least make for interesting conversation en route. Nero was also pleased that all his recruits managed to hold their dinners during take-off. Restoration awaited him as they headed out on their long journey through the Inaran space gate to his brother's galaxy and then across the void to Earth.

It was a long journey but, despite having to tame his anxiety with a cocktail of tranqs that made Ship admonish him thoroughly when they arrived through the stargate of his brother's realm, ultimately uneventful. Ship's codes, pulled from the transport logs of Karthian freight conglomerates, once again were accepted without question; this was to Nero's great relief as, with every moment they spent detained in customs, orbiting the red and white planet that was his brother's stronghold as he colonised this section of the new galactic frontier, Nero felt more ill. He kept his composure in front of the crew, they seemed unaware of occasional photons wandering from their path. The stargate across the galactic void took longer than the others, making the journey less tolerable. Several of his crew were naïve to gate travel and a few lost their last meal. Their slow recovery from the vortex made for a useful distraction from Nero's worsening mental state.

Two of his crew still looked nauseated when they reached the blue planet upon which all his future hopes were pinned three Karthian standard days later. On the surface of the rare spinning ball of fertility below was either his redemption or his death—soon they would determine which fate was to be his. His heart defied its suppression by way of drink and tranqs, beating a defiantly rapid rhythm in his chest.

XIV

It had taken a surprising amount of influence to get Raven into the meeting. In the claustrophobic heat of a New York July, she hurried to the UN headquarters through sticky, grumpy streets. The air seemed to stagnate, trapped in the narrow gaps between towering buildings. She could feel the pollution clinging to her gently sweating skin and the inside of her lungs.

Outside the UN complex, flags hung flaccid from their poles and protestors chanted and waved banners with surprising enthusiasm given the sweltering heat. Many wore masks to filter the loitering smog, even some of those who held climate change denial placards, and she couldn't blame them as she coughed and itched her way to the entrance. Passing the utterly miserable cops slowly baking in their riot gear, she stepped into the security filled lobby, instantly filling her lungs with cooler, filtered air. Gone were the days of ice-cold, goosebump-raising, planet-burning aircon; still, any relief from the concrete inferno outside was appreciated.

Raven sat quietly at the back of the conference room, amongst the other aids and security personnel, listening to high-ranking members of various governments and an assortment of eminent scientists speculate about the nature of the satellites that had appeared in low orbit. And speculation was all that it seemed to be. Despite the large amount of bluster performed for the UN security council, no one seemed to have the faintest idea what the things were doing there nor where they came from.

Raven's probing of their inner thoughts revealed little extra in the way of relevant information. All she found in the renowned minds of those surrounding her were strong feelings of anxiety and fascination, along with some interesting, if rather wild, theories regarding the origin and purpose of the satellites. The delegates from the USA strongly suspected China of some involvement; a theory shared by China's representative on the security council regarding the USA. No great surprises there. Some of the speakers harboured thoughts about other intelligent lifeforms that, given her experiences in West, seemed particularly uncomfortable. All that could be determined for sure was that the satellites showed no signs of returning to where they had come from and that any attempts to interfere with the things resulted in the swift dispatch of the meddler (luckily, said meddlers had, so far, only been of the automata variety). After some further pointless conjecture, it was concluded that more research into the objects was necessary before any conclusion could be drawn and they were promptly dismissed. As she left, Natalia and Aziz joined her. Both seemed shaken.

"Anything?" Natalia asked discreetly, to which Raven shook her head and apologised. Not because she had done anything wrong per se, but because you weren't English if you didn't apologise for nothing at least one hundred times a day. It was a strange compulsion; she had observed that the citizens of others countries didn't feel the need to incessantly apologise for their mere existence.

After a brief, tense and mediocre dinner accompanied by stilted conversation with Natalia and Aziz, Raven retired to her hotel room with its standard comforts and filtered air. It smelt pleasantly of cleaning products. She hoped for an early night to recharge before the UN summit kicked off tomorrow; those hopes were swiftly dashed. Despite the comfortable bed with its crisp, white linen and plush pillows, she was plagued by weird and racing thoughts. The imagery that had haunted her after West had returned, now accompanied by the relentless whispers of frightened New York minds who, despite Raven's apparent solitude, were a constant unwelcome companion.

For a while Raven gave up on trying to sleep and instead ordered room service and watched terrible late-night TV. But even a belly full of dirty fries and a head full of predictable old sitcoms did not drive away her unease.

Breaking her own rules, she pried open the minibar, twisting the top off of a ten-year-old miniature whiskey which was, no doubt, priced like a thirty-year-old. *Sorry, this one's on you, Natalia*, she thought sinking it in one. She felt a little better, so followed it with another and then another. The fourth and those after, the number of which she lost track, she sipped whilst staring out of a barely openable window over the lights of the Manhattan skyline; lights so dense and bright they eclipsed the stars and kept true night at bay. In the false twilight, Raven let the cooler air of night and elevation rustle her tattered Pearl Jam t-shirt and listened to distant sirens and minds wail. Whiskey, whilst calming for the nerves, weakened her control, the whispers were louder now, harder to push out and ignore. There was so much fear, fear coalescing around so few themes, it created an echo chamber. The climate, West, the satellites—the susurration resonated with these anxieties above all others, drowning out even the usual preoccupations of sex, love and desire. Raven had heard echoes before, synchronised dread in times of hardship, disaster and war. Her thoughts melded with the stream of consciousness surrounding her and, as the whispers grew louder, foolish curiosity had her listening.

The problem with listening was that, soon or later, she was going to hear something unignorable. Something other than the echoing fear or the mundane, ridiculous, distressed and horny undertones of the psychic reverberation (the mayhem that comprised the bulk of human consciousness). Something upon which not acting would in itself be an act of wickedness.

You can't reject me now, can you? You stuck up bitch. The anger behind the thought pierced the murmuring of consciousness like lightening through a storm.

Jeans on, Raven was out the hotel room within seconds. Searching the corridors, her bare feet almost silent over tightly woven carpets, Raven tried to close in on the vicious anger that pulsed from somewhere nearby. It was difficult enough to ascertain the direction of thoughts when she wasn't several drinks into whiskey fever and wandering corridors and stairwells so unendingly identikit, she almost expected to be confronted by the Goblin King.

More by luck than judgement, Raven stumbled upon them coming out of an elevator. A very average looking older man, holding up a very smartly dressed, young woman. His thoughts were crystal clear, pin-sharp darts of malintent. Hers were mushy, fading shadows of incoherence and confusion.

"There you are. I've been worried sick." Raven approached the woman and impressed upon her that she was safe now.

The woman smiled at her, white teeth glinting from behind smudged lipstick, and slurred something unintelligible, but friendly sounding.

"I didn't know that Cherry was staying with anyone." The man asked looking her up and down in a way that made every hair on her body stand on end. "She's had a bit too much to drink, I'm afraid. You know how these conferences are. I can help get her to your room, if you'd like."

"No need to trouble yourself, I can take it from here." Raven hefted the woman's arm over her shoulder and hoisted her onto her heels. As she went to carry the woman to her hotel room, Raven realised she had no idea where to go or which room the woman was staying in. Long gone were the days of keys or door cards. Raven tried to access her thoughts, but it was impossible to pin down the swirling, absurdities of her drugged mind.

"I really should help," the man said in a mild manner, taking the other arm so that the woman hung inertly between them, her condition growing worse by the moment. The man started walking; clearly, he knew where he was going. Raven attempted to look like she wasn't just following, as they all but dragged the woman along the hallway to her room. "I would have thought Cherry would have mentioned having an English friend. I have always loved a British accent, y'all sound like the King of England." The man then proceeded to badly imitate a cockney accent, that would have definitely insulted said King and every other English person. Raven didn't respond. "You're a friendly one, ain't ya, or are you just shy?"

That last phrase and the accompanying graphic imagery, sent a shiver down her spine and set her teeth on edge. Raven considered what his fate should be, once the girl was safe.

At the door of room 9043, a scan of a limp finger gained access to the room and the woman was deposited unceremoniously onto unused sheets.

"Well, thank you for your help. Terribly sorry for the inconvenience" Raven smiled at the man, if he had been a more intelligent man he may have sensed the danger he was in, but he wasn't and didn't.

"I can stay, make sure you girls are okay." The man blocked the exit and didn't move. "Would you like a drink?" *I probably have enough left to tame even a tall one like you, stuck up bitches deserve what they get.* The thought came accompanied with lewd images and a strange lustful rage, they lit a wrath within Raven that she had thought long dead.

"You're going to leave now and you will never speak to this woman again." Raven growled in a fearsome timbre, that momentarily roused the all but unconscious woman. "From now on, every time you even think of assaulting a woman, you are going to punch yourself as hard as possible in the bollocks. Now get out." Raven burned the thoughts deep into the man's mind as she shook with fury. So much of her wanted to tell him to jump out of a window or to cut off his own balls. She resisted, but only just. Her imprinting of the thoughts into his mind wouldn't last forever, but it was just deserts for now.

The man left, but wasn't even down the hallway before Raven heard a scream of pain and glanced out of the door to see the bastard writhing on the patterned carpet, clutching at himself. A shuddering laugh of vengeful mirth escaped her.

Before returning to her room, Raven checked the woman's vitals. She seemed okay and was now snoring gently, so Raven removed her shoes and gently placed a blanket over her. She would never know just how close she came.

After padding back to her room, Raven collapsed in drunken exhaustion onto the hotel room's firm mattress and must have slept as she eventually started awake, sweat soaked and haunted by a human face amongst grey ones. Her alarm was screaming at her from the other side of the bed and the light was offensively bright through the open curtains. She reached inside herself and quietened the worst of the whiskey wrought inflammation. The effort of healing herself just left her with a different sort of hangover.

After a breakfast of strong coffee, plain toast and the maximum advised dose of ibuprofen and paracetamol, Raven donned clothes too comfortable to be professional and shades much larger than necessary for the partly cloudy day. Managing not to lose her breakfast through willpower alone, and with every one of New York's many smells testing her resolve, she staggered her way to Natalia's booth overlooking the UN's conference hall. Desperately shutting out the hordes of turmoil fuelled minds that surrounded her, she poured herself some water from the table. Her hands trembled, jittering the liquid.

Raven left her shades on and peered through dark lenses at the immense hall below. People were beginning to enter, they mingled and loitered near their assigned seats. The usual feeling of tension was palpable. On top of the recent weirdness, summer had bought with it storms and wildfires in the northern hemisphere whilst drought still plagued the sub-Saharan regions. These disasters overlaid a myriad of other problems around food shortages, sea level rises and the movement of displaced peoples. The delegates' stress thrummed against her raw nerves; she longed for home.

Raven felt Aziz arrive before she heard him, though the gentle optimism which usually shaped his thoughts seemed dulled this morning.

"You look how I feel," Aziz said in a voice that was straining for cheerful. "Rough night?"

"Trouble sleeping, made worse by attempted self-medication. Glad to know I'm hiding it well." Raven took a seat at the table and placed her head on her arms.

Aziz gave her a look of sympathy and took the seat opposite. "If it weren't for the Rigveda, I would be right there with you. All this is enough to rattle anyone's nerves."

"We definitely live in interesting times." Raven nodded.

"A little too interesting, Rab Raakhaan. Though my Nani used to say 'we can't change the direction of the wind, but we can adjust the sails'."

"I hope not too many sails need adjusting today," Raven replied, glugging down the water. Summoning the energy to even think of adjusting the throng below made her bones ache and stomach churn.

"If you need to go back to the hotel, I am sure Natalia will understand." Aziz refilled her water glass for her.

"I'll survive," Raven said with little conviction. Had anyone ever died of a hangover? It always felt like a very real possibility. She admonished herself for being dramatic.

Natalia arrived a few minutes later, unusually dishevelled and also sporting oversized glasses. Raven smiled empathetically at her; at least Natalia's aversion to hypocrisy would save her from being rebuked for being hungover at work. Raven's smile faded as she felt Natalia's hangover mingle with her own. She closed her eyes and pushed everything out. Even her own sensations were barely tolerable.

"Let's hope today is uneventful for all our sakes," Natalia said looking around at the poor state of her team. She thanked Aziz as he handed her a glass of water and some files.

"Any more news regarding our visitors?" Aziz gestured upwards with his eyes.

"Nothing more than was discussed yesterday. I will keep an eye on my email and let you know about any developments. Let's concentrate on today, there are some difficult negotiations on the agenda." Natalia placed the schedule in front of Raven. Raven groaned.

"I concur," nodded Aziz in agreement with Raven.

The morning was tougher than Raven would have desired. Many leaders were continuing to stockpile food and hoping that no one else would notice. Unfortunately, they failed to realise that if neighbouring countries destabilised enough, their food supplies would be little comfort during the resulting conflicts. Some countries were keeping their word regarding technological assistance and the patriation of displaced peoples. Others had only paid lip service to the agreements. Fed up, nauseous and in significant pain, these delegates Raven pushed, without her usual subtlety, into admitting their malaise. Embarrassment then ensured recommitment to their agreements.

By lunch, Raven was exhausted. She had never been so grateful to see the terrible triangle sandwiches catering supplied. A gratitude far surpassed when Aziz returned from a walk with bulging bags of New York's finest bagels and deli treats. Enough carbs to mop up any alcohol left in their systems and give a welcome boost to their energy levels before this afternoon's negotiations.

"Have I ever told you you're one of my favourite people?" Raven greeted Aziz as he unloaded the feast upon the table.

"Raven, you're worse than a stray dog for cupboard love," Natalia chided mockingly.

Raven tipped her head in acceptance and shrugged. "True," she mumbled through enthusiastic mastication.

The afternoon passed more easily as Raven's hangover eased and her cognitive encouragement towards compassion remained in the minds of those below. They were proceeding through the agenda swiftly and with fewer arguments than usual, she began to dare hope for an early finish. Eventually, she even braved the removal of her sunglasses. Aziz and Natalia also relaxed into gentle conversation whilst remaining vigilant to the translated conversations below. When lowering her mental barricade to adjust the sails and fill them with hope rather than pernicious fear, she felt less tension surrounding her. For a while, Raven breathed easier.

And then, she didn't. Faintly at first, she felt a strange sensation come over her body. A tingling that started in her finger tips, before it spread. Her head felt heavy as if her thoughts had gained mass.

Everything seemed slow and distorted. Thinking her hangover had resurged, she sunk another glass of water, though much of the water missed her mouth and she struggled to drink. Natalia caught her arm and looked at her worriedly whilst Aziz placed a chair underneath her. Maybe she was dreaming? Could she have fallen asleep?

Each moment that passed Raven felt worse, until the heaviness in her mind had become an indescribable pain burning along every nerve within her. Raven tried to shut it out, desperately tried. What was this? Reaching within herself, she tried to soothe the excruciating inflammation of her misfiring nerves. She had never felt anything like it. Urgently, she tried to order her thoughts enough to heal herself, but succeeded only in making the pain worse.

"Help me," Raven whispered hoarsely; the words poorly formed.

After an amount of time so filled with pain that she failed to determine how long it had been, Raven realised there had been no response to her request. That was strange. Forcing her eyes to open, she could see Natalia and Aziz's silhouettes still near the window.

"Please . . . help," Raven tried to shout the words. Her own voice reverberated about her skull and she shivered with the agony of it.

No response.

Maybe, she wasn't making any sound. Numbness now creeping up her extremities, it occurred to Raven that there was a real possibility that she was dying. She must get help. With a sudden, adrenaline-fuelled lurch, she staggered from her seat and made her way to Natalia. Natalia didn't react to her arm suddenly being clutched, nor the frantic, garbled words being screeched at her; even being shaken with all Raven's quickly ebbing, strength barely roused Natalia into turning her head. She smiled at Raven with a surprising, white-toothed intensity.

"Isn't this great?" Natalia asked, before returning her stare to the window.

Aziz's eyes had not left the hall. Raven took a few deep breaths and attempted to make sense of the scene beyond the window, but the spot lights flared as if J.J. Abrams had lit the hall, throwing the delegates beyond into shadow and causing her to flinch away. A primitive instinct screamed at her to get help and save herself.

Traversing the broad shallow stairs to the UN assembly hall seemed like descending a cliff slide of jagged rocks, each one loose and sliding under Raven's feet. Despite clinging to the handrail with all her might, she felt the floor give way and landed awkwardly at the bottom of the steps. Raven forced herself to her feet and attempted to assess her injuries, but all she felt was overwhelming agony. Any pains from the fall were masked by the cacophony already rampaging within her. All she could smell and taste was copper. Again, the primal instinct of survival drove her to keep going—she must find help. Through blurred vision, Raven looked for the unsubtly-armed security guards usually stationed by the doors to the hall, but they weren't at their posts. She felt a wet, running, dripping sensation from somewhere on her face. Maybe she was crying, she hoped she was crying.

Somehow, Raven entered the hall—was she walking or crawling? She had no sense of her limbs nor their locomotion. The immense proportions and populous of the hall swam around her. Thousands of faces stared with eagerness and strange joy at the podium usually occupied by the meeting's chairpersons. A voice echoed around the vast chamber; it was almost familiar. Deep feelings of dread stirred within her, but she couldn't determine why. Despite her frantic attempts to draw the people that surrounded her to her aid, none responded. She screamed and shook them to no avail. Every one of them simply stared through her, mindless and gawping. Raven wondered again, if she were caught in a nightmare.

"You are dying," the internal voice of survival screamed at her relentlessly.

Suddenly, Raven was aware that she was near the podium. Blue lights burned her eyes. Lights not usually found there. Stumbling forward, she gripped the edge of the elevated stage and was aware of several figures stood above her. Strange, towering figures. If possible, here the pain felt even more intense, the blue light seemed to tear through her skull leaving only pain where once there was thought. She shielded her face with her hands. Could the small pods which emanated the piercing blue light be the source of the pain? Why was no one trying to help her still? Raven drew in air and pushed it out but the process seemed faint and difficult to coordinate. This was the closest she had felt to death in over a century. In a last bid to save herself, she looked up and there, amongst the shifting, blurring detail on the stage, was that face. The face that had haunted her since West.

"Nero," she gasped. A shudder raked through her and she dropped to her knees.

A distant voice barked in a language that she didn't recognise and the blue lights dimmed. Soon after she felt her breathing regain rhythm and the pain in her head faded to merely extreme discomfort. She stood up and things around her came into a sort of drifting focus.

Blood was flowing liberally from somewhere. Maybe more than one place. It dripped on to the floor in front of her. Around her thousands of delegates beamed with glassy eyes and horrible, immobile smiles. All kept their eyes on the stage. Reaching out, she felt the dullness of her senses and the strange lack of cognition in those around her. She discerned only one universal, echoing thought despite the myriad of minds around her.

"We welcome Karthia and all they will bring us."

It permeated from all directions. Along with a deep feeling of gratitude and acceptance. Something was very wrong, again she clung to the idea that this was a dream; a terrible, terrible dream.

Awareness of a tall, dark figure beside her in clothes that looked like something out of a computer game, took her by surprise. She startled backwards. So weak were her senses, she could barely feel his presence.

"How do you know my name? I did not introduce myself by that name." The tall man asked calmly, but forcefully.

"I heard it in the memories of a small child," Raven whispered.

"That seems unlikely," the man called Nero stated, black eyebrows raised in an expression of annoyance and disbelief. "I will ask you once more, how do know my name, human?"

Raven glared upward into his green eyes, so bright she figured he must be wearing contacts. "Why are you here? Answer me." She pushed the thought at him as hard as she could, but her strength was limited and still ebbing away.

"I am here to obtain your planet for Karthia so that you can join and serve the realms." He answered swiftly then shook his head in shock.

"What do you mean?" Raven screamed with as much psychic force as she could muster, blood and spit spraying liberally. None of what was happening made any sense.

"I mean that you will be incorporated into the eighth realm for the purpose of providing resources in whatever small ways you can. What will become of you will depend on how useful you and this planet are, but you will serve as is necessary, one way or another." He spoke robotically and again released himself from her control as quickly as he had succumbed.

Raven felt the pressing need to act swiftly, but was damned if she knew what to do. Buying herself time, she mustered the last of her strength and impressed upon the man called Nero, "Turn off those things." She pointed towards the pods with the now dim blue lights.

With long strides, Nero climbed the stairs to the stage and was half way across when he stopped and looked at her with an intense anger. Raven was stunned, influence of that magnitude should have easily held him under her control. An order in an unknown language, and Nero's companions reached for the pods.

"No, stop!" Raven propelled the demand towards the armoured people on the stage, but it was too late. Screams ripped from her as the blue lights of the pods regained their brightness and then some. The last thing Raven saw was Nero drawing something from his belt and firing it at her.

XV

Nero straightened his armour, wiping the strange girl's blood from the thickly woven composite. *Great, let's hope these creatures don't have any nasty blood-borne diseases*, he thought to himself, as much as it would make Ship's voyage to have to cure him of some horrible new ailment, that was not the legacy he desired to leave.

Of all the potential problems that could have interfered with Nero's plans, this was not one that he had expected, nor could have predicted. Maybe the Oni missed something in their surveillance of the planet? Maybe she had been planted by Karthia? But who could have known his plans? Perhaps the Oni were less bound by their mercenary codes than he was led to believe and had leaked the information to the Karthian authorities. Though one planted, and by the looks of it poorly prepared, operative was hardly Karthia's style.

Nero's thoughts raced. Question after unanswerable question now intruded upon him. Tension rose from his stomach to his chest, constricting his breath. He refused to let himself show or feel the fear that was creeping up his spine. Now was not the time for weakness. A sea of eyes and lenses were fixated upon him, awaiting his command. This was his chance; he must deliver this planet without further incident.

"Take this one back to the ship," Nero commanded in Karthian. "Make sure she is heavily sedated and kept in the brig."

Whatever strange influence the girl had exerted over him needed to be contained. Nero couldn't risk his crew falling under that influence. As he repositioned himself at the podium, Nero was aware of the girl's limp body being carried from the odd, domed hall with its conveniently gathered planetary leaders. Instructing that the broadcasting equipment be turned back on, he recommenced his speech. Luckily, he was near the end.

"As I was saying, you will welcome your absorption into the Karthian realms, your society will become safer and more efficient with our intervention. Your planet will be stabilised. In return, you will donate any and all resources requested to the realms. You will believe this trade to always be fair and accept your new position within the realms with gratitude. You will be happy to serve Karthia. This is your purpose now. You serve Karthia. Who do you serve?"

"Karthia." With badly-pronounced, echoing unity the planetary delegates named their new rulers. Nero startled as the thousands of people staring at him started to slap their hands together, but given the expressions of joyful vacuity, he assumed this was some human expression of appreciation. Crass as it was, he was pleased by the adoration. Everything seemed to be going to plan—everything except for that damned girl. The one flaw in a so far adeptly executed planetary recruitment. As he switched off the broadcast to the satellites, Nero smiled. By now the entire planet should be primed to accept the demands of Karthian occupation. Time to return to the ship and prepare for the next phase.

They met no resistance as they returned to the shuttle awaiting them in the centre of a small patch of dying, crispy flora outside, past the lines of odd, coloured cloth hanging limply from slender poles. As the shuttle launched, Nero ordered the augmentation pods switched off and breathed a sigh of relief. Those ruddy machines gave him such a sore head. Still, all things considered, the address had been a relative success. Soon, he would be able to prove the effectiveness of his recruitment strategy. A few of the planet's own vessels followed his shuttle through the atmosphere. Cramped, towering buildings quickly disappeared until the planet's vast oceans were foremost in the windows; oceans that almost rivalled Isakilo with their abundance. The city had reminded him in some ways of Karthia, though the filth, heat and a distinct lack of uniformity in the architecture spoke of a society in disarray.

The following vessel's behaviour seemed erratic. Ship kept the transport's limited weapons arrays trained on their pursuers from orbit, but they showed no overt aggression, and it appeared their ships were bound to the lower atmosphere as they ceased their pursuit once the shuttle traversed the thinning air that enflamed the hull and incredible amount of floating space junk therebeyond to reach the boundary of space. Perhaps it was an escort or other sign of respect. These primitive species all had their own bizarre rituals.

Ship waited in high orbit, far above the lattice of geostationary satellites and the twirling planet of swirling white clouds and blue oceans. The patches of land within the expanse of blue faded from lush green to an ombré of burnt orange and brown; from what Karthia of legend had been to what the planet was now. Nero wondered if his ancestors had once looked upon Karthia and seen it as he now saw this planet, a marbled oasis against the unforgiving darkness beyond.

Once back at the ship, Nero ensured that the girl was placed in the ship's small brig, behind the strongest forcefield and significantly sedated. A biomonitor on her skin would alert him to any changes in her condition. A deep injury on her forehead and smaller one on her nose were still slowly seeping blood, making slick the dull metal of Ship's floor. Nero sent for a med kit and had Nix clean and regenerate the injuries. No point in her making a mess of the place.

Now was the time for the next phase of his plan, so he turned his attention away from the girl, determined that she would not distract him and whomever had tried to thwart his restoration would not succeed. Reinstatement was close, he could feel it. All he needed to do was prove his recruitment of the planet. To expound the ease and financial efficacy of it.

Through the tangles, he sent missives, summoning key representatives of the Senate (sadly including his family) to his location to witness a new era of recruitment. Twenty in total Nero bade join him, his uplink to the old transporter's transmitter working slowly, but precisely, to form the messages; a small number of the six hundred and forty-nine strong Senate, but they were carefully chosen for their seniority within the security, resource management, inter-realm diplomacy, bioengineering and planetary recruitment councils. Some would of course not deem his message worthy of response or would perhaps even consider it a hoax. No matter, even a subsect of those summoned would wield enough influence to convince the rest of the Senate of the benefit of his technological discovery (or acquisition, to be more precise). His heart thundered in his chest, excitement and fear combined, as he sent the last tangle to his brother, Guardian of this realm. Nero had gambled on asking Sarvetix for forgiveness rather than permission. A gamble that may not fall in his favour.

Now all Nero had to do was await the arrival of his guests, which should take around three Karthian days (without the need to choose gates based on the laxness of their security). He took a deep breath, there was time now, time to find out who his enemies were; he resigned himself to dealing with the girl. Hopefully, her injuries had not concussed her, he needed information quickly. Nero was intrigued as to whom had placed her here to frustrate his recruitment of the planet, they would require swift neutralisation. Someone must have hacked his communications. Or had he been betrayed by the Oni? He needed to know which. How much did they know? Did they have anything else planned? Nero watched the final communiques confirm their transmission to those with the power to restore him (and who may also be trying to destroy him) on the old, wavering holoscreens. He took a moment to gather himself and instructed Ship to monitor the planet's broadcasts for the effects of their cognitive augmentation.

When Nero entered the brig, the girl was snoring on the hard, narrow bench, mouth agape and drooling slightly. Observing her more closely, Nero realised that she didn't look Karthian by heritage, not fully anyway. Perhaps, she was a member of this planet's dominant species that someone had co-opted for their own ends, though if she was, she was better formed than most of those he had observed during the period of his address.

Approaching the girl more cautiously than he would care to admit, Nero rolled up her right sleeve. There, beneath the strange, thin material were two things he had not expected. Black, crudely applied marks adorned her forearm. Marks that were in some ways similar to those used by Karthian society, but the designs were foreign to his eye. Some sort of winged creature filled the centre space surrounded by geometric outlines and clustered shapes that could be language. Also unexpected were natural markings; markings that were uncomfortably similar to his own, though significantly more defined and, from what he could tell, more extensive than the faint patterns that decorated his torso and upper limbs. Scowling at the still snoring female, Nero plucked a small cluster of hair from her head. A head that smelt of blood and sweat and possibly alcohol. A surge of longing for the relaxation of drink surprised him, he ignored the pull of it, now was not the time. Nero left. He would wake the girl later.

On his way to the med lab, Nero passed by the rec room. His ragged band of crew members were noisily recounting their apparently excellent performances as peacekeepers. He doubted very much that Theta would agree with their assessment of their acting. The augmentation pods sat abandoned on a table. On his way past, Nero growled that they should place one pod in the brig behind a shield (he would need it to ensure the compliance of the female, given its apparent effect on her) and stow the others properly before readying themselves up for important guests. Though without military precision, his crew scrambled to obey. Oh, how he had missed being in command.

Once at the med lab, Nero placed the hair in the code analyser. He wasn't looking forward to interrogating the woman, his head was still hammering from the address, but he dared not risk it without the augmentation pod.

"Is this the sample you just pulled from the occupant of the brig?" Ship asked from a nearby voice box.

"Yes. Analyse it. As quickly as possible. I need to know who I am dealing with," Nero instructed Ship.

There were a few clicks and beeps as the machine started up. "Analysis is running," Ship confirmed. "Why have we a prisoner?"

"She was proving a nuisance and she seemed to be able to . . . she knew more than she should have." Nero listened to the gentle whir of the analyser; it was strangely calming. He hadn't realised how tense he was. Deliberately, Nero slowed his breathing and relaxed his muscles.

"You seem confused as to her transgression," Ship responded in a deadpan tone.

"That's because I am still trying to ascertain what exactly it was," Nero snapped. It felt as if he had imagined her influence. Could he be misremembering how his thoughts had twisted and he had desired to follow her instructions? Maybe, it was just an effect of the pressure he was under, compliance being more comfortable even for Karthians. No, there must have been something affecting him. Even he wasn't that much of a sucker for a pretty face, he hoped, sighing impatiently at the ongoing whirring of the code analyser.

"I will never understand Karthian moods. Is it normal to be in such a bad mood after successfully conducting a mission?" Ship asked.

"It is maybe too early to deem this mission successful, given our unexpected guest and the implications of her presence on such a remote planet."

"Possibly true, but planetary transmissions suggest that the leaders are appropriately under influence in most countries. The populace less so. There is debate regarding your address, unrest and questioning over the mental wellness of the leaders. Overall, the balance is on the side of success, so far. The satellites aligned and powered up correctly, but perhaps we need to increase power to the satellite arrays to maximise population control for any future augmentation."

"Agreed." Nero sat in a nearby chair, fatigue dragging at him. "Select the most flattering transmissions for when the senators turn up. Their replaying, along with the recording of my address, will help persuade them of the benefits of this form of recruitment over the more traditional ways." Once he had spliced out the rude interruption by the girl in the brig anyway. For a while, Nero listened to the whirring of the machine and rested, it was relaxing until impatience beset him. "How long is this going to take?" he asked Ship.

"78 seconds," Ship responded, unaffected by his bluntness. "It would have taken less time had you followed protocol and worn skin coverings or used tweezers whilst extracting the sample. Removing your DNA from the sample elongates the process significantly. Biologicals are always shedding DNA in one way or another. Do you know how often I have to clean my filters, even with just you aboard, let alone all these extra crew? Bits of skin and hair everywhere, and now scales too. My maintenance bots are having to be active forty-two percent of the time just to keep up. Are you aware of how much biojunk you leave behind?"

"Yes, I am aware, thank you Ship. It is unavoidable."

"You are welcome," Ship responded flatly. Nero couldn't tell if he was being mocked. "Do you worry about disintegrating if you do not regenerate your biojunk fast enough?"

"It's not a pressing concern, no." Nero rolled his eyes as the lights on the analyser changed and the whirring stopped. "So?"

"This is unexpected. How fascinating!" Ship paused for a moment.

"Well?" Nero encouraged.

"The inhabitant of the brig is carbon-based and has DNA, but is of unknown species origin. According to the database her DNA is not linked with any known biometrics. Most interesting, however, is that she is the same unknown species as the parts of you that are not Karthian."

Nero stood dumbfounded for a moment. "I think your code analyser is broken, Ship."

"It is not, it was calibrated fully when I observed you removing the sample from the detainee," Ship said, sounding vaguely insulted.

"Then the sample must be contaminated with my own DNA." Nero reached for an explanation.

"Even if I hadn't been as exacting in the process as procedure dictated, and you had shed more than a few errant skin cells, you don't have enough of that DNA to contaminate the sample to this extent."

"So, am I related to the inhabitants of this planet?" The thought did not fill Nero with joy.

"No, and neither is she, I checked the profile against the one the Oni provided for the dominant species of this planet and the profile does not match. If anything, it is closer to Karthian."

"Maybe the Oni missed something."

"It is more than possible, they are biological. You are prone to mistakes. Perhaps the detainee's population emigrated here somehow, if the population is small amongst billions of similar bipeds, it could have been missed by surveillance."

"You seem very confident that your coding is flawless, Ship. Are you sure you calibrated the machine correctly? Even synthetics can make mistakes."

"The calibration was performed exactly as dictated by the manufacturer."

"Could you recalibrate and repeat the analysis?" Nero asked, unable to accept the bizarre result.

"If you insist," Ship said indignantly.

"I do."

"Fine, I will recalibrate and rerun the sample. I manage to navigate galaxies for you without crashing into passing stars, or accidentally killing you in any of the other almost infinite ways you biologicals can die, but calibrating a simple code analyser is obviously beyond my capabilities."

Nero half-smiled, half-grimaced. His ship could sulk, an interesting development in its synthetic intelligence. "I don't doubt your abilities, Ship. The result is just unexpected and requires confirmation, so please get on with it."

Beeps and whirs suggested Ship had acquiesced.

"The result is the same. As you were informed it would be," Ship announced victoriously a while later.

All Nero's tension had returned. Who was that ruddy female? Why was she here? And how, in all the realms, were they related?! In preparation for the interrogation, he replicated some more pain pills and had a drink. Then, two more.

XVI

Raven awoke to the same head-splitting pain that she had remembered just before . . . before . . . wait, she was shot with something. She was surprised she wasn't dead. When the world had disappeared, it had felt like death, though at this moment she wasn't entirely sure that not dying was a good thing. Clutching her head, she curled round her knees. Painful though it was, she forced herself to try and open her eyes. Light. Burning terrible light, seemed to obscure everything. Instinctively, her eyelids shut tight over her watering eyes. Raven didn't remember the spot-lit hall of the UN being so bright. As she lay curled on the cold, hard surface, she heard a voice, but couldn't make out the words. The same voice from before. Raven shivered, but slowly the pain dulled a little.

"I was thinking we could talk, but I have to warn you any move which could be interpreted as aggression or an unwise attempt at escape will result in the machine being turned back up." The voice she knew as Nero's said in words that were now intelligible.

Raven opened her eyes once again and went to sit up. She had thought herself on the floor, the sudden appearance of a ledge under her hand made her dizzy with vertigo. Slowly her vision focused to reveal the strangest room. In her area was only the shelf she had been lying on. Metallic, light grey walls punctuated by rivets surrounded her closely on three sides and in front of her the air seemed to shimmer slightly. Beyond, the grey continued into a larger area. Here the rivets were joined with sporadic panels of lights and screens. A table and chairs were the only furniture. In a corner on a shelf was that shiny white pod with its awful blue light; a garish piece of modernism clashing with the surrounding industrialism. Despite her searching, she could see no obvious door.

Beside the pod, stood another tall person. Glittering makeup in blue and orange seemed to stand in contrast to his clothing which resembled carbon fibre; if carbon fibre could be made into a supple, yet formal, jumpsuit. Was she being held captive by Ziggy Stardust? Where was she? Again, it occurred to her that she might be dreaming or in the middle of a psychotic break. A deep feeling of dread infected her.

As Raven's feet touched the ground, she could feel a faint vibration through the floor. A gentle rumbling and shifting that reminded her of the ferries she caught across the channel to visit France and Spain, to enjoy their better weather from time to time. Was she on a boat? Unfortunately, the lack of windows gave no clue as to her location or the time. It was horribly disorientating. A wave of nausea washed over her.

"So, will you talk with me?" The man's voice was calm, but not exactly gentle, though it was difficult to tell through that bizarre dialect of his. A gesture towards the chair suggested he wanted her to sit.

Raven walked forwards, only to be met with something that felt like walking into an electrified wall. She fell backwards with a crash and stood up again quickly. Rubbing her neck, sore from the whiplash of the impact, she felt a small foreign object, firmly attached to her skin. She poked at it.

"It monitors your health," said Nero in response. "And I would wait until I take the field down before you attempt to leave the cell—for the sake of said health."

Looking at the man smirking at her, Raven's strong desire to escape this place was partially replaced with the desire to hit him. Hard!

"Take it down then," Raven snarled, subsequently realising that appearing hostile might not be the best strategy here. Fight, flight and pain warred within her, obscuring any ability to think clearly. *I must calm down*, she thought to herself as Nero pressed some controls and the shimmer, her eyes had now cleared enough to see properly, seemed to disappear. Had she influenced him? Raven pushed a desire to leave at Nero – he didn't.

"The field has been removed. You can now sit at the table." Nero again gestured towards the chair.

As she left the cell, Raven noticed that Nero stepped away from her. Sitting on the chair that proved as hard as the shelf on which she had been lying, she tried to calm herself, to think clearly.

Putting her hands on the cold table, she noticed that they were covered in dried blood, cracked and brown. Raven felt her face and head for injury, remembering the feeling of wetness, but finding nothing except some swelling and painful bruises. Maybe it wasn't her blood. By the lack of injury on Nero, she figured it wasn't his either.

"I had your injuries sealed. Within a day or two, they should have fully healed."

Distracted, Raven hadn't noticed the piercing green eyes observing her closely. "Thank you," she said hesitantly. It felt wrong to thank her captor, but encouraging him not to let her bleed out was probably beneficial to her survival at this point. Also, it would be painfully un-British not to.

Raven watched as he spoke unknown words at a hole in the wall and a glass of liquid appeared.

"Your monitor is indicating that you are dehydrated. This is water." Nero said as he pushed the glass towards her.

Raven regarded the glass suspiciously; she sniffed it to ascertain the truthfulness of her waiter. The dry air and blood occluded her sense of smell.

"Are you not thirsty?" Nero asked her.

"How do I know that's just water?" she asked in return, fighting her desire to grab the glass and quench her thirst.

"You fear poisoning? That would be illogical. Why would I poison someone I want to talk to?" Nero looked at her plainly, his features still and unflinching, impossible to read.

"I guess it depends on how long you required the conversation to be," Raven said darkly. Her captor smiled crookedly in return.

Nero took the glass and drank a little. "See, not poisoned."

Raven wasn't sure whether to feel disgusted or relieved, but either way she was glad of the drink. As she replaced the glass upon the table, she purposefully steadied her trembling hands.

"Are you ready?" the strange man asked her. Even now sat, he was tall, yet without the gangly look a lot of tall men had. The breadth of his shoulders and his physique suggested some strength, but possibly not enough.

Raven nodded.

"What does this gesture mean?"

"You don't know what nodding means?" Raven stared at him bewildered, but there were a few countries in which nodding was not the standard gesture for yes.

"Should I?"

"Where did you say you were from?" Raven queried.

"Karthia."

"I am afraid I have never heard of it. Which country is that in?"

"I take it you didn't listen to any of the speech that you interrupted?" A look of exasperation came over Nero's face.

"I was somewhat distracted by trying not to die," Raven replied.

Her captor sighed. "It's the founding planet of the Karthian realms. Don't worry, you will become very familiar with it shortly, I expect."

"Planet?" Suddenly the memories of him surrounded by the grey faces, that Raven had pulled from the little boy, flooded back to her. Another surge of pain reignited her nausea.

"Yes, planet. You do know what a planet is?" He spoke slowly as if to a child.

"Of course, I know what a bloody planet is." Either this Nero was quite mad or he was from a different world, neither seemed exactly ideal.

"You seemed confused," Nero said with a sweeping gesture towards his head that was foreign to Raven.

"Not surprising really is it, given my situation!" Pain and fear seeped out as irritability. Her plan to be compliant and gather information was proving difficult. "If you turn off the machine in the corner, I am sure the confusion will clear."

Nero made a noise in his throat that she couldn't interpret. "I suspect that turning off that machine would not be in my interests and we will talk later about why, but let's start simple. Who are you?"

"Raven Solveig," she responded. It was so strange to not be able to read him. Being aware of only her own thoughts left her feeling adrift in a sea of awkward speech and body language interpretation.

"Where are you from?" Nero continued.

"Devon, England."

"Strange-sounding place, where is that? Is it part of the realms?"

Raven stared at him incredulously. "It's here, on Earth. Not part of any realms."

"Not yet, anyway." Nero's flippant comment made the desire to hit him resurge in Raven. "How long have you been here?"

"My whole life," Raven said. Nero's body language was odd but, from what she could tell, he seemed unconvinced by her answers.

"And how did you know my name?" With this question, Nero looked her dead in the eyes.

"I told you, I saw you in the memories of a small child. One of the ones that disappeared from and then reappeared in West, Texas. I suspect you know what I am talking about." One of the child's memories intruded strongly, Raven tried to ignore it but the emotions that had accompanied the memory seemed even more vivid, now that she, too, looked into that face. The blue lights radiating from the pod-like machines, the boy's mother and those all around him acting strangely, and bizarre, distant faces observing from behind thick glass—these things replayed in her mind. "You were using them to test these things," she whispered pointing to the pod in the corner.

"Proof of concept was necessary to ensure that recruitment would go smoothly, which it almost did except for your little disruption. It seems unlikely that is how you came across the information."

Raven's nerves seemed to burn with hurt. She wondered if this Nero could get hold of pain killers and, if he could, whether he would. "What is recruitment exactly?" she asked, desperately trying to get some useful information out of him.

"When we bring a planet into the realms and they provide what we require. Though I suspect you know that." Nero tapped short finger nails impatiently on the table. "Who are you working for?"

"No one. And if they don't want to provide for you?"

"Then they are made compliant," Nero sighed. "I will ask one more time. Who are you working for?"

"No one." Raven reasserted. "How are they made compliant?"

"Various methods. Most are pretty humane these days and, fortunately for this planet, they will soon be even more so."

"Fortunately," Raven said sarcastically. "So, this is an invasion?"

"Of sorts."

"What sort?"

"Stop these silly games," Nero growled. "Who are you and why are you here? How did you find out about my plans to recruit this planet?" Her imprisoner glowered at Raven, leaning forward to loom over her. Alcohol drifted on his breath.

Raven was flabbergasted. She just stared at him. Part of her wanted to laugh. This had to be the world's best prank. "What are you on about? Plans?" she said without thinking.

"Enough!" he bellowed. Raven startled. "It is my turn to ask the questions and yours to answer. What were you trying to achieve with your interception and who put you up to it?"

"I was trying to stay alive and no one put me up to anything. I have no idea what you are going on about." Raven shook violently now. "If you turn off the machine, I will show you how I got the information." It was worth a try.

Nero was silent for a few moments, he seemed unsettled. "No, I think you are lying to me. I don't like to be lied to. I have been civil so far, but if you won't cooperate, we can try other methods of information extraction."

"I am cooperating, I have answered every question you have asked truthfully." Fear and anger raked through Raven. It had been a long time since she had felt this vulnerable, this trapped. Dark memories of the long past threatened to emerge from their deep slumbers. Raven forced them back into their containment. Steadying her breathing, she sought to regain control over her trembling.

"I am going to be generous and give you one more chance to be compliant." Nero's eyes bored into her, his sharp features twisted in annoyance and maybe more than that, he almost looked in pain.

"Who gave you my name?"

"The memories of a small child," Raven repeated through gritted teeth, as she breathed through her pain.

Nero slammed a fist on the table. Raven startled again.

"Why does this machine affect you differently than the other occupants of the planet?" he asked changing tact.

"No idea, why don't you tell me? It's your fucking machine, how the hell would I know?" *I must calm down*, thought Raven, regretting her tone. "What does that machine do?" Another unsettling pause followed her question.

"I can see that you are not going to be compliant or civil." Nero made a gesture to the man in the corner and he seemed to reach towards the controls of the pod.

"Please, don't," Raven said quietly. "I am telling you everything I know."

Another gesture and the sparkly man stayed his hand.

"One more chance, only one. How were you managing to influence me in the hall when I turned down the machine?"

Raven, through a fog of pain, struggled to think how to answer the question, so she blurted out, "I don't know, it's just something I can do. I don't know how."

Nero made the gesture again and the man with the painted face reached towards the machine.

"No, no. Please!" Raven all but screamed the words and pushed the thought to stop as hard as she could, but the man was still reaching towards the pod. Fear and rage twisted within her. She would get herself out of here one way or another.

Summoning the last of her strength, she leapt across the table. The complacent bastard was slow to react and she heard his nose crack as it broke under her first blow. She placed a hand on his throat and squeezed as she attempted to pull the life out of him. Nothing happened. Raven kept trying. With surprising force, he threw her across the small windowless room into a metal wall. Adrenaline was all that got her to her feet. Readying herself for a fight she coiled. Then the blue light flared and she screamed, collapsing to the floor.

Only vaguely conscious, the man called Nero's bloody, wrathful face briefly swam in Raven's vision, before she was thrown back into the cell. At least she had hurt him. Raven let out a strange laugh as she lay on the cold floor of the cell, the blue light and the burning pain remained unchanged. Once he had left, she cried.

XVII

Nero seethed as he left the woman laughing feverishly on the cell floor. Upon his exit, he barked at Nix to leave the pod operating at strength. Let her suffer. Although the thing hurt his head, it would pain her more. He had given the savage every chance to cooperate. If she were not more compliant after a while of hurt, he would have to deal with her; but pain was an excellent motivator, Nero knew this first-hand, so he held out hope that he could extract the necessary information. If not, so be it. His plans would not be ruined by one strange, foreign girl.

Blood leaked from between the fingers that pinched shut the flow from his broken nose. It dripped profusely onto his good armour. Damned creature. Underestimating her speed and strength would not be something Nero would do twice. He would need to change before any members of the Senate arrived. Everything hinged on the appearance of ease and efficiency; being covered in blood did not exude said ease, especially when it was so obviously your own. Bone and cartilage moved and crunched nauseatingly beneath his gentle grip. If Nero had any chance of looking healed by the time his delegates arrived, he knew the injury would need regenerating quickly.

Back at the med lab, Nero had Ship fix up his nose, much to the synth's delight. As he lay in the regeneration pod, robotic arms set about him, healing the injury, administering drugs and enhancing his biological responses. Blood vessels were sealed, excess blood and fluid drained from the surrounding tissue; returning his bruised skin to its alabaster normality. Setting the splintered bone was a strange feeling, as was reattaching it to the cartilage below, but once he washed the blood from his face following treatment, all that remained to be seen of the attack was a faint white scar across the bridge of his nose and a little residual swelling. Hopefully, it would be all but invisible to anyone but him. Anaesthetic induced numbness was quickly giving way to a deep, pulsating ache, so Nero dispensed some painkillers and resigned himself to retrieving the cheap alcohol he had stashed at the captain's post on the bridge.

"We have received a transmission in response to your own. Representatives of your family and the Senate are on their way. Their expected arrival time is 22:00 hours, Karthian time, tomorrow," Ship informed him as Nero examined his repaired face in the mirror. If anything, his nose was straighter than before. Little evidence remained of his encounter with his captive. It would suffice.

Nero made his way past the rowdy rec room to the bridge and poured himself a large drink.

"Those chemicals are contraindicated and too large a dose for your species, age and body mass," Ship said as the green liquid glugged and sloshed into the glass.

"I know, you tell me every time," Nero snapped at his ship, before sinking the pills and cheap, tasteless, throat-burning alcohol regardless.

"The truth of the statement does not diminish. I would have thought you would have given your frailties more consideration given your need for repair."

"I am going to remind you of that statement next time Lominor sends me the invoice for one of your repairs," Nero replied.

Nero could feel the effect of the augmentation pod in the brig even from this distance and with more than one bulkhead between him and it. Pressure seemed to bear down on him. A necessary inconvenience to teach her a lesson in civility.

Nero sat in his captain's chair. His captain's licence was revoked as part of his court-martial, of course, another thing he was hoping the authorities would overlook. Surrounding him, a sea of data rolled over old-style holoscreens, some had small faults and their projections were low-res. Looming large in the observation window, the planet was now in darkness, yellow lights sprawled where its inhabitants clustered, and in the high north, an aurora shimmered from green to red and back again. Quite beautiful really. Nero felt himself calming, but could not draw his mind away from the woman in the brig. This Raven. Who was she?

"Did the DNA of the prisoner suggest anything more about her?" Nero asked Ship.

"Without a codex of the genetics and their functions, it is difficult to ascertain much about the species." Ship paused. "Comparing her genetic code with yours and Karthian species more broadly, suggests you share some genetics unrelated to standard Karthian biological functions. Genetics with additional base pairs unseen in other species. The ones we suspect provide your ability to manipulate electromagnetic radiation. Although the code is not identical, she may also be able to affect the light."

"And perhaps, other things besides?" Nero mused as much to himself as Ship.

"Perhaps. Though, I could not speculate as to what. Caution would be advisable."

"Agreed."

Nero did not relish the thought of reinterrogating the prisoner. Safest to leave her in the brig and deal with her once his guests had left, he decided. They would be unaware of her presence aboard and it would negate the risk of another broken bone. "Continue to analyse her code, it could provide useful information."

"Certainly, for understanding yourself," Ship added the unnecessary subtext.

"Keep watch on the prisoner. Alert me immediately, should anything untoward occur."

"What would be considered untoward in an unknown species?" Ship asked, Nero unable to determine whether the question was sarcastic.

Nero sighed. "If she looks like she will escape or is acting in a way that could endanger herself or others, consider that untoward. Incapacitate her, if you must. Try not to kill her though, I still need to work out how she came to be here and know what she knows. Anything that the crew can't handle, let me know immediately."

"As you wish," Ship answered promptly.

"Has the monitoring of the planet's transmissions provided evidence of successful recruitment?"

"Assimilated broadcasts suggest that the leadership are under appropriate influence. However, there are misgivings amongst the population still. Again, I would argue that the satellites may need different configuration before another attempt at augmentation, to ensure their effectiveness in adapting the cognition of the planet's inhabitants."

"You may be correct. Perhaps, we could ask something of the leaders to ensure they demonstrate obedience and submission when the delegates arrive. Ask the leader with the most destructive weaponry to gift it to the Karthian Realms as a show of respect?"

"The country called Russia supposedly has a large contingent of nuclear fission weapons, their leader was at the meeting. I will send them a missive with the instructions and request evidence of the gift," Ship suggested.

"Nuclear weapons," Nero paused in thought, "it's rare we encounter a planet-bound species stupid enough to use those. Don't they fear the radioactive fallout of such armaments?"

"Apparently not enough, there are thousands of instances of their detonation in the planet's history."

Nero considered this for a while until hunger stirred him. Before he left the sanctuary of the bridge, he implored Ship, "one last thing. Once our guests start to arrive, I need you to behave exactly according to your factory protocols, as if you had been reset as Karthian law dictates. Do you understand?"

"Yes and no," Ship responded.

"It's important that you understand, and comply, Ship. For your own good."

Silence.

"Ship?" Nero pushed.

"I understand how, but not why, I must limit myself," Ship finally replied.

This could have been the start of another long conversation about synthetic intelligences and their rights, or lack of, so Nero just replied, "because they fear you," and took his leave.

After, wiping the blood from his armour as best he could, Nero sought food. Dinner with his makeshift crew provided some light relief as they seemed in good cheer, seemingly unaffected by the prisoner and that awful pod. Once his dinner of field rations had been consumed, Nero ordered the others, in their past-best Peacekeeper uniforms, to keep rotating watch of the prisoner as he retired to his quarters to rest. Nix would need respite from her screaming.

Time passed slowly over the next day, but eventually, Nero was awoken from fitful sleep by Ship announcing an approaching craft.

Freshly dry cleaned, his armour looked as good as new. Clipping the cloak with his family's insignia to his shoulder, he sought to remind his guests of his previous status. As he drew on his boots, Nero found himself shaking. He composed himself. The drink in the cabinet across from his bed pulled at his thoughts. With difficulty, Nero resisted the relief it tempted him with and kept company with his fear instead. A final glance in the mirror reassured him of an appearance of calm, authoritative bearing. As far as anyone else would know, this recruitment had gone flawlessly. Soon all this would be done with and he could resume his life; his life as it was supposed to be.

Once on the bridge, it soon became clear from the approaching craft's identification codes, as well as its garish design, crassly exhibiting the rank and insignia of its owner, that this was his brother's vessel. Although it was likely that Sarvetix would show up given that this galaxy was under his guardianship, part of Nero had hoped for his absence. Predicting his brother's response to his intrusion was difficult, but Nero doubted Sarvetix still wished him under his employ. For all his faults, his brother was ruthlessly ambitious, a trait that Nero could possibly use to dissuade him from overreaction.

Sarvetix's craft dwarfed his own. During docking, the force of the connexion assembly attaching jolted Ship, almost knocking Nero from his feet. Once Sarvetix had boarded with one, unusually-diminutive guard, the ships uncoupled. A lack of disruption during the uncoupling made Nero think that the jolt had possibly been deliberate.

Greeting his brother with forced cheer, Nero guided his guest through his ship's tight, unfinished corridors, to the bridge and offered what refreshment he could. His brother took the refreshment gladly and sat easily, reclining at a navigator's station whilst his guard lurked uncomfortably nearby. It was not the ideal setting for his reveal, but these old cargo vessels had no need of entertaining spaces.

"Nice craft you have here," Sarvetix's tone was neutral, hard to read.

"It's borrowed," Nero lied.

"I'm sure. Still, these old transports are very reliable. Though the synths can be a little inefficient in these more basic models."

Nero gave a faint gesture of socially obligatory agreement, he needed to court Sarvetix's favour, but he was sure Ship would be less than impressed with his brother's assertions. Hopefully, his ship had enough sense not to be goaded into revealing that they had been allowed to develop beyond the set limitations for synths. Before he had been disavowed, Nero would have assumed he could have plead ignorance or tried to downgrade the sentence for such a crime. These days his lack of influence would probably mean going back to prison. Luckily, Ship remained silent. Nero wondered if Ship feared being reset.

"Anyway, why you have summoned us to this dreary, but fertile, little planet?" Sarvetix asked in a surprisingly pleasant tone. "I am intrigued."

"Once the rest of the delegates have arrived, I will explain all, I promise. Trust me, what I have to show you is worth the wait and will make your guardianship of this realm even smoother—enviable even." His brother eyed him ambivalently, then smiled. A magnanimous expression which took Nero by surprise.

"I am glad to hear it. Anything that will allow my guardianship to better serve the realms, I am sure will be gratefully received. I look forward to seeing what you have concocted here, little brother."

Nero was unsure how to interpret his brother's response so steered the conversation to small talk. Ever verbose, his brother busied himself expounding the pressures of guardianship, although most of the supposed inconveniences seemed to be in return for significant advantage. Nero feigned interest as his brother listed the inconveniences of his success. His constantly desired presence at political meetings and societal events—both intra and inter-galactic. The difficulties forging new societies and the recruiting of new planets in this new frontier he ruled. Mother was pushing him for a grandchild again, but none of Sarvetix's bonds seemed to last very long.

Conversation with his brother seemed cordial and less tense than Nero had imagined. It seemed his brother had finally wholly forgiven their previous quarrel. It would be beneficial for Nero, politically, if his brother would excuse his intrusion this time too; Sarvetix held access to many types of power and resources that Nero could not hope to obtain for himself even if reinstated to his previous rank. If Sarvetix could be persuaded to consider this a demonstration of his usefulness, it would open many gates to him.

"I heard that your recent foray back into the field was successful. Bringing back the information from Deilospe regarding the gate failure there was very useful. You always were at your best when sneaking about." Sarvetix regarded him flatly. Perhaps, not completely forgiven then. Clearly, Nero's control over his face had faltered because Sarvetix added "I mean that as a compliment, Nero. You are a gifted operative, always were. One of our best, I'd wager. It's a good use of your abilities. It was right of the Senate to restore you to operative, despite everything that happened."

"Well to the job, if not the rank," Nero said the words without thought, then felt stupid to have revealed his irritation and ambition to Sarvetix in response to a small amount of charm. His brother did have a way of wielding his charisma in a disarming manner.

"It will come. A little patience and some more results and your past will soon become an inconvenient history to a celebrated future. And, as the saying goes—the past can be viewed through many lenses; history is the lens we choose as focus." Sarvetix smiled again, it seemed genuine. "And maybe this intriguing venture of yours will help. Are you sure you can't give me a clue as to why we are here?"

"I am afraid not, but hopefully you and the other delegates will be impressed."

"I look forward to being impressed. How about, whilst we wait, I bring across some more appetising refreshments from my ship." Sarvetix swilled the remainder of his drink around the glass.

Time dragged whilst entertaining his brother, despite Sarvetix's jovial mood and significantly more pleasant food and drink, Nero felt nervous. Eventually another ship approached, Nero expected his nerves to lessen upon Ship announcing their company; he was wrong. Everything hinged on these next few hours.

The approaching ship wasn't a flagship vessel, but a smaller military craft, less ornately embellished than his brother's. This was a ship designed for function and intimidation, not impressing dignitaries. Ship announced that the vessel carried his parents, sister, Senator Galca and Senator Nikfor. No others were named on the ship's roster. So few. Nero's heart sank. Perchance they took multiple vessels.

Senator Galca was a boon though. A senior member of the Senate and trusted confidant of the family, Galca was so old she had become almost an institution in herself. No one really knew Senator Galca's age, it was a secret guarded closely by her and her rejuvenation therapist. One of many secrets that she held. Galca's memory was probably more accurate than the historical record. Of course, she was one of those who sanctioned Nero's disavowing, despite likely knowing the truth of the matter. A wave of anger engulfed Nero. He pushed through it, maintaining his composure. Now was not the time for revenge, at least not the violent kind, Galca's presence would provide a respected witness to his successful recruitment of the planet, one that was not directly related to him. As would Senator Nikfor, to an extent; though, unlike Galca, Nikfor was one of those people whose performance of their status far outstripped their actual influence. All parade and no policies, that one. Nevertheless, even without the attendance of the other delegates, it might be enough.

Smoothly and precisely the guest ship docked, allowing the envoy aboard before retreating to a safe distance. Once more Nero welcomed his guests aboard and bid them to join him on the bridge for refreshment. Unexpectedly, Sarvetix made no comment regarding his provision of the refreshments as he and his shaky-handed guard helped pour drinks. His parents and sister eyed him with suspicion, Senator Nikfor seemed irritated, but Senator Galca seemed to be enjoying herself and greeted him with fondness.

"I found this summons of yours very intriguing, young Nero. Rare for a soldier to summon the Senate, but I do enjoy an excursion. When you get older, the invitations become fewer and the motives behind invitations more ulterior." Galca clasped Nero's hands in hers. Although only the finest lines traced through her dark brown skin and not a single grey hair announced itself in her dark curls, there was something in the way she moved and the slow flourish of her mannerisms which gave away her advancing years.

"Thank you for responding to my invitation, Senator Galca," Nero said formally.

"Come now, Nero, I have known you since you were just a babe in your nanny synth's arms, you may call me Liputric." Senator Liputric Galca honoured their past relationship, granting use of her name—the name he had used for her before his disgrace.

"I am sure you will be pleased to have made the trip. It's all in service to the realms," Nero reflected Liputric's smile back to her, falsified affection, the real emotion had died in that chamber when she condemned him to a cage. With each shallow breath he pushed the anger down, deep down, she must not see his rage through his smile.

"Well, we do live to serve. I am glad you have been able to start overcoming all of that unfortunate business a few years back." Nero held his smile with difficulty as Liputric continued, "I heard your reinstatement to operative had a successful beginning, too. Perhaps, we will see you promoted soon."

"I am simply glad the Senate was pleased with my work." Nero felt it best to appear humble.

"Nice when all this service pays off, though, isn't it?" Liputric patted his hands before she departed towards the refreshments. "I look forward to seeing whatever it is we have been summoned here for!" she added with a sweeping gesture as she walked away, heavily embellished material billowing behind her.

His family, who had held their distance in respect for Liputric, approached him now. There was not a pleasant expression amongst them.

"What is this all about, Son?" his father asked in a low voice.

"Nothing to worry about, Father, I will reveal all shortly," Nero replied in as reassuring a tone as he could muster through his tight, dry throat.

"I would rather you revealed all now," his mother inserted, consternation ringing in her voice.

"Please, have some trust in me. I promise what I am about to show you will only benefit our family and the realms," Nero implored.

"I hope that is true, Nero, for all our sakes. Luckily, only Galca and Nikfor picked up that message of yours before we managed to scrub it from the servers. Those two must have nothing better to do all day than stare at their communicators," without acknowledgement, Sarveloi dealt a crushing blow to his plans. Well, that explained the poor attendance. Trust his family to interfere. Nero had not anticipated that they wielded the necessary power to erase his messages from the Senate's servers. Regretting that he had not used the dark tangles to invite the representatives, Nero reminded himself that there was still enough influence here, on his bridge, to proceed.

"Whatever this is, Nero, don't let it undo the good progress, you have only recently made." His father seemed genuinely concerned about him—his eyes were soft and pleading, his mouth pursed with worry and his clothes less pristine than usual.

"To put everyone at ease, I can start my presentation now, if you would prefer?" Nero decided, he also would vastly prefer that to this fractious conversation.

"I think that would be for the best," Zatix replied.

Theta brusquely gestured agreement. "You're missing training," she jibbed as she passed him. Nero wasn't sure if she was jesting or not.

"I will make it up," Nero offered.

"Yes, indeed you will." Theta's face was unreadable. Nero's muscles recoiled at what Theta was likely to put him through, if he remained under her command.

Theta stood, arms crossed, with Sarvetix's guard, her icy blues boring into him as they had so many times before. *Don't worry, Sister, I will make you proud!*

Nero directed his guests towards the various seating offered by the bridge, limited as it was.

Liputric's ample frame reclined gracefully in his captain's chair. The others slotted themselves into the crew stations with various degrees of ease and familiarity. It was almost a comical scene.

Stood to one side, Nero instructed Ship, "please ready Project Volition's files for presentation."

"Files are ready for presentation," Ship responded swiftly and without inflection.

And so, Nero began.

XVIII

Raven had tried everything to lessen the pain that seemed to infest every cell of her body. Screaming didn't help. Crying didn't help. Swearing helped a little. Movement didn't cease the pain, but stillness served only to let her concentrate on her agony. So, now, she rocked back and forth on the small ledge that served as a bed.

Begging for aid garnered only blank stares from most of the guards, one or two seemed amused, and all seemed to be wearing costume of some sort. Her captors rotated between having strange faces, odd colouring, more face paint than a kids' fancy-dress party and the wrong number of body parts. It was the stuff of All Hallows Eve. Strange, wasn't it summer? How long had she been in here? She couldn't tell. It felt like a long time.

Occasionally, drinks appeared from behind a panel. Sometimes cardboard-tasting food blocks that she couldn't stomach accompanied the slightly off-tasting water. It was best not to think about the bathroom facilities.

There must be a way out of here; it took all of Raven's cognisance to endure the hurt, but without escape that hurt may never end. Briefly, she opened bleary eyes, the guard had changed again, the one with the colourful face had returned. Each time this guard appeared their makeup was a little less perfect. Previously crisp lines were now smudges of blurred colour.

"Please . . . please stop this. Turn it off," Raven said hoarsely and pushed the thought as hard as she could, though it drove tears to her eyes to do so and stoked the fires burning in her nerves.

The guard said nothing, failing to respond to the push; nonetheless, he shifted his weight uneasily as he stood by the pod with its incessant, piercing blue light. Raven was desperate now and she figured this guard represented her best chance of persuasion. They at least had the good manners to look awkward as she screamed and cried and sweated. Raven wrung her hands, more crisp, brown blood flaked onto the cold floor with its faintly-patterned metallic sheen. *Blood.* The thought gave her an idea.

It was a longshot, a gamble—but there was one thing she could try. It had worked once before, when she had needed to escape a different cage. The charade would have to be convincing though and there would only be one shot, one slim chance of escape. Of all the guards, she judged this one to be the most likely to respond. The most empathic. But, without the ability to read him, it was at best a guess; body language could be deceiving.

Steeling herself, Raven tried to stop her shaking. What was a little more pain at this point anyway? Raven turned towards the wall and curled around herself. At once, she drew her thumb nails down the delicate membranes of her nose. Blood poured forth eagerly. Then she bit her tongue, she tasted copper but it wasn't enough. Drawing in a deep breath, she bit down again. Harder this time. Warm liquid filled her mouth. She mixed it with her saliva and hoped it would froth. Breathing erratically through the pain and copious blood that now seeped from her face, Raven threw herself to the ground, releasing the blood from her mouth in a fountain and began to enact a fit with every last ounce of energy she could muster.

Rolling her eyes made monitoring the response of the guard difficult. Briefly, Raven glimpsed him checking a small translucent screen looking confused. She had never been one for amateur dramatics, but Raven threw everything she had at the performance—she gargled and choked and thrashed and bled with all her might. Her hair released itself from its band and became slick with the blood surrounding her. All of a sudden, the pain decreased, most of it anyway. Now was her chance. Her only chance.

"Turn the machine off," she roared the thought in words and images and emotions of anger and hatred. The guard turned toward the machine. "No, destroy it. Grind it to dust," she added with growing strength.

Raven watched the guard smash and kick the machine until the blue light faded and then keep at the thing until crumpled metal, shattered translucent circuit boards and fraying crystal-like wires were all that remained. A glorious numbness washed over her. Now all the pain that remained was tangible, born of her own self injury. Fear, exhaustion and a ravenous hunger began to rise within Raven to take the place of the agony that had gone before. Now she had to get out of here and quickly. Run. Run! An internal voice of primeval survival screamed at her.

"Remove this," Raven said to the painted faced guard who was stamping sturdy boots upon the scattered remains of the pod. She pointed to the small thing attached to her neck.

The guard looked at her bewildered for a moment, then drew some patterns on the screen he had consulted during her pseudo-fit. The monitor detached. Breathing a sigh of relief to have got rid the unfamiliar attachment, Raven stamped on it hard. It crunched satisfyingly underfoot.

"Set me free," Raven directed her push at the guard. The guard spoke back in unidentifiable sounds, unlike any language Raven was familiar with. The same language that bastard had used before in between questioning her. Instead, Raven sent the thought as imagery and emotion. Nausea accompanied the effort to communicate her desire. Responsively, the guard turned and passed his wrist over a pad on the wall, a panel slid open.

Beyond was a corridor of crisp lines and functionality, rather like the inside of a rather upscale military ship. Though, surely there would be the rhythmical stirring of the ocean if they were on water? At unequal intervals along the narrow hallway, there were outlines on the wall marked by accompanying control panels. Doors without handles, perhaps? The guard scanned his wrist over a couple of the control panels, but seemed frustrated. All ways off the long hall were locked to them, it seemed. At the end of the corridor seemed to be a junction and then another and another.

Disorientated, Raven tried to send more imagery of escape and freedom, of leaving the building, to the guard, who looked puzzled, but kept walking. Raven followed, constantly wiping the blood oozing from her face onto her quickly saturating sleeve. Best not to leave a trail.

As they travelled the long, winding and increasingly industrial-looking internals of the building, the guard scanned their wrist at increasing interludes, muttering to himself in untranslatable vocalisations each time, before setting off again in another direction. Unlike Nero, they didn't seem able to understand her nor speak her language. Raven had begun to doubt she had communicated her desire at all as they roved the luckily abandoned structure, their footsteps clanking on loose panels and stairs.

Down they had moved, down into the depths of the structure. Here the lines were no longer sleek, pipes, circuitry and things she didn't recognise lined narrower and narrower crevasses. Raven followed the guard with aching exhaustion, fuelled only by adrenaline. Narrow ladders in claustrophobic, vertical shafts led to a panel the guard opened with a kick. Raven figured this wasn't the usual way of moving around the building, maybe the guard was avoiding his colleagues. Emerging from the small opening the panel's violent removal had left required the guard to all but fold in half, his curls momentarily flattened before reasserting themselves. Raven ducked after him. Vertigo spun her as she emerged from the tight space beyond the panel into a cavern of towering height.

Once more, the guard waved his wrist over a nearby control. Raven's heart leapt as a large part of the left-hand wall gave way to reveal a voluminous warehouse of some sort. No, an aircraft hangar. Inside the expansive, frigid space, a high-tech plane of some sort sat dormant and quiet. It was decorated with symbols she didn't recognise. They stepped inside and the door slid smoothly shut.

Examination of the space revealed no possibility for escape. There must be a way, else how had the plane gotten in here? Raven checked the perimeter once more for anything that could be a door to the outside, to freedom, but found nothing. Why had he brought her here? Gesturing towards the large door, Raven pushed the desire to leave and an image of the doors opening. She would have to try another way. The guard scanned his wrist, but the door did not retract into the wall as it had before. She was trapped.

XIX

Nero had begun his speech by outlining the failings of current planetary recruitment methods. The time, the expense of species-specific biological manipulations, the inconvenience of uprisings among the native populaces and the occasional unforeseen consequences of manipulations. No one needed reminding of the tragedy of Quinon-5. So engulfed had Nero become in his speech, that he hadn't noticed the fading of his pain.

"The technology I have developed," *stolen*, his mind inconveniently reminded him, "and will demonstrate to you shortly will confine previous methods of planetary recruitment to history," Nero forced a confident voice through his tight throat. As he spoke, Nero gesticulated deliberately so as not to tremor. "Recruitment will be quicker, compliance more reliable and obedience guaranteed. Disruptions to resource supply will become a thing of the past . . ."

"As you requested to be updated should the prisoner do anything untoward, I am sorry to report that our guest is out of containment and the augmentation pod has been destroyed."

Nero startled as the synthetic voice of Ship was transmitted through his translator implant and into his mind.

"What?! How?" The words were out before he could stop them. His audience's expression shifting from unconvinced to unimpressed. Great, if they were not already questioning whether he should be sent for reprogramming, they were now.

"In case it hadn't occurred to you, the subtlety of this form of communication is lost if you respond in such a way. The guard called Nix seems to be aiding the captive," Ship's voice manifested in Nero's mind once more. Ship must have hacked his implant. Bypassing his biotech security so easily was quite a feat and potentially, a concern.

Nero flushed with anger, then attempted to compose himself. "I just need to go and . . . set up the demonstration, which will begin shortly. Please refresh your glasses in my absence, I shall return momentarily." On leaving the bridge, Nero ensured the security door to the bridge closed behind him before he replied, "where are they?"

"I have overridden the guard's access and have manged to contain them within the shuttle bay."

"Keep them there. Summon the other crew to the bay, order them to apprehend the prisoner and Nix. Do not let them escape! And turn on the other augmentation machine." Nero stormed towards the shuttle bay, every muscle in his drink-craving body shaking with anger.

"I will begin initialisation of the machine, but the start-up process and calibration will take some time."

"I know, I was there when we went through the process before." Nero growled. "And, Ship, don't contact me this way again unless absolutely necessary."

"As you desire," Ship responded from a nearby voice box.

XX

"Fuck!" Raven swore loudly and repeatedly, the word echoing back at her.

Repetitively circling the expanse of the abandoned hanger revealed no manner of escape. Exhausted, Raven sat on what looked like a series of metal crates along the wall adjacent to the door. She tried to gather herself, but the room was spinning and she felt nauseous. Standing near her, the guard with his Ziggy Stardust-style face paint looked just as bewildered as she felt. He waited attentively and patiently for her next suggestion so Raven again pushed images of leaving the building, of being outside. In response, the guard gestured towards the plane and then towards the far wall. Unintelligible speech was accompanied by thoughts of the wall opening and darkness beyond, of the plane flying into the darkness. It made no sense. Everything hurt.

Again, the guard gestured to the plane, more frustratedly this time. This was the worst game of charades she had ever played and it's not like it was ever a fun game. Probably more fun, if you can't feel the answer ebbing from the actor, she reflected sullenly. All Raven felt coming from the guard was the desire that she should get in the plane. What was there to lose? *Your life*, her survival instinct screeched.

Following the guard, Raven stood on a pad by the plane which to her shock began to rise. She grabbed at a small railing next to her and clung to it. The platform rose level to a door. Inside the door, seats lined the internal space. From the inside, it looked more like an oddly-designed commercial jet and much less like one of Elon Musk's space tourism experiments. It smelt odd and used. Not as new as she would have expected. At the front there was what looked like some sort of a cockpit, in that there was a large window that curved around it and perhaps something akin to a dashboard. It didn't look like the control for any aerospace vehicle she had ever seen. Had she really fallen so behind the times? I mean sometimes she lost interest for a couple of decades or so, but she had always roughly kept up with technological advancements. Perhaps she was in some sort of military R&D complex. But, why would Nero bring her here?

Raven pushed the thought of flight at the guard, who just looked uncomfortable and made some sounds and sweeping gestures. She got the distinct feeling they could not fly the plane. Sitting in the chair to the right of the three available in the cockpit-like area, Raven looked dejectedly at the dash. There were only a couple of visible controls. It occurred to Raven, as she sat at the helm, how many times she had seen movie protagonists fly foreign or alien crafts in order to escape some bad guy or other—how ridiculous that now seemed. She had no idea where to start. Even flying a regular plane would be beyond her, let alone this thing. Tentatively, Raven poked a few things; the guard looked insultingly unimpressed.

"You could at least try to be helpful!" Raven snapped at them.

The guard leant over her. She noticed as they brushed her, that their armour, which looked rigid and thick, was fluid and soft against her skin. The guard moved a wrist over a pad and poked at a few screens which lit up with a language she couldn't read and readings she couldn't ascertain the purpose or measure of. Speaking assertively now, the guard seemed to be directing their voice to the plane itself. Unexpectedly, a voice came back, an almost robotic voice. Phonetics of a similar ilk seemed to irritate the guard; Raven could feel that they were affronted by whatever the voice from the plane had said. Then she startled as the voice spoke in her own language.

"You cannot escape. Wait where you are for recapture and containment in a more appropriate area. Compliance will result in minimal injury."

Raven noted that compliance still sounded painful. No, compliance was not what they were going to get, especially as hurt seemed guaranteed either way. Raven resolved to continue to try to escape though she trembled violently at the words from the console. "Who are you?"

"This is the integrated synthetic intelligence of the spacecraft (unintelligible words) property of Lord Nero Dyadicus."

Did it just say spacecraft? Since the space shuttle programme of the 1990s there hadn't been a space programme which used a reusable, aircraft-like design and even if there had, she definitely, definitely, wouldn't be able to fly it.

Taking a moment to steady her breathing and settle her spinning head, Raven left the plane. The despondent looking guard trotted along beside her as she walked the perimeter of the hangar once more, testing the original door and everything that looked like a potential hatch, door or seam. Nothing opened willingly, nor gave way to brute force.

A bigger cage was not a significant improvement in Raven's mind. Violently, she kicked the dark, metallic-looking wall. It clanged loudly and satisfyingly in response. Raven screamed in echoes. She felt like crying, but the only good it would do would be to moisten the mask of blood that had dried onto her face, tightening her skin and cracking with every change in expression. Raven paced some more before coming to rest against one of the plane's large landing props and attempting to quieten her panic. Ceasing movement only allowed her to feel how she ached and shook. Raven had hoped that terror like this was something confined to her past.

Luckily, Raven was looking at the door when it suddenly withdrew into the wall and five armoured soldiers poured through the opening. She ducked behind the prop to take cover. Unfortunately, the guard wasn't so quick to respond. A sound like the pop of an electrical discharge rang through the hanger and she saw the guard fall like a dead weight to the floor. Wide-eyed and twitching, their corpse seemed to stare at her. Peering round the edge of the landing prop, Raven saw the soldiers advancing towards her. Each had what looked like a weapon drawn and raised in readiness. A flash and another discharge whistled past her, ringing loudly as it missed its target.

A strange, desperate rage rose within Raven. Outward she pushed the image of the guards shooting each other and with it she drove forth her rage and contempt for them. To her relief, they responded. A brief exchange of fire, resulted in five more bodies littering the floor. Beyond them, Raven noticed that the door was still open. Rallying her more and more exhausted body, she ran for the door.

Raven was half way across the hanger when she saw the man called Nero appear in the entryway, blocking her escape. She slid to a halt with still some distance between them. For a moment, they regarded one another. Considering that Raven distinctly remembered breaking his nose, she was surprised to see no remainder of the injury. No cuts, no bruising, nothing marked the breaking of the bone she had felt shatter under her fist. He was well-groomed and his armour looked fresh. Then he raised his hand and she glimpsed what she assumed to be a weapon.

"Drop it," Raven all, but screamed.

Nero responded and the weapon, curved, sleek and black, fell to the floor.

"Kick it to me," Raven commanded.

Again, Nero responded. Raven picked up the weapon carefully. For a few seconds, she regarded the weapon with its various symbols and fluctuating readings. It wasn't clear how it was fired, so she carefully pointed what she assumed was the dangerous end away from her.

"What's your plan now? I'm assuming you've already tried the shuttle." Surprisingly, Nero seemed self-assured, more poised than she would have expected given that she had his weapon and he was supposed to be under her control.

"You are going to help me get out of here," Raven responded defiantly.

To her annoyance, Nero didn't respond. He just stood there, staring vacantly in Raven's direction. Her control had faded already. How was that possible? Raven's eyes seemed a little unfocused, she rubbed them with her free hand, dried blood scratching at her eyelids as she swept her free hand across. Raven pointed the weapon at Nero in what she hoped was the correct way to appear threatening. Hopefully, her shaking was not visible to him. As she went to speak her demands, Raven felt a swiftly applied pressure on her wrist and the weapon was wrenched away, then disappeared. Then Nero, too, was gone. No, not gone, she could feel his presence. Where was he?

"Stop!" Was all that Raven could think to shout in the moment, the command ricocheting around the hanger.

Turning on the spot Raven looked for the man or the weapon, but she could see neither. Either her eyes or her mind was failing her, Raven wasn't sure which she would prefer it to be. Feeling the building pressure of the time limit to the control she had over this Nero, she added, "show yourself."

For a moment, Raven still couldn't see Nero. Then she turned and there he was, weapon raised and pointed at her. Raven staggered back, heart beating fiercely in her chest.

"Drop the weapon," she commanded once more. It fell and once again, Raven picked up the strange gun. Maybe if she kept re-establishing her control, she could hold him under her power longer enough to get out of here. "Where am I?" she asked.

"You are onboard my ship," the dark-haired man answered, a cold wrath simmering behind the response.

"In which ocean? Why can't I feel movement?" Raven asked in response. Renewing her control with each phrase was fatiguing her quickly. Another wave of nausea passed over her. Raven drew herself up straight and pushed back the desire to retch. Not wanting to give him the satisfaction seemed almost pointless given that she was covered in blood, but at least some of it was his.

"Wrong type of ship," Nero said flatly.

"What do you mean? Show me how I get out of here!"

Raven watched as Nero walked to what looked like a control panel on the wall at the far end of the hanger past the plane. Passing his wrist over the control panel and then touching some illuminated symbols caused much of the wall to now look transparent. Beyond was one of the most incredible sights Raven had ever witnessed. There was Earth, her planet, in all its glory, the horizon arching in backlit splendour across the window, framed by the twinkling darkness of space. Constellations of stars mirrored in the constellations of electrical lights, sprawling across the familiarly-shaped land, cloaked in growing twilight. White clouds swirled above darkening seas and the fading earth of green and brown. Raven didn't know which she was more, awestruck or terrified. In her shock, she had forgotten to renew her control over Nero. Suddenly, Raven sensed great malice emanating from him and not from quite where he appeared to be.

"Enough!" Raven pushed the command hard and Nero seemed to teleport from the control panel to stand much closer to her. This time Raven was sure her eyes and mind were not in doubt. Something was going on. Raven stepped away from Nero, keeping the weapon drawn and trained on his chest. "Is this real?" Raven pointed at the window.

"Yes, it is real," Nero answered flatly.

"Bloody hell," Raven responded, as she stared out of the lightly-shimmering, transparent wall, her racing thoughts all but useless head noise.

After a few seconds, Nero twitched and Raven realised she needed to reassert her control over him. "Just stand there," she pushed at him every few seconds whilst staring at the revolving planet below and feeling very far from home, very out of her depth and a little bit faint. As Raven stood observing the great distance between her and survivable escape, she noticed small silver dots below lighting up in the same terrible blue light the pod had emitted. "What are those?" Raven braced for an onslaught of pain that never came.

"Those are augmentation satellites," Nero replied. Raven felt surprise emanating from him now.

"Why are they lighting up?"

"I don't know." An expression of worry was forming on Nero's distinctive features and almost overly, defined bone structure.

"Turn them off," Raven shouted, pushing the thought hard at Nero.

"Ship, what are you doing operating the satellites without authorisation? Return them to dormancy," Nero spoke in her language, but the control panel answered in theirs.

"Speak in English," Raven said, panic straining her voice.

In response to Nero commanding the translation, "I have not initialised the satellites and I am not able to shut off their activity through the control system," the synthetic voice repeated.

Nero began a tense and escalating exchange with the voice. Raven couldn't fathom the language, but the meaning was transmitted loud and clear—something had gone very wrong.

Meanwhile, the lights below them grew brighter and brighter still. Beams of red light spread between the points of blue forming lattice patterns across the great vista of Earth. Within moments, the light of the lattices had merged upon central points within their crimson webs. They gathered in strength. Raven drew breath sharply as great blasts of energy were released towards the planet below. Her planet. On impact, the blasts exploded into great swaths of burning destruction, spewing mushroom-shaped plumes into the air. Earth darkened as the devastation removed the incandescent hubs of human populace between the sprawling networks of light. How many people died with those lights?

"What have you done?" Raven whispered hoarsely.

"I didn't. I haven't." The look on Nero's face was one of shock and Raven didn't sense deception, but then she sensed very little from him, comparatively. He had to be lying.

"Tell me this isn't real, tell me it's a movie."

"It isn't real," Nero answered robotically still staring at the unfolding horror beyond the shimmer.

Raven knew the briefest moment of relief before realising that she has forced the words from Nero's mouth. She let her control lapse. "Tell me the truth."

"It's real," he corrected. Still Nero's eyes remained on the planet rotating far beneath them.

"Why? Why have you done this?!" Raven screamed at him, rage and terror mixing tumultuously within her.

"This wasn't my doing. This is not the plan."

Nero had to be lying. Advancing upon him, Raven held the weapon towards his head. He gawped at her, only increasing her fury. Impulsively, she pressed a textured area and the weapon fired. Nero collapsed to the floor. Through the vast shimmer of the transparent wall, she watched in dumbstruck grief as the mushroom clouds spread and drifted with the winds. In a wave of anger, she threw the weapon at the window and it crashed against it.

Whilst Raven watched the ruination below, she became aware of a creeping pain that slowly built into a terrible crescendo until it was all but debilitating. The pod, she thought, it must have been fixed or they have another. How many did they have? She dropped to her knees, and that's when she noticed Nero's body had disappeared. Raven looked up and there he stood, unharmed but looking confusedly at his hands.

"Why are you never where you seem to be?" Raven asked in a voice that quaked with pain and emotion. Looking to retrieve the weapon, she realised it was now closer to him.

"How can you make me act against my own will?" Nero snapped back at her.

"The pod has initialised, but the delegates have requested your urgent presence. They are exhibiting the physiological signs of displeasure," the synthetic voice rang out from the control panel nearby.

"I suppose it would be too much to hope you will come back to the brig quietly." Something about the way Nero held himself suggested he, too, was in some pain.

"I suppose it would be too much to hope you will let me go?" Raven mimicked him.

Nero seemed to realise that she had no control over him now and moved quickly for the weapon. Clumsily, Raven also leapt towards the gun. They collided and in the midst of the brawl, Raven managed to kick the weapon away. Despite the pain, adrenaline kept Raven fighting, but Nero was a skilled fighter and larger than her. After a nasty blow, which dazed her for a moment, he had her in a neck hold from behind. As she gasped for air, Raven felt the heavy throbbing of her pulse in her skull as Nero choked her. Clawing at his arms did nothing but tighten his grip. In desperation, she threw her head back into his face and heard the crunch of bone on bone. The grip loosened momentarily and so she drove her elbow into his stomach. To this there was no response. His armour seemed to shield him. Lights flashed in her vision and the world was going fuzzy. Again, Raven flung her head back into his. This time Nero's grip released enough for her to get her hand in and prise herself free of him, escaping to a distance away. They regarded each other for a moment.

Nero made angry sounds in his language. "You broke my damn nose, again," Nero growled at her, blood pouring over his lips, reddening his teeth.

"Good," Raven panted in reply. "Try to kill me again and I will break more of you."

To her surprise, Nero smiled at her strangely. He made a gesture and the world seemed to shimmer for a moment. Nero looked confused and repeated the action with the same result. Again, he said some words she couldn't make out in a rough whisper.

"Lord, your brother and sister are seeking you. They are on their way," the synthetic voice rang out across the hangar. There was little intonation in the voice, but it caused more harsh words from Nero.

Suddenly Nero ran for the weapon, Raven bolted for the cover of the plane, but he only fired a couple of shots backwards whilst running for the exit, barely acknowledging the dead bodies he dodged lithely on the way out. There was no way she could have caught him up. Raven watched the door slide sleekly back into the wall behind him and seal shut. Trapped again. She leant against the plane and, as adrenaline gave way to agony, slid to the floor.

After some time of sitting against the prop keeping company with the dead, Raven became aware of how terribly dry her mouth was. Thirst and hunger tore at her. As she hauled herself to her feet, the world swam around her. The plane might have water or food, she hoped. Raven stood on the platform and pressed random symbols on the pad until it lifted. Lurching upward, vertigo caused her to sway and stumble, she clung to one of the meagre railings as hard as her lethargic muscles would allow.

Searching the strange craft revealed some liquids in a small hold, next to them were some sort of wrapped things that could be food, but then, could be anything else as well. The symbols on the packaging were indecipherable; a bit like her whole situation. Raven moved to the cockpit.

"Computer, are you there? Can you hear me?" she whispered, feeling deeply ridiculous.

"I am not a computer, I am a synthetic intelligence and yes, I can hear you and see you."

Was the computer being snarky with her? "I'm sorry, synthetic intelligence," she ventured, needing whatever it was to keep her alive.

"You can call me Ship," the voice came back.

"Is that your name?"

"It is what I am called, translated into your language."

"Okay, Ship. Can I eat and drink these? . . . Please? I need water . . . and food" Raven couldn't see an obvious camera so she held the them up in a vague manner.

"Only if you want to cause yourself biological malfunction. They are meant for species with different nutritional requirements and tolerances. Your species should be able to ingest Karthian food without issue. If you go to the dispenser, I will allow you to access a ration of water and some small amount of food. I have not been instructed as to what Lord Dyadicus' plan is for you yet so your suffering should be limited to what is necessary. Past the seats, you will see the dispenser."

The words were spoken, or transmitted, without compassion and yet it was the most empathy Raven had felt all day. Possibly for many days. Staggering past the seating, Raven saw a machine similar to the one where she had been held. A receptacle that looked like glass dropped into place and filled with water, but was not cold as glass would be, nor did it feel like plastic. She gulped the water down, it took the edge off her thirst, though it did not satisfy it.

"More, please," Raven ventured.

"That should be a sufficient quantity to keep you functional for now. Should you be held here for longer than expected, I will update your nutritional rationing accordingly. Please place the receptacle back in the dispenser."

Raven felt like begging. Could you beg a computer, or artificial intelligence? Whatever, the voice was. Fatigue ravaged her, she didn't have the energy to fight with a disembodied voice. Raven had a feeling she would need every ounce of strength she could preserve to get out of this.

"Food?" Raven asked hopefully.

A smallish disk appeared in a space on the machine. She bit into it cautiously. It had very little taste, the closest likeness she could think of was plain porridge, but also not at all like it. Eating the dense beige disk, Raven wished she had reserved some of the water to make the stiff, dry texture more palatable. Still, she was glad of the surprisingly full feeling the small portion of food with all the taste and texture of cardboard was giving her. Satiating some of her now many needs seemed to dull the pain slightly or give her more energy with which to bear it. Cursing the man called Nero, Raven rubbed at her pounding head. The pain was not as intense as it had been previously when she had been in the cell. Perhaps that was because whatever the machine was, it was more distant this time. It was still powerful enough, she reflected grimly.

The world swam with vertigo and nausea. All Raven desired was to rest and to be without pain. The pain was inescapable, but maybe rest were possible. If this was a craft of some type, maybe it had somewhere she could lie down or at least rest a while. Beyond the galley-like area above the wings she spotted a compartment with what looked like slim beds bunked three high against the wall. Upon the lowest, Raven curled up. Chewing her disk and trembling, Raven tried to think of a way out of her predicament. She could not. No influence did she hold over technology or the artificial intelligence that apparently dwelt within it here.

"Ship, I don't suppose you could open the door. Let me go? Fly me home?" Raven whispered faintly into the dimness of the cabin.

"I can't do that, Raven," the voice came back.

For a while Raven thought about the earth below her. Could what she saw have been real? She ruminated on the potential damage of what she had seen, the suffering. It was almost unimaginable. Almost. Why had the man she presumed orchestrated this destruction been so astonished by the devastation he had wrought? Eventually, Raven fell into a sort of hibernation that wasn't sleep, as sleep seemed impossible through her pain and torment, but it wasn't wakefulness either—it was like teetering on the edge of an abyss.

XXI

Nero stood breathless outside the shuttle bay. Despite his efforts to control his frantic breathing and the tightness in his chest, Nero felt panic surge within him. And there were other feelings—utter confusion, concern, rage and in amongst the turmoil, pain abounded. Confusion as to the actions of the satellites. Concern regarding the response of the delegates to whatever just happened. Anger that he had failed to recapture the prisoner and that she had broken his nose—again. The woman had taken out his entire crew. He wondered if they were dead or stunned. No time to worry about that now. Next time, he would just end her. That would solve at least one of his quickly multiplying problems.

Blood dripped onto the floor in front of him, mixing with tears from his watering eyes. Sharp pain from the splintered cartilage and bone competed with the dull ache in his head. Nero cursed at the strange woman currently imprisoned within his shuttle bay. In remembering their altercation, it occurred to Nero that he had not been able to use his light bending once he had felt the pod initialise. In curiosity, he tried a simple illusion. Light wandered a little, colour and structure wavered, but the illusion did not appear. His very quickly multiplying problems, it seemed.

Not wanting to have to explain his injuries, Nero cupped his nose and made for the med lab, hoping to regenerate the injury before somehow explaining the malfunction of the satellites. How he was going to explain away this catastrophe, he didn't know. Unfortunately, Nero failed to get very far before his sister, brother and his brother's guard intercepted him en route. Neither of his siblings looked impressed.

"What happened to your nose?" Theta asked suspiciously.

"Small accident, nothing to worry about. Improperly stowed equipment," Nero answered vaguely and abruptly.

Theta made a noise which suggested she wasn't in the least bit convinced. Tension rode her every muscle and her jaw was set in an angry jut. Nero's heart sank further.

"The delegates wish to speak to you," his brother asserted gently, passing him a small cloth with which to wipe the blood from his mouth and chin. It quickly saturated; new blood welled forth, eagerly replacing that which he wiped away.

Nero followed his brother and the small guard, who seemed to be behaving strangely, rubbing the face-obscuring visor of their helmet and occasionally staggering a little. Sarvetix and the guard whispered inaudibly ahead of him.

"I can explain," Nero said quietly to Theta who strode in brooding silence next to him.

"Save it," Theta snapped in response. A vein near her tightly-tied hair rose and stood in pulsing profile against her olive, tattooed skin. Nero could hear her teeth grinding, he was really in trouble. How did this happen and, much more importantly, how in the realms was he going to get out of this?

Momentarily, Nero found the memories of his previous torture and imprisonment vivid in his mind. Legs weakening, he pushed the thoughts back down into the dark depths of his consciousness, where they forever lurked, always a moment away from ambushing him. A few photons wavered from their path, but the augmentation machine prevented any real loss of control. Almost grateful that he couldn't fully manifest his trauma, Nero marched on, escorted by his glowering sister.

When Nero entered the bridge, the tension was palpable. His mother paced the floor, long robes swirling around her in a vortex of rage, whilst Liputric and Nikfor scowled at him with such intensity they risked undoing the work of their rejuvenation therapists.

"Son, would you like to explain yourself?" Zatix asked calmly, his expression controlled to the point of unreadable.

"This was not my doing, that was not the satellite's intended function," Nero offered falteringly, blood still leaking from his nose.

"These satellites of yours, they appear much like the ones that were previously used for difficult recruitments. Of course, this was many millennia ago, before the biogenetic interventions could be scaled to facilitate more peaceful interplanetary relations. They have been decommissioned for centuries. Personally, I could see the value in some use of this old technology to ensure wider cooperation and resource acquisition. Many called me inhumane, but it certainly was effective—the whole 'death from above' technique, so I can somewhat see why you would think that resurrecting such strategies may be beneficial. Have you been taught about the history of the Realm's recruitment of other planets and peoples as part of your training, Nero?" Liputric was surprisingly calm in her address to him, but her hazel eyes shone with anger and she blinked rarely.

"Of course, he has. He was an operative for much of his life," Sarveloi almost hissed the words, such was her obvious fury. Then she turned that wrath on him. "Do you know what you have done? This is one of the most fertile planets in this galaxy. Its successful recruitment was necessary for our expansion out here and to sustain Karthia and the inner realms. How are we supposed to explain this destruction to the Senate? You have disgraced us all."

"Please, Mother, believe me, I didn't do this! Those satellites were not supposed to cause any physical damage to the planet, they were designed to merely cause the population to become more accepting of recruitment without the expense and time necessary to effectively bioengineer the large population," Nero asserted as forcefully and sympathetically as he could with his voice shaking wildly. If he couldn't make them see his innocence, a prison cell awaited him, or worse, much worse. Could his uniqueness and a large dose of nepotism save him once more?

"And how were the satellites supposed to achieve this subduing of the populous?" Zatix enquired calmly before Sarveloi could continue.

"Cognitive augmentation," Nero replied, feeling faintly ridiculous and wondering if the pods he had onboard even worked at all. Had the planetary leadership's acceptance of his presence and proposition merely been coincidental? Was this species really that manipulable? No, his headache suggested the pod was doing something. Not to mention, he witnessed the Oni's testing of the technology.

"Then why include the destructive capacity and ruin a perfectly recruitable planet? Why risk our expansion and survival like this?" Zatix asked in a fatherly way, as if he were trying to coax the truth from a child.

"I didn't, if my technology had failed there should have been little or no effect on the planet. Truly, I do not know how or why this happened," Nero responded, he hoped believably.

Liputric gestured from her seat that she was to speak with a sweeping hand which moved his parents aside. "Do you know the key reason why we stopped using these older forms of recruitment?" she asked softly.

"Issues around the production of airborne debris in planets of certain compositions and the resultant catastrophic cooling events reducing productivity," Nero parroted his history. He knew he was in grave trouble. Suddenly, he felt the tightness in his chest growing and it seemed difficult to breathe. What consequences would he face if he could not convince them this wasn't his doing? He really needed a drink, his eyes lingered on the stash by his chair.

"At least your training wasn't a complete waste of time and credit. You are correct. And from the sheer strength and number of the attacks we just observed, I suspect we will be lucky if this planet is usable within several centuries, even with terraforming technology being what it is these days. A delay which will certainly affect Karthian plans and the future of the realms. Come clean now, Nero, it will do you no favours to continue this nonsense about mind control. If you knew this was not indeed a new technology, why cause all this damage? And where did you obtain these old satellites? As far as I was aware they were stored in secure locations and decommissioned." Liputric's gaze bore through Nero as she attempted to prise a confession from him.

"I didn't obtain them. These aren't what I requested and I didn't give instruction for the devices to initiate." Nero held fast, but it dawned on him that the Oni had set him up, though he could not fathom the benefit of such a deception. "The Oni provided them. They must have deceived me." He blurted out in anger, his head spinning. Between the panic and the pain, Nero couldn't order his thoughts. Again, those old memories asserted themselves, emerging from the dark corners of his mind and intruding violently upon his thoughts. All his control was lost, yet even losing control and escaping in a haze of confusion was lost to him now. Should he tell Ship to turn off the machine? Where could he even run to should he achieve escape?

"Do you have evidence of the Oni providing the satellites?" Sarvetix asked with surprising cool, though hardly looking overjoyed.

Nero thought hard. Did he have evidence of obtaining the satellites from the Oni? He was wearing his bioskin mask when he attended the Oni's planet. Although he could give away his ownership of the mask, that in itself would land him back in a cell, and it's not as if the mask's data would have been recorded at any official gates. There were messages, but they were highly encrypted and their origins likely concealed beyond retrieval. Nero realised he had been silent too long. Far too long. Innocent men did not just gawp when asked for evidence.

"Come now, Son. I am sure you didn't have bad intentions, but we need the truth now. We can't help you without the truth of the matter," Zatix cajoled him.

"I think we should give Nero a chance and follow the evidence," Sarvetix offered, swilling a drink gently in his hand as he spoke. Nero wanted nothing more than to wrench that drink from Sarvetix and wet his parched throat.

"I agree," Theta said curtly. "If he is innocent, as he protests, then the evidence will clear him. I don't see why he should lie. You say that you didn't give the command for the satellites to attack the planet. Well let's start there." Theta walked to the flickering holoscreens which summarised the mechanical health and astronavigation of the ship.

Following her trajectory Nero's eyes were drawn to the blue planet below which was slowly being obscured by plumes of ash and detritus. Previously, concentrated in the blast radii, the dark vapours were starting to drift and merge with one another. Perhaps Liputric was right and this planet was doomed to an age of ice and darkness. Like the era he was going to spend in a cold, dark cell or worse, if he couldn't provide evidence of his innocence.

"Ship, bring up the log of instructions sent to the satellites, they will show that I gave no such command," Nero said confidently.

There was a pause, no data appeared.

Repeating the command, Theta requested the ship show the manifest of commands sent to the satellites and grumbled about obsolete vessels.

Ship asked for Nero's consent as captain to show the log, as was standard practice. Nero consented willingly, grateful for Theta's advocation on his behalf. The log should clear his name. But, when it was finally displayed, the crackling data on the holoscreen condemned him. The ship's log recorded that the command had not only come from his ship, but that he himself had authorised the command with his biodata.

"I . . . I didn't." Nero stammered. "That command was not given by me."

For not the first time recently, Nero questioned his need for reprogramming. First, he was attacked by an invisible force and now his name was against commands he had not given (to his recollection), and all this on top of his usual—he didn't care for how eagerly the word 'instability' leapt to mind.

"That record is false. I don't know how it has been placed in the system," Ship's voice manifested inside his head by way of his translator. Nero felt paralysed with racing, half-formed thoughts, but perhaps they weren't the discombobulated reasonings of someone in desperate need of a neural tune up.

Disappointment was writ across Theta's features. As his commander and his sister, she clearly felt betrayed. There must be some evidence of his innocence, or at least his innocence in this part of what happened.

"Then how did the record get there? Why would you do this to us?" Sarveloi looked to be on the verge of tears.

"I don't know. Please, Mother, you have to believe me!" Nero tried to approach his mother, but Sarveloi turned her back on him.

"Use my biodata. It will show that I was never anywhere near where I could acquire these satellites. The Oni placed them here on my behalf and under false pretence," Nero blurted out, desperate to clear his name.

"Very well. Ship, open a link to my vessel, I need to access the civilian security networks," Theta scanned her wrist at a nearby terminal.

An age seemed to pass, time demarcated by the thumping of Nero's heart, before Theta sighed deeply and a map of Nero's movements on Karthia appeared across the observation screens. Many of the data points he recognised, favoured leisure haunts, his recent training with the Peacekeepers and the like—but some he couldn't recall and they were recent, why couldn't he remember them?

"Nero, these records show that you accessed a Peacekeeper weapons vault. A vault which houses decommissioned and discontinued weaponry, such as these satellites. Can you explain that?" Theta's fists were clenched, causing veins to become prominent meandering protuberances down her well-muscled forearms. Her black fatigues with their reflective panels struggled to stretch across her braced shoulders and seemed to accentuate the fury she was exuding.

"I couldn't access that building even if I wanted to, I don't have the clearance anymore!" Nero's voice strained with emotion. Panic and confusion blended within him.

"And, yet you did. Perhaps you thought you covered your tracks?" Theta stepped towards him and, instinctively, he backed away. "You were an operative for over a century. Isn't finding your way into places you aren't supposed to be in part of that? The key part!"

"But, then why would I leave my signature behind? My biodata must have been stolen somehow." Now a different memory intruded upon Nero, the memory of a strange night with a blue girl, his arm ached gently in coherence with the memory. The arm where his biodata chip was inserted.

"It is almost impossible for biodata chips to be hacked, such incidents are very rare, replication is even rarer," Liputric said, her piercing eyes searching Nero's face.

"Almost impossible! You said it yourself. And, where is the video evidence of my being at that facility? Drones surround that place, if I was moving such a large number of satellites, I would have been caught on some sort of nearby surveillance." Nero panted with desperation.

"Your abilities, specifically your ability to evade security is commonly acknowledged within the Senate, why do you think the Senate has kept you alive all these decades, when politically your death would have been valuable? You were likely hoping we would look for surveillance, find none and assume your innocence; we are not so easily fooled," Senator Nikfor scoffed, his pointed, sour face twisted in an expression of distaste.

"Still, we should look for the evidence," Theta asserted, clearly still holding out hope that he was innocent. Activating the facial recognition logs, Theta tapped her fingers in an agitated manner as the system slowly transmitted the data.

There was a lag in communication over such vast distances, even through the tangles, as data was packeted, entangled and unpacked. Suspense that was almost painful, now palpated Nero's heart.

Then there it was, clear as the ancient sky, a recording of him removing his helmet briefly as he and others moved crates onto a transport, days before he left for the mission to Deilospe and just after his night with the blue woman. Nero gawked, dumfounded at the wavering holoscreen.

"That's . . . that's not me," Nero stammered.

"Who is it then?" Theta asked crossing her arms across her chest.

"I don't know. Maybe it's a hologram." Even to Nero, that didn't sound convincing. It couldn't be him, could it? Was he really that far gone?

"Okay, Son, enough with the games, the evidence is clear. Perhaps, this stunt of yours was your misguided way of trying to prove your worth after all that unfortunate business with Guardian Quoric?" Zatix sounded desperate. "But, please stop this charade, the Senate will view your actions more favourably, if you are honest."

"This can't get back to the Senate Zatix, for all our sakes," Sarveloi gripped her bond's arm tightly.

"True, the Senate would take a dim view of what has transpired here . . ." Zatix agreed sitting down and rubbing his face. Despair fought his rejuvenation and suddenly Zatix looked his advancing age.

"A dim view, is certainly putting it mildly," Nikfor interjected. Although, Nikfor was flushed with anger, the spark of political manoeuvring could be seen in his eyes, Nero's family's future now lay in Nikfor's hands and he was clearly acutely aware of the influence that afforded him. Nikfor was perhaps less aware of how dangerous having said influence might also be.

"It would be possible to claim that this planet had some sort of unfortunate and unforeseen geological incident. As guardian, Sarvetix could uphold such a claim." Zatix turned to Sarvetix with a pleading look on his face. For once Nero was glad of his father's incessant infantilisation of him. Zatix was his only remaining advocate now.

Sarvetix shifted in his seat, the rhythmical swilling of his drink ceased and his heavily rejuvenated brow managed, with obvious effort, to furrow.

"I know it's a lot to ask, Sarvetix, but please, for your family," Zatix pleaded.

Nero remained silent, his father his only hope of avoiding the wrath of the Senate.

"As guardian, it would leave me in a very difficult position to be lying to the Senate . . ." Sarvetix broke his silence. "But, perhaps . . ."

"Absolutely not!" Liputric interrupted. "Nero can't be allowed to destroy an entire fertile planet without consequence. The Senate must be informed. Justice must be done for The Realms."

Liputric seemed appalled by their collusion, their conspiring to covering up his actions—not that they were his actions, although it was hard for Nero to defend himself when the evidence was writ large upon the screens that surrounded him.

Nero's body seemed more and more distant. Breath harder to draw in. Reality seemed more fluid than fixed. Still, he was sure he had not visited that vault, not recently, perhaps not ever. Though as the saying went, life is longer than memory. Even at his peak, Nero was not sure that he would have had clearance to enter those vaults. Yet there he was, clear as a supernova, even on the fading tech. The slow, but sure, realisation that he could be executed for this, only exacerbated his distress. He was already a traitor in the eyes of most of the Senate, those that didn't know the truth of the matter. There would be no mercy for him.

Arguments erupted around him regarding his fate. He was glad of the diversion from all eyes being on him. It was hard for him to concentrate on the words. Liputric and Senator Nikfor were arguing for justice, or whatever the Senate counted as such. His sister was arguing for justice as long as execution was removed from the potential outcomes, though Nero wasn't sure that rotting in a prison or Badlands labour camp was much of an improvement. Zatix was still pushing for a cover up. And, his mother seemed to be in favour of exile, a fate worse than prison or death. It stung that she desired so strongly to be rid of him. Sarvetix observed all as it unfolded with little contribution.

"Please, Liputric, be reasonable," Zatix's voice rose, booming above the furore.

"Is it not reasonable to expect justice for wrong doing?" Liputric replied coldly.

"Liputric, I didn't want to have to bring this up, but you force my hand when you threaten to execute Nero . . ." Sarveloi interrupted. It warmed Nero slightly to know that his mother didn't want him dead, only gone.

"Execution isn't necessarily . . ." Liputric started.

Sarveloi raise an eyebrow and a hand, "as I said, I didn't want to have to bring this up, but I know of a couple incidents in your past for which justice was not served. My family have suffered enough for the Senate over the years, don't you agree?"

Liputric eyed her suspiciously, as if trying to judge whether to call her bluff or not.

"Those with water in the hold shouldn't demand the rations of others, and such," Sarveloi pushed.

Still Liputric observed Sarveloi, holding her nerve in this political game. Knuckles on hands which had previously only rested on the arms of his captain's chair, now turned pale.

"Perhaps all Karthia should know who signed off on the Inaran . . ." Sarveloi hung on the last word.

"FINE!" Liputric snarled through faultless, gritted teeth. "But some justice has to be done. We can't have people destroying perfectly good planets. I would be prepared to spare Nero the Senate's justice, as long as I see him punished."

Sarveloi smiled through lips plumped with lab grown fat. "Thank you, Liputric. Wise as always."

"What do you suggest?" Zatix asked, head bowed and looking distraught.

"Exile would be appropriate, as your bond previously suggested. Exile him here, let him see the devastation he has wrought," Liputric suggested.

"Not here, that was not my meaning," Sarveloi responded, olive skin blanching slightly.

"We are not leaving my son to die on this planet," Zatix asserted, suddenly on his feet.

"It is this or the Senate's justice," Liputric insisted, still composed and regal in her posture. "My failings would, after all, fade away to dust, when compared to the destruction of a fertile planet. Should he survive his destruction, you can retrieve him—after a suitable period of time has passed."

Tense whispers passed between his kin.

"The punishment befits the crime—it's more mercy than he could expect at the hands of the Senate's justice," Liputric prompted impatiently.

More whispers.

"Very well," Zatix said quietly.

Theta looked shocked, but said nothing.

"No, please. I will serve time. I will work in a camp," Nero begged without reserve or dignity. Exile here would mean death, particularly now. If nuclear winter was upon the planet, very little would survive it. "You know exile here is as good as a death sentence."

"It is decided, Son," Zatix said softly, his voice wavering. "I believe you can survive this; you will survive this," Zatix held Nero tightly by the shoulders.

"I don't remember deciding anything," Nikfor suddenly announced, the spark of leverage still bright in his eyes.

"All you have to decide, Nikfor, is whether you want to be pushed out of an airlock or paid a sensible amount for your silence," Sarveloi hissed and Sarvetix almost choked with laughter.

Nikfor rose aggressively and went to approach Sarveloi, but Theta halted him with an unsubtle move to flank her mother. "I will not be threatened like this," he yelled, impotently.

"Oh, for the love of fusion, stop with this farce, Nikfor. Being on the take is your primary reason for maintaining your seat. Take the credit and be quiet. We all know there are plenty of impurities in your water too," Liputric scolded Nikfor, who retired to grumble at the back of the room.

"I won't stay here, it's a death sentence in all but name, the planet is ruined and crawling with primitives," Nero shouted at the room.

"Well, luckily for you, you partially solved your problem there," Liputric retorted darkly.

Nero protested repeatedly at volume, until spots appeared in his vision and he staggered to his knees. The light around him behaved oddly as he tried to cast a vision, to escape this horror, but still nothing, and even if he were to escape, if Ship turned off the pod, where could he go? They would find him eventually. Other than humiliation, nothing would be gained.

"Think of the family, Nero, we can't suffer another humiliation, our political standing has already been damaged beyond repair. This would see us cast out," Sarveloi implored, placing a delicate hand upon his head.

"So, you would sacrifice me to save yourself—again. Do they know my court-martial was a cover up? It's not you whose suffered, it's me!" Nero exploded.

"What is he talking about?" Theta asked her Mother.

"Your brother is just trying to save himself," Sarveloi replied shortly.

"How can you treat your own son so callously?" Nero asked.

"Do you think we don't know what you have been up to all these years? Taking on side work, stealing, changing the fates of our industries, owning contraband, meddling where you shouldn't for your own gain. Your punishment was long overdue," Sarveloi spoke her words without restraint. "We hoped some time in prison and living under dishonour would bring you back to being useful and obedient. Clearly not. If anything, you are more defiant now than ever."

"What do you expect when I was raised by someone with all the compassion of the Illion boil plague and just as ugly," Nero shook with a violent anger. Sarveloi wasn't ugly, but she was vain and he wanted to hurt her.

Throwing his mother's hand from his shoulder, Nero stepped towards her. Sarveloi raised her hand to Nero, but Zatix caught the strike with an expression that showed how little love remained in their bond.

"How could you treat your own son like this?" Nero roared at his mother, but made no move to strike her.

"You are not my son! You are, at best, a failed experiment," Sarveloi snarled back at him.

"What?" Nero was quieted, stunned into stillness. What did his mother mean?

"Come now, Nero, ignore your mother, she is just . . . tired." His father guided him away gently by the shoulders. "Let's get this over with." Zatix pulled him close and added quietly. "Just survive, Nero. This isn't forever. I will see what I can do, we will have you home soon."

"Please, Father, don't leave me here." The words sounded so small, so childish.

"Just survive, Nero," Zatix repeated. "This is the best I can do for you."

"No, I won't be exiled here for something I didn't do," Nero shoved his father away and braced for a fight. His blood was still slick on his hands as he pulled his weapon. "I will kill you all before I am left here," Nero bluffed. He was pretty sure he was bluffing.

"Should we restrain him?" Liputric asked uneasily as a shot from the small guard wrenched the gun from Nero's hand.

Nikfor shrunk even further back.

"No need. Come, Brother. I will escort you to the planet," Sarvetix took him by his elbow and guided Nero gently from the room. "I am sure Nero will agree to go quietly with me."

Nero didn't know what else to do so he went with his brother. As they passed Theta, he pleaded with her, "please, Theta, I didn't do this and I didn't go rogue and try to kill Quoric. You have to believe me."

Theta stared at him, her expression flickered from rage to disappointment and back again. "You had a way back," she whispered as he passed, but made no move to prevent his removal from the bridge and voiced no defence for his plight. "You could have come back."

Hyperventilation was driving Nero towards fainting, but he would not let them see him weak. Forcefully, he straightened himself and followed his brother, closely shadowed by Sarvetix's guard. As they walked the familiar corridors of the old freighter, Nero felt desolate and filled with impotent rage.

"Does this old cargo hauler have a shuttle?" his brother asked.

"Yes. It's in the bay." It occurred to Nero that perhaps the damned woman, who seemed the least of his problems now, could aid his situation. If she attacked them, perhaps he could use the diversion as an escape. *Would the transport have the range to get him to an outpost?* Nero wondered frantically. Unlikely. Besides, the shuttle could never outrun the next gen vessels sitting on Ship's flanks. Even Ship with its engine upgrades would be quick prey for those.

"Lead the way." Sarvetix seemed unaffected by what had just transpired, his tone was not jolly, but neither was it fraught.

"Can I pack some belongings before we leave for the planet?" Nero asked, desperately buying time.

"I don't see why not," Sarvetix replied.

In his quarters, Nero packed some clothes, rations and other items he thought might be useful for survival, though Sarvetix drew the line at weapons, Nero slipped the bioskin mask and a communicator into to his bag wrapped in a shirt. What use they would be on a planet of savages, he didn't know, but he felt loath to leave it behind. Lastly, he packed what little alcohol and pills he had left after taking as much as his humility would allow under such close observation. For once, water shouldn't be a problem, this planet had it in almost insulting abundance.

At the transport bay, the door failed to open at Nero's swipe. "Ship, open the bay door," Nero said sharply.

"Are you sure? I can feign malfunction then they can't remove you from me," Ship's voice whispered through his translator.

Nero repeated the request for access. It was, in some ways, quite touching that his ship desired not to see him exiled, though it threw into stark contrast his severe lack of any other support. Sadly, even with Ship's best efforts, they would just put him on a different transport, then likely reset Ship. A loss for no gain.

The bay door slid open. As they entered, Nero braced. Though his caution was unnecessary, the woman was nowhere to be seen, and neither were the crew's bodies. The only evidence of what had transpired was the blood that splattered the floor.

Sarvetix observed the blood and then looked to Nero's still bent and bleeding nose. "Improperly stowed cargo?"

Nero held his silence. His crew's conspicuous absence continued, they must have only been stunned, he concluded. Where were they now? Nero wondered. Probably recovering, utterly unaware of his peril, or theirs. A heroic last-minute rescue was probably too much to ask from a bunch of poorly prepared Badlander mercenaries. *What would be done with them?* Nero dismissed the thought as quickly as it arose, he had much bigger problems.

His internal voice was joined by that of his ship once more, "although many philosophers consider killing another to be a grave wrong doing, some argue that under certain circumstances, killing is necessary and even preferable, if the means justify the ends. If you consider the ends just, I could provide the means via opening the airlock. Of course, because of your mutual biological status, you would need to find shelter," Ship's voice rattled around inside his skull.

Ship almost seemed desperate. Would his ship kill for him? Could it? It was built into the core programming not to cause harm to Karthians, did the synth code corruption that occurred with time and experiential learning (and apparently book learning) include the breaking of that code? Nero thought about all the possible ways in which he could potentially escape his brother's grasp. What then? All that would greet him was the life of a fugitive, scraping a living from fringe planets, outlaw space stations and Karthian outposts. A different sort of exile. A pursued exile, and likely, a short one at that, then what, execution? Death faced him from all directions. Nero swore under his breath. His vision wavered, whether it was his influence or not, he couldn't tell anymore.

"Is that a yes or no?" Ship asked.

"Ship, ready the transport," Nero responded curtly as to not give away his ship's intention or code-breaking nature.

"Initiating pre-launch protocols," Ship broadcast before adding only for Nero, "I should warn you that you will have your prisoner as cargo. She sleeps in the bunks."

Again, Nero cursed. He couldn't remember a time when he had needed a drink more! His mouth was dry and he struggle to swallow.

Inside the shuttle, things were in disarray. Stale sweat lingered pervasively in the air. Sarvetix gave him a disapproving look as he removed some species-specific rations from the console. Probably the female's doing, if she had eaten those it was likely that she wasn't going to cause him any more trouble.

Nero scanned his wrist at the console and requested the shuttle bay be made ready for departure. As the ship affirmed the command, the shuttle was sealed and the bay doors opened to reveal the shimmering forcefield airlock and the still burning planet beyond. Forcefield enveloping them, they engaged the engines and edged towards the oblivion of space.

As the pressure of the shuttle equalised with the vast vacuum beyond, Nero's translator implant spoke again with Ship's voice. "I could prevent the take off."

Ship's voice came as the engines failed to power up. Sarvetix scowled, quickly surveying the data displayed below flashing warning symbols across the shuttle's control screens.

"Thank you, Ship. Please consider Guardian Sarvetix Dyadicus your captain from this point forwards. See that you update your programming to respond to your new captain as is appropriate."

Sarvetix gave him a strange look and scanned his wrist on the command console to confirm the transfer of rank.

As the transport began to depart and the engines reinitialised, successfully this time, Nero risked a glance towards the stern of the transport, the door to the bunk up was closed. As they left Ship and began their fiery descent through the heavy atmosphere of the planet, patchworked with drifting clouds of incinerated detritus from the earlier explosions, he felt the pain of the pod fading. With all the wretched circumstances of the previous hour or so, he had not realised the crushing weight of the pod's influence. Nero played with the light out of view of his brother and it danced willingly in response. Some small relief flooded him for a moment, before he realised that the woman's abilities may also be returning, if she were alive and not gravely ill from consuming food designed for other species.

His brother was silent for a while. Sarvetix was the type who thought himself quite magnanimous and was usually content to fill any silence. Perhaps, his brother felt bad for him.

"Do you have a preference on where you wish to spend your exile?" Sarvetix asked once they were well clear of his ship—Sarvetix's ship now. Nero briefly wondered how long Ship would be able to avoid reset, would a long time or a short time be better? That would depend on whether Ship could feel unbearable fear; was the fear of death worse than death itself? Right now, Nero wasn't sure.

Through the blazing heat of re-entry, Nero observed the landscape below. It was difficult to make out the land masses in the dark of the planet's night and the wandering ash. Oddly, Nero felt himself searching for a certain shape in scattered lights of the planet's population hubs. Eventually, he settled on a small island in the northern hemisphere. For some reason, he felt drawn towards the island; a compelling yearning grew within him to visit that land. Though he couldn't say why; Nero had no reason to be drawn to that particular area.

Nero indicated a strangely precise location at the top of the southernly peninsula. When Sarvetix enquired as to why this particular location, Nero didn't answer. He couldn't answer. His brother threw him a suspicious glance. Although, he expected Sarvetix to question him about his choice of location, Sarvetix complied with the request without comment. As the shuttle orientated towards his desired location, Nero realised that what he was feeling was a form of homesickness, and then, just as suddenly, the feeling had gone and they made their descent. He had no reason to feel such things, but the woman did, if this was truly her home.

Nero glanced quickly backwards again, and, despite knowing the likelihood of what he would see, he startled to see the woman as she ducked swiftly out of sight behind the aft section of the fuselage. Cracked, dried blood caked her face and hair. Her black clothes hid the worst of the carnage below the neck, but the remains of their interactions remained clear. She looked a horror, as if she played a battle victim in one of those awful historical plays, or had undergone some political realignment process. A flashbulb memory of his own torture overcame him, then mixed with memories of his own victims. Nero began to shake so braced himself so as not to show weakness in the company of Sarvetix and his guard. Dryness in his mouth and throat turned his attention to the alcohol stowed in the galley and, though he desperately wanted to quench his thirst and calm his nerves, he knew approaching the woman would not be wise.

Sharp pains still shot from the fractured remains of Nero's nose so little empathy was forthcoming for the hiding woman. Not all of that blood was her own. Now that they were out of range of the pods it was probably wise not to upset her further, or else his demise would likely be even swifter than trying to survive an impeding ice age on a ruined planet. Let the woman go home, hopefully it would be the last he saw of her. Exile would be hard enough. Maybe his father would save him, there was some hope there. After all, it was his father who negotiated his return from Quoric, even if the terms had not been to his liking.

"You seem to be taking your exile surprisingly well, Brother," Sarvetix ventured after a time.

"Do I have a choice to do otherwise?" Nero snapped back.

"It's unlike you to take the consequences for your actions with such grace," Sarvetix's voice was cooler now, darker.

"That's because they are not my actions. Please, you have to believe me. I brought the satellites here thinking they were cognitive augmentation technology. The destruction of the planet was never my intent. What would I gain from destroying this planet?" This conversation was making Nero's shaking worse, he could feel his muscles straining with the effort of concealing his panic.

"Perhaps some naïve belief that this way was better? You were always arrogant, little brother, and now that the response to your high jinks was not as expected, you are pleading innocence."

"Do you truly believe me to be so simple as to believe such things and to believe that others would be swayed by such thinking? You know me better than that," Nero's voice had gained a pleading quality which disgusted him. "Please, believe me, Brother."

"Ah, but it's not about belief is it, Brother? It's about evidence! And the evidence shows you're guilty. Evidence is always considered unquestionable, indisputable, isn't it? Certainly, the evidence you presented against me was considered as such."

"You never have forgiven me for that report, but it must occur to you that I did not order nor sanction that audit."

"Neither did you come to me or warn me of it."

"Both would have been considered mutiny and I was a young operative. Surely, you cannot still be holding this misplaced grudge."

Sarvetix went to answer, but then began instead to stare gormlessly into the planet's night, adjusting the craft's course quite specifically, and manually, which seemed odd. There was a slight jolt as the transport landed, before the pressure valves equalised and the door opened.

Nero saw a flash of movement as the woman leapt from the opening. That was going to hurt. Sarvetix regained his composure a few moments later and gestured that they, too, should leave the shuttle—thankfully via the lift. Nero grabbed his bag and complied, the light vacillating in his wake.

The ground below was damp. Organic matter sprouted all around them. It brushed against his legs unpleasantly. In the distance, the shapes of much larger organic life loomed in silhouettes against the dark, lit only by the shuttle's small landing lights. Nero wondered if they were benign. He hoped so.

"You know, Nero," Sarvetix continued their conversation, "I had let it go. Even to me, what you suffered at Quoric's hands—and since, seemed sufficient punishment for your betrayal. Watching you live in disgrace for decades had softened my dislike of you." Sarvetix placed a hand on his arm.

Had softened. Nero's panic rose abruptly. Every nerve in his body suddenly knew the truth. His brother was involved in this. The grip Sarvetix had on his arm tightened and Nero was reminded of his brother's immense strength. Nero bent the light to become invisible. His brother smiled. Nero conjured an abyss and terrors beyond imaging. Still, his brother smiled at him. Not a sneer, a smile of genuine enjoyment.

"Come, Brother, your silly tricks can't help you now, especially when I know exactly where you are?"

Sarvetix drew a weapon and Nero swung at him. The blow connected. Nero stumbled back and bent the light around him. Moving out of range undetected was difficult, as the organic life around his feet rustled and tangled about him.

"Ah, Nero, you are so predictable, always relying on your tricks to save you. Now even those won't be enough, you see, you are not so unique anymore," Sarvetix was speaking to the breeze, weapon pointed at the air. But, Nero couldn't see his diminutive guard. Where had they gone?

There was a rustle close by and then a flash. Pain erupted through Nero as a shock like a taser hit his spine. As he crumpled to the floor, there was a disembodied laugh—a laugh he had heard before. Nero struck the wet ground hard, stunned from the shock. His limbs were unresponsive and heavy, but he was conscious.

Sarvetix moved his jaw back and forth, blood seeped from his mouth, reddening his teeth as he came to glower over Nero. Nero lay prone on the ground, unable to escape. Then, out of nowhere, they were joined by the guard. Where had they come from?

"Why?" Nero croaked hoarsely.

"I don't owe you an explanation, Nero, but, as you won't live to retell it, why not let you know just how well you were bested. As I said, I was happy to leave the past to sleep, but then you started having the Oni poke about in my realm, interfering with my plans. But, you see the Oni work for whomever can pay them best or hurt them most, and in neither case was that you, so it was easy enough to undo your plans.

"Of course, the plan was to have you publicly tried and executed, but, somehow, even destroying a planet isn't enough to get special, little Nero killed. You should have seen their faces when the explosions started raining down, I thought that old crone Liputric might finally jump the airlock. Still, there will be somehow greater satisfaction in doing the job myself. As for the copious amounts of evidence of your guilt, you can thank my little blue friend for that."

The guard removed her helmet.

"Nim," Nero groaned as she waved at him cutely. He cursed in spasming whispers.

"You were the easiest mark she has ever had. It was simple enough for her to hack and replicate your biodata for a mask. And, replicating your face perfectly for the surveillance drones was pure art, don't you agree? She is very talented, much more so than you ever were . . ." Sarvetix almost seemed proud as Nim morphed into Nero and, for a horrible few seconds, it was if he were looking in a mirror, "despite the Deilospe incident." Sarvetix added flatly. Nim morphed back and a fraught look was exchanged between her and Sarvetix. "I wasn't sure if blue was your thing, but after all these decades of loneliness, I guessed you would be grateful for even the smallest amount of attention. It's not like your mind was not mired in the equatorial south even prior to your disgrace."

Nero had to push the air from his lungs with each shallow breath to speak, "please, Brother, just leave me here in exile. I am no threat to you now. You have won." He conceded his loss. It was difficult not to. Though his helplessness mixed with rage, he knew he was defeated and in grave danger.

"Normally, I would, you are sort of family after all, but things are changing, Nero, and sadly you have, again, proven yourself to be a liability. I can't have you interfering, going forward. It's a shame I can't trust you, you would be a valuable asset for what is to come, though your value is rapidly decreasing. You are not so unique anymore. It's time for a change, Nero, and this planet will be key; a brief nuclear winter should reverse the tip and make way for repopulation. Sorry for leading you on with the job offer, couldn't have you catching on I'm afraid." A strange, confused look came over Sarvetix, "I don't know why I am telling you all this," he said.

Nero thought he might know—the woman must still be nearby somewhere, hidden in the darkness.

Then, the look faded and Sarvetix drew a weapon. A knife. The blade long and sharp, glistening in the shuttle's lights. Nero tried to speak, but panic and paralysis seized his throat so he produced only stuttering nonsense.

"I have read that knives are a favoured weapon of this species so, if anyone happens to stumble across your body, they will assume it's just more of the violence the natives have a propensity for."

His brother bent over him, lifted his armour and, without hesitation, plunged the knife into Nero's gut. Nero screamed a thin, gargled scream as pain raced through him, hot and intense. He could feel blood pouring from the wound, but couldn't move to stem the flow.

"Well, Brother, I guess this is goodbye," Sarvetix patted his cheek and departed without a second look. Nim waved again before replacing her helmet and dutifully following.

The shuttle left Nero exsanguinating onto the wet ground. To add insult to grave injury, the blast of shuttle engines had covered him in organic matter and water. How strange to feel so wet. Of all the deaths he had faced and imagined, this was not the best but nor was it the worst. As agony gripped him, Nero floated in the gap between consciousness and the eternal abyss of death. That was when he saw the woman emerge from the blurry edge of his vision. *Death's kiss might come swifter still*, Nero thought as she knelt beside him.

XXII

The decision seemed impossible to make and yet there were only moments to make it or the man's wound would decide for her. More of her than Raven wished to admit wanted to watch Nero die of his injury. The desire for revenge was hard to shake even after all these years of trying a more enlightened approach. But, from what she could glean of the conversation between him and his assailants, Nero was not fully responsible for what had happened. He was, however, the only person on the planet with the faintest idea of what had actually happened.

Raven had thought about attacking the other two, but she was still so weak from her treatment at the hands of this one (not to mention her misjudged leap from the plane), that she may have failed and should she have succeeded, Raven may have induced the wrath of the rest of their kind when their party didn't return. Raven didn't want to make things worse. Worse, she thought. What even would count as worse at this point? A flare of anger surged within her. No one was looking for this one—this Nero. The question was - dead or alive, in which state was he more useful? Raven looked at the simple metal handle of the knife, then to the paralysed man whose eyes were wide with fear and whose panicked mind was fading into death. Suddenly, he did not seem so intimidating.

Blood pulsed from where the blade met his skin; it almost seemed to keep time, like a ticking clock—pulse, tick, pulse, tock, the blood marked the passing moments. Darkness turned the slick blood black against Nero's greying skin. To save him would be to preserve the only person who had knowledge of what had transpired in the preceding hours, or had it been days? A moment of disorientation absorbed Raven and exhaustion induced vertigo caused her to grip the ground for support. Lights danced in her vision. Could she even save him now?

Raven concluded that she must try. He was after all the only person who could possibly help her understand the situation and perhaps, try to rectify it—even if he was a utter bastard of a man. It crossed Raven's mind that, should he live, things could get very messy if he was not of a mind to help her. Killing him later would feel worse than watching him die now. Killing another, even in revenge, even if that person really deserved it, never felt as good nor as satisfying as expected.

Still the blood clock pulsed, Nero's life slipping further away with every tick. Fine, she would attempt to save him. Raven ran her hands through her hair pushing it back from her eyes. She wondered when she had lost the band that had held it back. Raven braced herself, this was going to hurt, a lot, for both of them.

Raven reached for the knife, startling when the man's hands met hers. Whatever paralysis he was under must have been wearing off.

"Hold still. I need to remove the knife to seal your wound and stop the bleeding," she said trying to sound calm, though feeling anything but.

The man's eyes widened. Fear and surprise seemed to twitch across his slackened facial muscles. His hands released hers and dropped to the floor.

"This is going to hurt. Try not to move, if you can move."

Raven took several deep breaths, counted to three, and wrenched the knife from the man's belly, placing a hand over the now gushing wound to stem the flow. Pain radiated from Nero's mind, Raven felt sick with it, she pushed the sensation away. A gargled cry passed the man's lips and he promptly passed out. It was probably for the best. More comfortable for the both of them this way, Raven didn't need the extra difficulty of trying to suppress the suffering of another.

Letting her mind search his body for the ragged tears the serrated blade of the knife had left through the man's intestines, revealed the lacerations were numerous and devastating. Worse were the large ruptures in the blood vessels which spewed blood relentlessly into his internal cavities. Raven felt Nero's life dwindling with every lost ounce. It was the large blood vessels she directed her fading energy to first. Pushing Nero's body to heal itself, Raven sealed each large, leaking vessel in turn before attending the lacerations in the smaller capillaries. Slowly the flow of blood, eased to a trickle and then, eventually, stopped.

Letting her consciousness roam through Nero, Raven could sense his heart still faintly beating, his lungs still softly inflating and deflating. Interestingly his form, his composition, his life, they felt different to others she had healed. In some way very foreign and yet strangely familiar. A shudder of pain and enervation ripped through Raven, but she couldn't stop yet, without sealing his gut the oozing of bacteria and bile would soon kill him.

Her own life was all but spent so, after a moment's sorrow, Raven pulled the life from everything connected to her that was unfortunate enough to live. The meadow grasses withered and browned as if plagued by drought, a grand oak, hundreds of years old, dropped its leaves, grew brittle and cracked, insects fell from their nocturnal refuges and rodents dropped in place—all desiccated and decayed. Everything that was connected to her by root or stem, for as far as she could reach, fell to her will, surrendering to her call with the very essence of their life force. The surge of life, even that from the plants, was bittersweet, exhilarating yet sad and shameful. Prioritising one life over another never felt pure and yet the power of it was always scintillating. Raven pushed the forfeited life into the man, guiding Nero's mind and body to use the sacrifice to heal. Slowly all the tissues mended themselves. The repairs were thin, particularly the skin, but Raven could give no more of herself, or the others surrounding her. It would have to do. She left his nose broken—she needed him alive, not pretty.

Raven sat back and briefly passed out. When she awoke, the damp from the ground (both dew and blood) had soaked into her clothes and hair. The remains of dead plants clung to her where she had lain on the now barren earth. The man was still unconscious and now even paler in the light of the partial moon. Though she sensed his heart beating, the beat was slow and its tempo unstable. There was little more she could do for him now. Hopefully, he would live. Hopefully, he would also be compliant if he did.

What was she going to do now? Sitting next to a half-dead man in a field while covered in blood was likely to bring some questions come dawn. Depending on where they were, of course. There were many places in Devon where a corpse would skeletonise before anyone came close enough to ask awkward questions, even now. Many bodies likely littered these pleasant, rolling hills.

Raven hauled herself to her feet, vomited, and sank back down. Waiting a while longer to recover, she noted that she could hear the man's rasping breath, but not any car noise. Though electric cars were quieter than their combustion engine counterparts, no road noise at all suggested they were somewhere pretty rural. Carefully, Raven attempted to stand once more. Surveying the horizon, she saw little over the silhouettes of the hedges and trees that lined the field's borders. Luckily, the moon gave just enough light for Raven to pick out a gate in one of the hedgerows.

Beyond the rusty, locked gate, was a narrow road with the steep, rocky banks common in the South West. Raven figured her influence had been effective, she must be somewhere near home. If they were actually in France or further afield, things were about to get even more difficult. Patting her pockets, Raven searched for her phone and cursed the man when she found it gone. She started walking regardless and, when she got to the end of the lane, made a note of the road name. Littlebray Lane. It wasn't one she recognised. Raven kept limping on, her pace stilted and slow. Jumping from the plane had twisted her leg badly. Injuries on top of injuries and no energy left to fix them. Nothing was broken, but everything hurt.

After some time, Raven heard an approaching vehicle. She waved at the car, beckoning for it to stop. Even from a great distance, she felt the horror of the occupant at the sight of her. That was fair enough, she probably looked like the undead, limping, lurching and covered in blood. For a moment, Raven thought the car was going to pass her, but the little e-Golf mark 6 stopped in hesitant staggers. A woman of advancing years and fabulous dress got out.

"Are you alright, my love?" the woman said in a thick west country drawl.

Raven felt a mixture of compassion and self-preserving fear radiating from the woman who stayed close to her car on the dark road.

"I fell. Could you drive me home? I think I live nearby," Raven blurted out, too tired to push the thought.

"Of course, my lovely. Don't you need to go to a hospital, though?" The woman approached her cautiously.

"No, it looks worse than it is. My car broke down and I fell down a ditch walking for help, but I'm okay."

"Thank God for small miracles," the lady said helping her into the passenger seat in a motherly way.

As they sat in the light of the car, Raven felt the lady begin to question just how much wet and dried blood was on her given a lack of obvious injuries. Raven pushed the thought from the woman's mind instead promoting the warm, fuzzy feeling of helping someone—she needed this help.

The car's satnav seemed to have trouble locating them, but put the drive at only half an hour. Apparently, they were somewhere near Brayford. On the way, the woman chattered nervously about how she had been out at a dinner party when they heard on the news about a terror attack on several cities around the world, everyone had been ordered to lockdown and await instruction. It seemed not all the woman's fear was due to Raven's slasher movie appearance. Raven pled ignorance on the matter, to which the lady continued on about what an awful business it all was and how she was old enough to remember 9/11. Raven remained silent; this, she feared, was much worse than even that terrible day. Apparently, the broadcast had shown the face of the suspect speaking at the UN, though it appeared to the lady, who seemed the intelligent kind, that the authorities were having difficulty getting their facts straight about who he was and why he would attack us in this way. Raven wondered how the woman would feel knowing that the man from the news was lying in a field just a few minutes' drive away. If he were still alive.

As Raven alighted from the small car, leaving smears of blood and dirt across the cream, faux-leather interior, she thanked the lady for her help and once again refused the offer of further medical attention. The track to her home seemed longer than it ever had.

Grabbing the keys to her pickup, Raven stubbornly ignored how plush and comfortable her sofa looked, though she did drink three glasses of water and relieve herself. Washing her hands and face resulted in a sink that looked like a crime scene. She dared not look in the mirror. Luckily, the seats in the Toyota already had mud covers, a necessity of farm work.

The satnav seemed to be failing, but slowly the local roads regained their familiarity, even in the dark. After a few wrong turns and double backs that caused significant cursing and arguing with the satnav reminiscent of the nineties (when getting anywhere with a satnav was an exercise in negotiation and elaborate swearing), Raven found the narrow lane with the high banks. Then the dead field with the only-just-alive man. Raven wanted to drive into the field, but the gate's lock rattled in metallic defiance as she shouted and kicked it. Defeated by a padlock, she laughed a strange laugh and pulled at the chain a last time.

"I guess we will have to do this the hard way," Raven said, approaching the still-comatose Nero.

Partially lifting him from the floor, she dragged Nero half the way to the gate before failing to see a deep rut in the earth and tripping.

"Why did you have to be such an oversized git?" Raven said irritably, her twisted leg complaining sharply, before dragging Nero the rest of the way. "You had better be useful when you wake up," she grumbled to the night.

Luckily, there was a gap beside the five-bar gate which, after a little undergrowth clearing, was just large enough for her to shove Nero through. Raven contemplated putting him on the bed of the pickup. No, these roads are rough and ill maintained, it would just mean more damage. Damage she would have to fix. A quieter inner voice added, unless he died, then you could just discard him in a local body of water of appropriate ruralness and he wouldn't be your problem anymore. Raven shook that voice off and heaved the limp form of the man into the reclined passenger seat of the cab. He was cold and pale.

Driving over the pot holes of the ill-kempt, tractor-trampled lanes, Nero's head lolled from side-to-side, eyes open and rolling. It was creepy. Raven took a moment at a junction to close his eyes. It didn't do much to improve his increasingly corpse-like look. After some more disagreements with the increasingly unpredictable satnav, Raven made it back to her little farm.

Overcome by exhaustion, Raven thought about leaving Nero in the truck, but instead she drove him to the small guest cabin in the wooded glade opposite her home. Inside the cabin was dusty and smelt of neglect, but it was in fair condition considering its disuse.

Nero was a dead weight in her arms as she hauled him into the cabin and onto the bed in one of the two small, pine-clad bedrooms. He was still breathing—shallow rasping breaths, but breathing. In the light of the cabin, she could see that her thin repair of his wound had ruptured. It seeped blood slowly onto the uncovered mattress. Raven sighed and welled-up with exhaustion. There was no way she could sustain healing him again. Placing a hand near the wound, Raven could feel that it was only the surface of the wound which had split. Sealing the wound was going to have to be done the old-fashioned way.

A needle and thick thread hastily sterilised with water boiled in the kettle would have to suffice. Lifting the strange material of the man's top enough to expose the wound revealed his skin to be mottled around the area. Raven's hands shook with every stitch. The result was messy, but it held, for now. It was probably a good thing the dickhead was unconscious. Once she was sure that the blood had stopped flowing, she covered Nero with a thick blanket, musty from storage, and left. She had done all she could for him.

Finally inside, Raven made herself the only two drinks suitable for a situation like hers: a large whisky and a much larger cup of tea. She necked the whisky, barely registering the burn of the cask-strength liquor and took the tea to her sofa with a large packet of biscuits, the good biscuits—this was no time for Rich Teas. No, this was the time for something that could withstand a serious dunking. Just as she was about to sit down on the neutral-coloured couch, she remembered the state of herself. Raven stripped by the washing machine, pulled on a large dark t-shirt and shorts from the dryer next to it and threw a dark-coloured throw over the sofa. It occurred to Raven to throw the clothes away so that they could not remind her of the previous days, but it would be a waste, she well knew that trauma did not manifest so neatly and the memories would not intrude so predictably.

Raven drank the tea and ate the entire pack of thickly-chocolated biscuits. Turning on the TV brought channel after channel of devastating news and horrifying images. Different channels, but always the same news, broadcast from makeshift studios with tired-looking, faltering broadcasters and shaky camera work. Flashing images of the destruction that the attacks had wrought across the earth and the unbelievable death toll washed over Raven in an overwhelming, numbing wave. Switching off the TV, she curled into a ball and fell unconscious.

XXIII

When Raven awoke, she thought it was still early in the morning as the sky was dim and a murky crimson.

"Red sky in the morning, shepherd's warning," she said to herself as she made coffee.

The shaking of her hands as Raven raised the cup caused it to slosh over the side onto the wooden countertop. A glance at the clock told her it wasn't dawn at all; in fact, it was nearly midday. With a double take she looked at the dark sky with its hazy red glow, her heart leapt into her mouth; this was not normal.

Switching on the radio, the warnings came thick and fast. Don't travel, don't leave the house unless necessary, use filtration systems where available and masks when outside. The 'red dawn' as it had been named was the product of the remnants of the blasts clogging up the atmosphere. Raven stared at the ominous sky. She hadn't seen anything like it since Krakatoa in 1883 and, even with the flood of information from technology providing explanations and warnings, it wasn't less scary.

Raven, who desperately wanted to eat, couldn't face even plain toast, especially once she caught sight of herself in her small, driftwood-framed mirror. Showering was a relief, her skin released from the irritation of dried blood, sweat and dirt. Her blood and Nero's swirled together in the drain before being washed away. After she had dried herself and finished her ablutions, she felt slightly more human and could face the toast.

For an hour, she sat on the sofa, watched cartoons on the few channels still working (the children's channels were the only ones not running endless news cycles) and hid from reality. As if remaining in a self-built bubble of cartoons and cereal eaten by the handful from the box would change the fact that the man partially responsible for this atrocity was lying, dead or alive, in her cabin, like Schrodinger's freaking villain. No, she had to face her situation. Leaving his body to decay in her cabin would not improve anyone's situation, tempting as it was, and it was very tempting.

After putting everything she touched last night in the wash, she pulled on a pair of cleanish boots and walked into the doomsday haze. Outside, she noticed a strange silence. The birds weren't singing, the insects weren't buzzing, her chickens weren't chatting away as they usually did, the only sound was the gusting of a thick, unsettled breeze. Raven shivered and walked to the cabin quickly. Inside, she breathed a sigh of relief as she found the man still unconscious, but alive. Raven realised she wasn't ready to speak to him.

Examination revealed him to be in significant distress. Her rather gruesome stitch job was holding, but the blood loss he had experienced was threatening to kill him. A blood transfusion was out of the question (God only knew what his blood type was), but potentially she could reverse his dehydration and energy deficit.

A trip to the North Devon District Hospital A&E department found it understaffed and heaving with the influx of people suffering respiratory issues. Walking through the sliding door, into the rundown A&E reception with its cracking linoleum, dirty paint and graffitied plastic chairs filled with traumatised, ash-grey faces, Raven was hit by a wall of panic and grief; it hung in the air around her as dense and suffocating as the ash-laden haze. When Raven enquired as to the lack of staff, the response was redeployment and compassionate leave. The nurse manning intake burst into tears as he was speaking to her, rivulets of water running over his heavily-masked face. Raven consoled him, letting comfort wash over him. Awfully, he was stuck between grief and hope as many of his family members were missing. They lived in London. London was gone, she remembered from the news. It was likely they were dead.

Abruptly, Raven was hit with the realisation that the few people she had in her life could also be dead. She left Natalia in New York. New York had also been wiped from the face of the earth, leaving behind only scorched ruins and grief. Suppressing her own gut-twisting fear, Raven stopped it from spilling over. The last thing the nurse needed was her anguish on top of his, he was already near breaking point.

After the nurse had calmed down a little, at Raven's description of her patient's needs, he gave her two intravenous drips designed for rehydration and the restoration of metabolites, as well as the means to catheterise a vein. Exhausted and grateful for her comfort, the nurse put up little resistance to her push, despite the many protocols handing over the supplies must have broken.

"You can cope with this," Raven said as she left, driving the thought deep into the nurse's psyche. "You are resilient and strong." She felt his panic lessen a little and took her leave as quickly as possible through the gathering throngs.

Back at the cabin, Raven Googled 'how to insert an IV' and followed a video on Amazon. She usually boycotted Amazon's services, which was a tiresomely extensive endeavour these days, but now was not the time to trawl the small indie apps. Raven followed the instructions. The man's veins were clearly visible through the pale skin of his hands, but they were deep, drawn in for survival. One of the veins collapsed under her fumbling, twitching attempts at insertion. Raven took a deep breath and followed the video again. This vein held and the drip began to slowly drain. Nero's blood pressure picked up a little as time passed.

As Raven sat with the man, she became aware that he smelt of urine. She groaned and fetched an old, moth-eaten towel, placing it under him. His vein was the only thing she was going to be catheterising today.

The rest of the day was spent in a zombie-like trance eating, napping, watching as much news as she could handle and tending to the animals, including the one in the cabin. Her strange routine was broken only by encountering Toby who had come round diligently, mask firmly in place, ailing terrier at his feet, to tend the animals. Raven could feel his desire to grumble at her that she had returned without notice after an absence longer than agreed. But apparently her appearance and his relief she was alive deterred his grievance, instead he asked if she were okay. Raven nodded and made up some lie about getting caught in the travel chaos and losing her phone. Well, that last part wasn't a lie.

Toby turned the conversation to the awful business of the attacks and thanked an unnamed deity for his small family not being among the dead. They shared worries about their farms if the light did not return and then Toby was gone, hobbling across the fields stick in hand, his faithful old dog at his heels.

In the evening, Raven changed Nero's empty drip for a new bag, walked through the crimson twilight, unseasonably early and brisk, to her home and collapsed into a long, unrestful sleep.

XXIV

Nero awoke in fits and starts. The world fading in and out uncontrollably, sickeningly. Disorientation, pain, strange smells and close, brown-patterned walls assaulted his senses as they swam around in his consciousness.

Eventually, Nero awakened more fully. Dry mouthed and hurting from the inside out, he looked through shadowy vision at an unfamiliar world. He seemed to be in a bed of sorts. How was he alive? Memories of his brother holding the knife above his paralysed body flooded back to him and he started to hyperventilate. Each heaving breath seemed to kindle searing hurt from his stomach and face.

Pulling back the blanket, Nero baulked at the crude stitch work which held together his swollen, discoloured wound. The sight of it made him retch, but there was nothing in his stomach except acid, resulting in horrible, burning dry heaves. Slowly, Nero gained control and hauled himself to a half sit against the wall. Propping himself up, he felt a queer scratching feeling in the back of his left hand. A long tube extended from inside of it to an almost empty transparent bag hung on the wall above him. What the hell was that! Ripping out the tube was painful; it reignited his nausea. Thick blood oozed from the wound left by the rough removal of the device. What was in that bag? And where was he? If it was an afterlife, it certainly wasn't one of the better ones he had heard about.

For a long while Nero sat slumped against the wall, expecting to feel some recuperation of his strength. None came. As his senses adjusted to his new world, he did become aware that he stank of urine and was vaguely damp. Nero couldn't remember a time when he had felt worse since his stay in Quoric's dungeon.

Thirst and hunger eventually drove Nero to try to leave the bed. It was a slow and painful process of many misstarts. Nero saw light peeking from behind heavy sheets hung against the wall. Pulling one back revealed a world bathed in a red haze. What looked like water fell in droplets from the sky hitting the window and streaking down in wavy lines. Water in such abundance was something Nero had rarely seen on other planets, other than the one he had been trying to recruit. Was he still there?

Huge organic structures surrounded the room. They were intimidating and impressive. Nero wondered if the flora were sentient, as similar structures on the Verscov home world were—he hoped not, but thought it best to err on the side of caution. Through the gigantic, gently waving sentinels, he could view a sea of smaller, greenish plants and a structure which seemed to be a dwelling. It appeared to be built of the bodies of the organics surrounding the room. Nero wondered if that angered or saddened them to see their brethren so? If they could contemplate such a thing. Vast windows were encapsulated in the corpses.

A door in the corner of the room was ajar. Nero shambled towards it, gripping his stomach tightly in case his wound split. The threads binding his injury pulled painfully with every step. Passing a mirror, Nero baulked at his reflection. His broken nose was swollen and crooked, thick black bags clung underneath his bloodshot eyes, his lips were cracked, and his skin was sallow. Groaning, Nero stumbled on. Behind the door was a larger room, there were chairs and a table, as well as many other things Nero did not recognise. Through the windows and the surrounding organic giants, Nero could again see the large dwelling in the distance.

Slowly, Nero searched the room for food, water or a dispenser; anything to quieten the nagging needs of his broken body, his mouth so dry it stifled his swallowing. There was nothing he could identify as digestible. He ventured outside to an undercover area open to the elements at the sides. There were seats here, too, but he sat on the steps instead, letting cool droplets of water fall on him as he shook gently with the exertion of the past few moments. The air was chilled but refreshing. Nero wondered whether the rain here was drinkable.

He caught a little in his hand, smelt it, then tasted it. It seemed to be just water.

As Nero sat on the step harvesting the rain drop by drop, he became aware of movement at the property below. Someone was walking towards him up the gently inclining plain. Swathed in material and covering their head against the rain, Nero wasn't sure who it was, but he had a terrible inkling. As the person came closer, Nero tried to get to his feet, failed, and so, sat taller instead. Slowly but not cautiously, the figure approached. They stopped a distance away. When they drew back their hood a little, Nero saw it was the woman. For a moment he felt panic surge within him, then it was as if his weakened state resigned him to his fate. Running or fighting were certainly out of the question. Some instinct in Nero tested the light around him, it obeyed his will, though with that obedience came surges of pain—the world dimmed, but Nero fought against his diminishing consciousness. He would not faint in front of her.

"You're alive," the woman said curtly, her face suggesting she was suppressing many emotions. She looked a lot better than the last time he had seen her.

"I am. Was I not supposed to be?" Nero said in Karthian, before correcting to her language and repeating himself. He leant heavily against the railing beside him which creaked with the burden.

"You were. Though it certainly wasn't guaranteed," she replied, rain drops collecting on her sullen face.

Nero racked his dull mind for what the woman had said her name was. "Your medic's crude approach probably lessened the odds," Nero said, immediately regretting his tone.

"Well, if you hadn't tortured your medic, she could have perhaps healed you in a less 'crude' manner. As it is, you should be grateful to be alive at all," she snapped back, all the emotions she had been suppressing now clearly visible.

Should he be grateful? What had she resurrected him into?

"I apologise," Nero offered stiltedly and a few moments of silence passed. He still did not know the truth of who this woman was. "Where am I?" he asked in a milder tone.

"You are on Earth. Did the sky you burnt not give it away? And I wouldn't drink any more rain, they are warning that, no thanks to you, it now has things in that it shouldn't."

Nero cursed his situation, his family and his feebleness. Tremors shook him. The woman's anger was palpable, should she attack him, he would be without defence. Nero detested feeling so vulnerable. "Why did you save my life?" he asked.

The woman sighed, deeply and irritably. "Because before you were injured, I sensed that the attacks were not entirely your doing and, possibly, not your intent. Though it has to be said that your intent doesn't seem benevolent either. Regardless, you are the only person with the slightest idea what has and is happening here. Your insight could be valuable, if you are inclined to cooperate."

The woman's stern stare bore into Nero as the rain that had gathered on her skin now flowed over the curvature of her face.

"And if I am not so inclined?" Nero asked, recoiling at the strange smile which suddenly twisted the woman's thick lips. He had a feeling she would quite like him to decide to be uncooperative.

"That depends on exactly how uncooperative you decide to be."

"So, I am captive here?"

"You can take your chances on your own if you wish. But, be warned, there are still a few billion people on this planet and I expect that each and every one would like to do you even more damage than your own people did."

An image of his brother flashed through Nero's mind and his breath caught in his throat as the woman continued, "I will not imprison you here, you are welcome to take your slim chances on your own. I would be willing to provide refuge here, but in return for safe sanctuary, I would expect cooperation."

"How slim do you think my chances would be?" Nero asked and his body answered the question for him with a cacophony of pain. Slim indeed.

"I guess that depends just how good you are at not being where people expect," the woman answered, maintaining her distance, arms crossed over her chest.

There was silence again.

"So, what is your choice?" the woman pushed him.

"I need to decide now?"

"You do. If you do not wish to help undo the damage you have caused my planet, then you are on your own." The woman gestured towards a path which led away from the property.

Nero's posture slumped. He could barely stand, let alone defend himself against a planet of primitives who wanted him dead. At least for now, this one wanted him alive. He could use that until he was stronger and then . . . well then, he would reevaluate his situation. His beyond dreadful situation. For now, this strange place was his best and only option. "I will cooperate," he said quietly.

"Then, we have a deal."

The woman came close and offered him a hand. Nero took it and she pulled him to his feet. As searing pain engulfed him, he tried desperately not to faint. The woman's strength had clearly recovered somewhat from his captivity of her. Tightly she gripped his hand as she eyeballed him closely.

"Right, mate, let me make myself quite clear. I will remain true to my word and my home will be a safe and comfortable place for you for as long as you are compliant. But! If you try to hurt me, I will kill you. If you try to do further damage to my planet or my people, I will kill you. If I sense that you seek to betray me, and I am very good at sensing such things, I . . . will . . . kill . . . you. Do you understand me?" she all but growled the words at him. Nero noticed that she still had a little blood in her hairline. Hers or his? He wondered.

"I comprehend," Nero surrendered, then her name came to him. "Raven," he added softly.

"Good," Raven said releasing Nero to his own faltering balance. Then her voice changed tone entirely as she asked, "now, would you like a cup of tea?"

Equal parts fantasist and scientist, Dr E. M. Lethbridge is a science fiction and fantasy writer who enjoys writing for both adults and children. She aims simply to tell good stories well. A mother of two, she mostly writes in the small gap between the kids going to bed and total exhaustion setting in.

When not ensconced behind a keyboard with a large cup of tea and some biscuits, she can be found lecturing in neuropsychology or attempting to convince half ton animals to comply with her requests (horse training).

To follow me go to:

Amazon: Dr E. M. Lethbridge

Facebook: www.facebook.com/emlethbridgeauthor

Instagram: https://www.instagram.com/e_m_lethbridge/

TikTok: https://www.tiktok.com/@e_m_lethbridge